Lecture Notes in Computer Science 2196

Edited by G. Goos, J. Hartmanis, and J. van Leeuwen

Springer
Berlin
Heidelberg
New York
Barcelona
Hong Kong
London
Milan
Paris
Tokyo

Walid Taha (Ed.)

Semantics, Applications, and Implementation of Program Generation

Second International Workshop, SAIG 2001
Florence, Italy, September 6, 2001
Proceedings

 Springer

Series Editors

Gerhard Goos, Karlsruhe University, Germany
Juris Hartmanis, Cornell University, NY, USA
Jan van Leeuwen, Utrecht University, The Netherlands

Volume Editor

Walid Taha
Yale University, Department of Computer Science
51 Prospect St., New Haven, CT 06511, USA
E-mail: taha@cs.chalmers.se

Cataloging-in-Publication Data applied for

Die Deutsche Bibliothek - CIP-Einheitsaufnahme

Semantics, applications, and implementation of program generation : second
international workshop ; proceedings / SAIG 2001, Florence, Italy, September
6, 2001. Walid Taha (ed.). - Berlin ; Heidelberg ; New York ; Barcelona ;
Hong Kong ; London ; Milan ; Paris ; Tokyo : Springer, 2001
    (Lecture notes in computer science ; Vol. 2196)
    ISBN 3-540-42558-6

CR Subject Classification (1998): D.3, F.3, D.1, F.4.1, D.2

ISSN 0302-9743
ISBN 3-540-42558-6 Springer-Verlag Berlin Heidelberg New York

This work is subject to copyright. All rights are reserved, whether the whole or part of the material is
concerned, specifically the rights of translation, reprinting, re-use of illustrations, recitation, broadcasting,
reproduction on microfilms or in any other way, and storage in data banks. Duplication of this publication
or parts thereof is permitted only under the provisions of the German Copyright Law of September 9, 1965,
in its current version, and permission for use must always be obtained from Springer-Verlag. Violations are
liable for prosecution under the German Copyright Law.

Springer-Verlag Berlin Heidelberg New York
a member of BertelsmannSpringer Science+Business Media GmbH

http://www.springer.de

© Springer-Verlag Berlin Heidelberg 2001
Printed in Germany

Typesetting: Camera-ready by author
Printed on acid-free paper   SPIN: 10840656   06/3142   5 4 3 2 1 0

Preface

This volume constitutes the proceedings of the second International Workshop on the Semantics, Applications, and Implementation of Program Generation (SAIG 2001) held on 6 September, 2001, in Florence, Italy. SAIG 2001 was held as an ACM SIGPLAN workshop co-located with the International Conference on Principles, Logics, and Implementations of High-level Programming Languages (PLI).

As the commercial production of software systems moves toward being a traditional industry, automation will necessarily play a more substantial role in this industry, just as it plays a key role in the production of traditional commodities. SAIG aims at promoting the development and the application of foundational techniques for supporting automatic program generation. A key goal of SAIG is to provide a unique forum for both theoreticians and practitioners to present their results and ideas to an audience from a diverse background.

This year we are fortunate to have three influential invited speakers: Krzysztof Czarnecki (DaimlerChrysler), Tim Sheard (OGI School of Science and Engineering), and Mitchell Wand (Northeastern University). The proceedings include abstracts of the invited talks, and an invited paper by Tim Sheard.

Seven technical papers and two position papers were presented at SAIG 2001. The technical papers cover a wide spectrum of topics, including:

- A rigorous, operationally-based treatment of the correctness of an important program transformation (*Johann*)
- A schema-based approach to generating solutions for maximum multi-marking problems (*Sasano, Hu, and Takeichi*)
- An elegant method for the generation of machine code without chains of jumps (*Damian and Danvy*)
- A uniform approach to the compilation of goal-directed programs using partial evaluation (*Danvy, Grobauer, and Rhiger*)
- The integration of partial evaluators into interpreters (*Asai*)
- A software design method for Haskell based on the Unified Modeling Language (UML) (*Wakeling*)
- A novel approach to dynamically adaptable software using staged languages (*Harrison and Sheard*)

The two position papers tackle novel application areas:

- Global computing through meta-programming (*Ferrari, Moggi, and Pugliese*)
- Optimizing functional programs using size inference (*Herrmann and Lengauer*)

We thank the participants for their excellent contributions.

July 2001   Walid Taha

Scope

SAIG welcomes contributions on or across any of the following facets of program generation:

- Software engineering methods and processes,
- Domain specific languages,
- Deductive program synthesis methods,
- Computer algebra and symbolic computation,
- High-performance/high-reliability systems,
- Specialized support in traditional programming languages,
- Novel accounts of traditional compilation and linking techniques, and
- Specialized semantics-based methods and approaches.

Review Process

A call for papers was announced on several mailing lists and newsgroups. The workshop accepted regular technical submissions and position papers, and featured an open panel discussion at its conclusion. All papers are reviewed for presentation, clarity, interest, and coverage of related work. In addition, regular papers must contain novel technical contributions. In contrast, position papers must provide a clear description of a problem, survey existing approaches, and give a clear description of and argument for the proposed approach.

Fifteen submissions were received this year, twelve of which were technical papers and three position papers. Of these submissions seven technical papers and two position papers were accepted. There was a drop in submissions from last year, where there were 20 submissions in total. The most likely explanation for this drop is the occurrence of two related multi-day events earlier this year, namely PADO II and Reflection. That SAIG received this number of papers is an indication of a sustained interest in this research area.

All accepted papers are of the same high quality as the papers accepted last year. Most papers received three reviews. The final decisions were made collectively by the Program Committee based on all available reviews. In cases where Program Committee discussions were of benefit to the authors, the discussions were summarized and included with the reviews. One submission received a conditional acceptance, and the authors addressed the concerns of the reviewers in time for publication.

To promote further development of the works presented at the workshop, a special issue of a journal on the theme of SAIG will be organized after the event.

Advisory Committee

Don Batory, Texas at Austin   Tim Sheard, OGI
Eugenio Moggi, Genova   Walid Taha, Yale (Chair)
Greg Morrisett, Cornell

Program Committee

Gilles Barthe, INRIA   Eugenio Moggi, DISI
David Basin, Freiburg   Greg Morrisett, Cornell
Don Batory, Texas at Austin   Flemming Nielson, DTU
Robert Glück, DIKU and Waseda   David Sands, Chalmers
Nevin Heintze, Agere Systems   Walid Taha, Yale (PC Chair)

External Reviewers

Reiner Hänle, Chalmers   Perry Wagle, OGI
Dino Oliva, Agere Systems   Ed Walter, Agere Systems

Acknowledgments

SAIG 2001 would not have been possible without the support of the PLI organizers. We would especially like to thank Betti Veneri (PLI Workshop Chair) for her help in organizing the workshop, Carole Mann (Registration Systems Lab) for her quick response to our last minute requests, and Alfred Hofmann (LNCS Editor) and his team for their continual support during the preparation of these proceedings. Richard Gerber provided us with the START software and a lot of assistance while we tailored the system to our needs. Chuck Powel and Mark Wogahn (Yale CS Workstation Support) provided us with a lot of timely help.

Finally, we would like to thank the Università di Genova, Yale University, and ACM SIGPLAN for providing financial support for this workshop.

Table of Contents

Generative Programming and Software System Families
Abstract of Invited Talk

Krzysztof Czarnecki

DaimlerChrysler AG, Research and Technology,
Software Technology Lab, 89081 Ulm, Germany
czarnecki@acm.org
www.generative-programming.org

Today's software engineering practices are aimed at developing single systems. There are attempts to achieve reuse through object- and component-based technologies with two specific goals: to cut development costs, and time-to-market and to improve quality. But current research and practical experience suggest that only moving from the single system engineering to the system-family engineering approach can bring significant progress with respect to these goals [3,6,7].

Generative programming builds on system-family engineering and puts its focus on maximizing the automation of application development [1,2,4,5]: given a system specification, generators use a set of reusable components to generate the concrete system. Both the means of application specification, the generators, and the reusable components are developed in a domain-engineering cycle. This talk introduces the necessary techniques, notations, and processes using examples. It also outlines our vision of how the software industry can be transformed in a similar way the traditional industries moved from manual craftsmanship to automated assembly lines, and the role generative techniques can play in this transition.

References

1. D. Batory and S. O'Malley. The Design and Implementation of Hierarchical Software Systems with Reusable Components. In *ACM Transactions on Software Engineering and Methodology*, vol. 1, no. 4, October 1992, pp. 355–398.
2. J. C. Cleaveland. Building Application Generators. In *IEEE Software*, no. 4, vol. 9, July 1988, pp. 25–33.
3. P. Clements and L. Northrop. *Software Product Lines: Practices and Patterns.* Addison-Wesley, to appear in 2001.
4. K. Czarnecki and U. Eisenecker. *Generative Programming — Methods, Tools, and Applications.* Addison-Wesley, Boston, MA, 2000.
5. J. Neighbors. Software construction using components. Ph. D. Thesis, (Technical Report TR-160), University of California, Irvine, 1980.
6. D. Parnas. On the design and development of program families. In *IEEE Transactions on Software Engineering*, vol. SE-2, no. 1, 1976, pp. 1–9.
7. D. M. Weiss and C. T. R. Lai. *Software Product-Line Engineering: A Family-Based Software Development Process.* Addison-Wesley, Reading, MA, 1999.

W. Taha (Ed.): SAIG 2001, LNCS 2196, p. 1, 2001.
© Springer-Verlag Berlin Heidelberg 2001

Accomplishments and Research Challenges in Meta-programming

Invited Paper

Tim Sheard

Pacific Software Research Center
OGI School of Science and Engineering
Oregon Health & Science University
sheard@cse.ogi.edu,
http://www.cse.ogi.edu/~{}sheard

1 Introduction

In the last ten years the study of meta-programming systems, as formal systems worthy of study in their own right, has vastly accelerated. In that time a lot has been accomplished, yet much remains to be done. In this invited talk I wish to review recent accomplishments and future research challenges in hopes that this will spur interest in meta-programming in general and lead to new and better meta-programming systems.

I break this paper into several sections. As an overview, in Section 2, I try and classify meta-programs into groups. The purpose of this is to provide a common vocabulary which we can use to describe meta-programming systems in the rest of the paper.

In Section 3, I describe a number of contexts in which the use of meta-programming has been found useful. Some knowledge of the areas where meta-programming techniques have been developed helps the reader understand the motivation for many of the research areas I will discuss.

In Section 4, I motivate why meta-programming systems are the right tools to use for many problems, and I outline a number particular areas where I believe interesting research has been accomplished, and where new research still needs to be done. I do not claim that this set of issues is exclusive, or that every meta-programming system must address all of the issues listed. A meta-programming system designer is like a diner at a restaurant, he must pick and choose a full meal from a menu of choices. This section is my menu.

In the following Sections I elaborate in more detail on many of the areas outlined in Section 4. I will discuss many ideas from many different researchers that I think are important in the overall meta-programming picture. For some areas, I have outlined proposed research projects. My proposals are at the level of detail I would assign to a new student as a project, and I have not personally carried the research to its conclusions.

If we continue using the food metaphor, in these sections we discuss the general preparation of menu items; which ingredients need special handling; and

W. Taha (Ed.): SAIG 2001, LNCS 2196, pp. 2–44, 2001.
© Springer-Verlag Berlin Heidelberg 2001

special techniques that apply to broad areas of cooking. Not so much a cookbook that describes how to make each item on the menu, but a cooking class in general techniques of building and understanding meta-programming systems.

Finally, in Section 21, I discuss a number existing meta-programming systems. My understanding of what they were designed to do, and where in the taxonomy of meta-programming systems they lie. In this section I also discuss the MetaML system, which is my attempt at building a useful meta-programming system. In the world of meta-programming meals, MetaML is only one full course meal. I look forward to many other delightful meals in the future, especially those where I am the diner and not the chef.

2   Taxonomy of Meta-programs

In a meta-programming system, *meta-programs* manipulate *object-programs*. A meta-program may construct object-programs, combine object-program fragments into larger object-programs, observe the structure and other properties of object-programs. We use the term object-program quite loosely here. An object-program is any sentence in a formal language. Meta-programs include things like compilers, interpreters, type checkers, theorem provers, program generators, transformation systems, and program analyzers. In each of these a program (the meta-program) manipulates a data-object representing a sentence in a formal language (the object-program).

What kind of meta-programs are there? Meta-programs fall into two categories: program generators and program analyzers. A program generator (a meta-program) is often used to address a whole class of related problems, with a family of similar solutions, for each instance of the class. It does this by constructing another program (an object-program) that solves a particular instance. Usually the generated (object) program is "specialized" for a particular problem instance and uses less resources than a general purpose, non-generated solution.

A program analysis (a meta-program) observes the structure and environment of an object-program and computes some value as a result. Results can be data- or control-flow graphs, or even another object-program with properties based on the properties of the source object-program. Examples of these kind of meta-systems are: program transformers, optimizers, and partial evaluation systems. In addition to this view of meta-programs as generators or analyzers (or a mixture of both), there are several other important distinctions.

- **Static vs. run-time.** Program generators come in two flavors: static generators, which generate code which is then "written to disk" and processed by normal compilers etc. and run-time code generators which are programs that write or construct other programs, and then immediately execute the programs they have generated. If we take this idea to the extreme, letting the generated code also be a run-time code generator, we have *multi-stage programming*.

Examples of run-time program generators are the multi-stage programming language MetaML [69,79], run-time code generation systems like the Synthesis Kernel [46,67], 'C [64], and Fabius [44]. An example of a static program generator is Yacc [39].

- **Manually vs. automatically annotated.** The body of a program generator is partitioned into static and dynamic code fragments. The static code comprises the meta-program, and the dynamic code comprises the object-program being produced. Staging annotations are used to separate the pieces of the program.

  We call a meta-programming system where the programmer places the staging annotations directly a manually staged system. If the staging annotations are place by an automatic process, then the meta-programming system is an automatically staged system.

  Historically, the area of partial evaluation pioneered both the technique and terminology of placing the staging annotations in an automatic way without the intervention of the programmer. Write a normal program, declare some assumptions about the static or dynamic nature of the programs inputs, and let the system place the staging annotations. Later, it became clear that manually placing the annotations was also a viable alternative.

- **Homogeneous vs. heterogeneous.** There are two distinct kinds of meta-programming systems: homogeneous systems where the meta-language and the object language are the same, and heterogeneous systems where the meta-language is different from the object-language.

  Both kinds of systems are useful for representing programs for automated program analysis and manipulation. But there are important advantages to homogeneous systems. Only homogeneous systems can be n-level (for unbounded n), where an n-level object-program can itself be a meta-program that manipulates $n+1$-level object-programs. Only in a homogeneous meta-system can a single type system be used to type both the meta-language and the object-language. Only homogeneous meta-systems can support reflection, where there is an operator (`run` or `eval`) which translates representations of programs, into the values they represent in a uniform way. This is what makes run-time code generation possible. Homogeneous systems also have the important pedagogical and usability property that the user need only learn a single language.

3   Uses of Meta-programs

Meta-programming provides various benefits to users. We explain some of these benefits here.

- **Performance.** A common objective of many meta-programming systems is performance. Meta-programs provide a mechanism that allows general purpose programs to be written in an interpretive style but to also perform without the usual interpretive overhead. Rather than write a general purpose but inefficient program, one writes a program generator that generates an efficient solution from a specification. The interpretive style eases both maintenance and construction, since a single program solves many problems. One program is easier to maintain than many similar individual programs. The use of the parser generator Yacc is an illustrative example. Rather than using a general purpose parsing program, we generate an efficient parser from a specification, i.e. a language grammar.

- **Partial evaluation.** Partial evaluation is another meta-programming technique used to improve performance. Partial evaluation optimizes a program using a-priori information about some of that program's inputs. The goal is to identify and perform as many computations as possible in a program before run-time. The most common type of partial evaluation, *Off-line* partial evaluation, has two distinct steps, *binding-time analysis* (BTA) and *specialization*. BTA is an analysis that determines which computations can be performed in an earlier stage given only the names of inputs available before run-time (the static inputs). Specialization uses the values of the static inputs to produce an improved program.

- **Translation.** Perhaps the most common use of meta-programming is translation of one object-program to another object-program. The source and target languages may or may not be the same. Examples of translators are compilers and program transformation systems.

- **Reasoning.** Another important use of meta-programs is to reason about object-programs. If the object-programs are sentences in a formal language, an analysis can discover properties of the object-program. These properties can be used to improve performance, provide assurance about the object-programs behavior, or validate meaning preserving transformations. Examples of reasoning meta-programs are program analyses such as flow analyses and type checkers. Reasoning meta-programs are also used to build theorem proving systems such as LEGO [66], HOL [33], Coq [7] and Isabelle [57] and the study [36] and implementation [24] of logical frameworks such as Elf [60], Twelf [62], LF [61].

- **Pedagogy.** A pedagogical use of meta-programs is program observation. Computation often proceeds in stages. Inputs arrive in several stages and the computation comprising each stage is a program that incorporates the current inputs, and anticipates the next stage. Higher order functions provide a convenient mechanism for structuring staged programs. In a higher-order language solutions proceed by accepting some input, then producing as a result, a function that can deal with the next stage. Since functions are extensional (they can be observed only by noticing how they behave when applied to inputs), it is hard to explain or understand programs written in this style, since the intermediate stages cannot be observed.

A meta-programmed solution alleviates this problem. Instead of each stage producing a function as output, each stage can produce the code of a function as output. The code is observable and its structure is often quite illuminating. We have used this to illustrate several very complex algorithms to great effect, for example, the continuation-passing-transform, monad-transformers, and combinator parsers

- **Mobile code.** Recently meta-programming has been used as means of program transportation. Instead of using networks to bring the data to the program, networks are used to bring the program to the data. Because of security reasons, intensional representations of programs are transported across the network [38,82]. These representations can be analyzed for security and safety purposes to ensure that they do not compromise the integrity of the host machines they run on. The transported programs are object-programs and the analyses are meta-programs.

Why is meta-programming hard? Meta-programming is hard because programs are complex. Large computer programs may well be the most complex entities ever constructed by humans. Programmers utilize many features to manage this complexity. These features are often built-in to programming languages and include: type-systems (to catch syntactically correct, yet semantically meaningless programs), scoping mechanisms (to localize the names one needs think about), and abstraction mechanisms (like functions, object hierarchies, and module systems to hide irrelevant details). These features add considerably to the complexity of the languages they are embedded in, but are generally considered worth the cost. When we write programs to manipulate programs we must deal with this complexity twice, once in the programs we write, and again in the data they manipulate.

A good meta-programming system knows about and deals directly with the complexities of the object-language. If the meta-language does not deal directly with the type system, scoping discipline, and abstraction mechanisms of the object-language, the meta-programmer must encode these features using some lower level mechanism, complicating an already difficult task.

How can a meta-programming system help? A meta-programming system is supposed to make the manipulation of object programs easier. It should be easy to use and understand by the programmer; interface the meta- and object-languages seamlessly; provide high-level abstractions that capture both the details of the object-language and the patterns used by the meta-programs; be blindingly fast; and in the case of program generators, generate blindingly fast code. There is utility in providing general purpose solutions to these needs that can be reused across many systems. There has been lots of good work in addressing many of these issues, but it is not always clear how they fit together, or what is still missing.

4   Research Areas

Meta-programming as an area has been around for a long time. The LISP hackers had it right. Programs are data. But as a formal area of study, meta-programming has become an active area of research only in the last decade or so. There is a huge amount of work that remains to be done. Enough to supply legions of Ph.D. students with thesis topics for the next 10 years. The work varies from highly theoretical proofs to the nitty-gritty engineering problems of systems building. All of it is important, and worth doing. An overview of a few areas is presented in the itemized list below. In the rest of the paper we discuss many of these items in more detail.

- **Representing Programs (Section 5).** Programs are data, but they are complex entities. How do we represent them to hide unnecessary details, yet make their important structure evident, and their common operations easy to express, and efficient to implement?
- **Presentation (Section 6).** Presentation is the interface to the object-language that the meta-programming system provides to the programmer. Presentation can have immense effect on the usability of a system. Our experience with MetaML shows that object-language templates that "look like" object language programs are a great boon to the meta-programmer.
- **Integrating automatic and manual annotation (Section 8).** Partial evaluation systems save the user the bother of placing staging annotations, but the user of an automatic system loses some control over the structure of the output. Manually placing staging annotations provides complete control, but in many cases is tedious and error prone. Can the two techniques be married in a harmonious relationship?
- **Observing the structure of code (Sections 9 & 10).** There are many techniques for representing code as data. Many make code an abstract type. This is done to support its dual nature, or to provide a more usable presentation. Since these representations hide the internal structure of code, some other interface to the internal structure of code is necessary if code is to deconstructed or observed. A good interface that is both easy to use, and which reflects the user's logical view of the object-code's structure (rather than a view of how it is implemented) is hard to obtain.
- **Manipulating Binding constructs (Section 13 & 14).** Many object-languages include binding constructs which introduce and delineate the scope of local variables. As far as the meta-program is concerned, the actual name of these variables is immaterial. Any name could be used as long as it is used in a consistent manner. When generating programs one needs to invent new local names that are guaranteed to be different from existing names. This is necessary to prevent the possibility that one will introduce a scope that will inadvertently hide a necessary variable. In program transformation or analysis, the flip side of the coin must be dealt with. When deconstructing programs how can we ensure that locally scoped variables never escape their scope and become unbound?
- **Manipulating typed object-programs (Sections 15, 17, & 18).** When we write programs, many of us find the discipline of a typed programming language too valuable to ignore. Type systems catch errors sooner and facilitate writing good programs. Why wouldn't we want the same benefits for our object-programs? A typed meta-programming system can catch type errors in object-programs at the compile-time of the meta-program. Our MetaML system (see Sections 7 & 21) has made a good start in this area. Problems

still to be addressed include meta-programs that generate (or manipulate) object-programs with different object-types, that depend upon the meta-program's input, issues involving polymorphism inside object programs, and the issue of type-safety and the use of effects in meta-programming.

- **Heterogeneous meta-programming systems (Section 12, 18, & 19).** What do we do about heterogeneous systems where the meta-language and object-language are different? Heterogeneous systems bring a whole new set of challenges to the forefront. For every object-language, a new and different type system must be defined. If the type of the meta-program is to say something about the type of the object-programs it produces, then it must be possible to embedded the type system of the object-languages into the type-system of the meta-language. There is no guarantee that the object-language type systems is in any way similar or compatible to the meta-language type system. The two type systems may be incommensurate. For example, the meta-language may be the polymorphic lambda calculus, and the object-language Cardelli's object calculus [4], so a simple embedding is not always possible.

- **Building good implementations (Section 21).** Implementations of meta-programming systems are rare. We especially lack good implementations of run-time code generating systems. There are many competing needs in such systems. Should we generate code quickly? Or should we generate fast code? Either is hard to do. Sometimes, doing *both* seems nigh on impossible. How can we control the tradeoff?

  General purpose program generators should be able to generate code that interacts with several different object-program environments. Do we really need a Yacc for every language? How do we build meta-systems with the ability to produce object-programs that interact with differing environments?

- **The theory of meta-programs (Section 20).** Reliable systems are only possible when we understand the theory behind the systems we wish to build. Meta-programs have subtle semantic difficulties that just do not occur in ordinary programs. A good theory of meta-programming systems is necessary to isolate these problems and understand their interaction with other system features. Good theory leads to good tools.

In the following sections I discuss many of these areas in more detail. In many of the sections I give example programs, some times in imaginary, not-yet-existing languages. I have a choice here of which language style to use for these examples. On one hand, I have built a large system (MetaML) with great care to adhere to Standard ML's syntax and semantics, so I might like to give my examples in an ML style language. On the other hand, ML's style of using postfix application for type-constructor application (i.e. int list), its use of quoted variables (i.e. 'a) to represent type variables, and its inability to give type declarations (where the programmer gives a type for a function, but not its definition), push me towards using a style more akin to Haskell, with its typing prototypes and qualified type system.

So in the end I choose to do both. When giving examples that are actual MetaML programs, I adhere to the ML style. In all other places I adhere to the Haskell style of program definition.

5 Representing Programs

Many meta-systems represent object-programs by using strings, graphs, or algebraic data-structures. With the string encoding, we represent the code fragment f(x,y) simply as "f(x,y)". While constructing and combining fragments represented by strings can be done simply, due to their lack of internal structure, deconstructing them is quite complex. More seriously, there is no *automatically verifiable* guarantee that programs thusly constructed are syntactically correct. For example, "f(,y)" can have the static type string, but this clearly does *not* imply that this string represents a syntactically correct program. The problem is that strings have no internal structure corresponding to the object-language's structure.

Using PERL as a meta-language for object-language (say HTML) manipulation moves all the work of implementing language manipulations to the user. It is better to move common tasks into the meta-language implementation so the programmer does not need to solve the same problems over and over again.

The lack of internal structure is so serious that my advice to programmers is unequivocal: *No serious meta-programmer should ever consider representing programs as strings.*

LISP systems, and their use of S-expressions, add internal structure to program representations, but this does not really solve the syntax correctness problem. Not all S-expressions are legal object-programs (unless, of course, the object-language is S-expressions). LISP also lacks a static typing mechanism which is extremely useful when meta-programming.

An algebraic approach can be used to capture an object-language's structure in a more rigorous manner. One solution in this vein is to use a data-structuring facility akin to the algebraic datatype facility of Standard ML or Haskell. With the datatype encoding, we can address both the destructuring problem and the syntactic correctness problem. A datatype encoding is essentially the same as *abstract syntax*. The encoding of the fragment "f(x,y)" in an Haskell algebraic datatype might be:

```
Apply (Variable "f") (Tuple[Variable "x" ,Variable "y"])
```

using a datatype declared as follows:

```
data Exp = Variable String | Apply Exp Exp | Tuple [ Exp ]
         | Constant Int    | Abs String Exp
```

Using a datatype encoding has an immediate benefit: *correct typing for the meta-program ensures* correct syntax for all object-programs. For languages which support pattern matching over datatypes, like Haskell and Standard ML, deconstructing programs becomes easier than with the string representation. However, constructing programs is now more verbose because we must use the cumbersome constructors like `Variable`, `Apply`, and `Tuple`. The drawback is the requirement that the meta-programmer must be aware of the detailed mapping of the concrete syntax of the object language into the data structuring component of the meta-language. If at all possible, it is better to manipulate a representation with the more familiar feel of the concrete syntax of the object language.

6   Presentation

A *quasi-quote* representation is an attempt to make the user's interface to the object-language as much like the object-language concrete syntax as possible. Here the actual representation of object-code is hidden from the user by the means of a quotation mechanism. Object code is constructed by placing "quotation" annotations around normal object-language concrete syntax fragments. Inside quotations, "anti-quotation" annotations allow the programmer to splice in computations that result in object-code.

I am told that the idea of quasi-quotation originates in the work of the logicians Willard V. Quine in his book *Mathematical Logic* [83], and Rudolph Carnap in his book *The Logical Syntax of Language* [15].

A description of the early use of quasi-quotation appears in Guy Steele's *The evolution of LISP* [73] where he describes various dialects of MacLISP which supported a feature he calls *pseudo-quoting*

- *Pseudo-quoting allowed the code to compute a replacement value, to occur within the template itself. It was called pseudo-quoting because the template was surrounded by a call to an operator which was "just like quote" except for specially marked places within the template.*

In LISP back-quote begins a quasi-quotation, and a comma preceding a variable or a parenthesized expression acts as an anti-quotation indicating that the expression is to be treated, not as a quotation, but as a computation that will evaluate to a piece of object-code. A short history of *Quasiquotation in LISP* [8] can be found in an article of that name by Alan Bawden in the 1999 PEPM proceedings as an invited talk, and describes this in much more detail.

In LISP, quasi-quotation is unaware of the special needs of variables and binding forms. Quasi-quotation does not ensure that variables (atoms) occurring in a back-quoted expression are bound according to the rules of static scoping. For example `'(plus 3 5)` does not bind `plus` in the scope where the back-quoted term appears, nor does it treat the x in `'(lambda (x) exp)` in any reasonable way that respects it as a binding occurrence.

It wasn't until much later in the design and implementation of the Scheme Macro system [23,22], that quasi-quotation dealt properly with these issues. MetaML also fixes this problem and employs a static typing discipline, which types quasi-quoted expressions with object-level types, a useful and important extension.

A quasi-quote presentation is a mechanism with the benefits of both a string and an algebraic datatype representation. It guarantees the syntactic correctness of object programs using the type correctness of the meta-programs, but maintains the ease of construction of object-programs.

7   A Short Introduction to MetaML

MetaML is a homogeneous, manually annotated, run-time generation system. In MetaML we use angle brackets (< >) as quotations, and tilde (˜) as the anti-quotation. We call the object-level code inside a pair of angle brackets, along with its anti-quoted holes a *template*, because its stands for a computation that will build an object-code fragment with the shape of the quoted code. Along with the syntactic correctness guarantee, MetaML's template mechanism also guarantees type correctness at the object-level, and treats object-level variables in a manner that respects static scoping. We illustrate these features below:

```
-| val x = <3 + 2> ;
val x = <3 %+ 2> : <int>
```

```
-| val code = <show ~x> ;
val code = <%show (3 %+ 2)> : <string>
```

In this example we construct the object-program fragment x and use the anti-quotation mechanism to splice it into the object-program fragment code. Note how the definition of code uses a template with a hole.

We introduce a new type constructor < t > (pronounced *code of t*) to type meta-level terms which evaluate to object-code. Note how each code fragment is assigned a code type, where the type inside the angle brackets indicates the type of the object-program. For example <3+4> has type <int>, because 3+4 has type int.

The type system helps the user construct well formed object-programs. One of its most useful features is that it tracks the level at which variables are bound. Attempts to use variables at a level lower than the level at which they are bound makes no sense, and is reported by the type checker. For example:

```
-| fun id x = x;
val id = Fn  : 'a -> 'a
```

```
-| <fn x => ~(id x) - 4>;
Error: The term: x   Variable bound in stage 1 used too early in stage 0
```

In the above example x is a stage 1 variable, but because of the anti-quotation it is used at stage 0. This is semantically meaningless and is reported as a type error.

In MetaML, a quasi-quoted template involving variable binding automatically alpha-renames bound variables in a manner that precludes inadvertent name capture. Note how the bound variables x are alpha-renamed from x to a and b.

```
-| <fn x => fn x => x - 1>;
val it = <(fn a => (fn b => b %- 1))> : <'a -> int -> int>
```

This is particularly useful when computing the body of a lambda-abstraction using an anti-quoted computation. If the computation places the variable bound by the lambda-abstraction in a context where the same variable is bound in another way, inadvertent capture can result.

```
-| fun plus x = <fn y => ~x + y>;
val plus = Fn : <int> -> <int -> int>
```

```
-| val w = <fn y => ~(plus <y>)>;
val w = <(fn a => (fn b => a %+ b))> : <int -> int -> int >
```

Note how plus splices its argument in a context where y is locally bound. Yet if we use plus in another context where another y is bound, MetaML does not confuse the two.

MetaML also statically scopes free variable occurrences in code templates. This results when a variable is used in a level greater than the level where it was bound.

```
-| fun f x y = x + y - 1;
val f = fn : int -> int -> int
```

```
-| val z = <f 4 5>;
val z = <%f 4 5> : <int>
```

```
-| let fun f x y = not x andalso y in run z end;
val it = 8 : int
```

Note how the free variable f in the code template z refers to the function f:int -> int -> int, which was in scope when the template was defined, and not the function f:bool -> bool -> bool which was in scope when z was run. The code pretty printer places the percent-sign (%) in front of f in the code template z to indicate that this is a statically bound object-variable.

The **run** operator in MetaML transforms a piece of code into the program it represents. It is useful to think of **run** as indicating the composition of run-time compilation with execution. In the example below, we first build a generator (power_gen). Apply it to obtain a piece of code (power_code). Run the code to obtain a function (power_fun). And then apply the function to obtain an answer (125).

```
-| fun power_gen m =
     let fun f n x = if n = 0 then <1> else <~x * ~(f (n-1) x)>
     in <let fun power x = ~(f m <x>) in power end> end;
val power_gen = fn : int -> <int -> int>
```

```
-| val power_code = power_gen 3;
val power_code =
<let fun power x = x * x * x * 1 in power end> : <int -> int>
```

```
-| val power_fun = run power_code;
val power_fun = fn   : int -> int

-| power_fun 5;
val it = 125 : int
```

In MetaML we use run to move from one stage to the next. Because it is legal to use the anti-quotation under a lambda-binding, there is the possibility that run may be applied to variables that will not be bound until some later stage. For example:

```
-| val bad = <fn x => ~(run <x>) + 4>;
```

will cause an error because the object-variable x will not be bound until the whole piece of code is run, and then finally applied. This kind of error just does not occur in normal programs, and complicates both the semantics and type systems of homogeneous meta-systems. There has been much thought put into devising type-systems which will disallow such programs [74,49,77].

MetaML has one more interesting operator lift. It evaluates its argument to a constant (any value not containing a function), and produces a piece of code that represents that value. For example:

```
-| lift (4 + 5);
val it = <9> : <int>

-| lift (rev [1,2+3]);
val it = <[5,1]> : <int list>
```

In MetaML the angle brackets, the escapes, the lifts, and the run operator are staging annotations. They indicate the boundaries within a MetaML program where the program text moves from meta-program to object-program. The staging annotations in MetaML are placed manually by the programmer and are considered part of the language. In MetaML the staging annotations have semantic meaning, they are part of the language definition, not just hints or directions to language preprocessors.

It has been argued that manually staged programs are hard to write, and are much larger than their unstaged counterparts that could be input into a partial evaluation system, thus saving the user a lot of work. With the advent of modern meta-programming systems with quasi-quote staging annotations it remains to be seen if this argument still holds. Our experience has been that manually annotated programs are (within a few percent) the same size as their unstaged counterparts. Still it would be nice to have the benefits of both systems.

8   Partial Evaluation

Off-line partial evaluation is an automatic staging meta-system. Consider a simple partial evaluation function PE. It takes the representation of a program with one static parameter and one dynamic parameter and returns an answer. It analyses this program and automatically produces an annotated program which when given the static parameter as input produces a representation of the function from dynamic parameter to answer. From this description we can infer that PE should have the type (<s -> d -> a>) -> (<s -> <d -> a>>) For example consider the program:

```
-| val ans = PE <fn s => fn d => d + (s + 3)>
ans = <fn s => <fn d => d + ~(lift (s+3))>> : <int -> <int -> int>>
```

which evaluates to a new two-stage program. This step is called binding time analysis. When this two-stage program is run, and then applied to 5 (the specialization stage) it produces a new specialized program:

```
-| val special = (run ans) 5;
val special = <(fn a => a %+ 8)> : <int -> int>
```

Note how the static addition (s+3) is performed at specialization time.

The integration of a function like PE into a manually staged language could provide the benefits of both manually and automatically staging a program. Since both partial evaluators and staged languages exist, it remains an interesting engineering problem to integrate the two.

9   Intensional Analysis of Code

MetaML, as originally designed, allowed the construction and execution (see Section 7) of code. Observation of the structure of code, and its decomposition was not originally supported, and has never been included in any of the formal property studies we have performed.

Consider the problem of implementing the PE function from the previous section. What tools do we need? Its obvious PE needs to observe the structure of its argument. Is the argument an lambda-abstraction (<fn s => ...>), is it an application (<s + 3>), is it a constant (3), or is it a variable (s)? If it is a variable, then is it statically scoped like %+, or is it an object-bound variable like d?

In MetaML, code is implemented as an abstract datatype. The interface to this datatype includes only the quasi-quote template notation, and the function run. Internal to the interpreter, code is implemented as an algebraic datatype along the lines of the Exp datatype used in Section 5. This internal representation is not visible to the programmer, as we wish to insulate the programmer from the details of the internal structure, allowing him to construct object programs using the same syntax (via the template mechanism) used for meta-programs.

In order to allow intensional analysis of code we must either make explicit the internal representation, or supply some other interface to the abstract code type. The actual MetaML implementation is far too complicated to deal with in this short section, but if we consider the Exp datatype as defined in Section 5 we can illustrate the key ideas.

```
data Exp = Variable String | Apply Exp Exp | Tuple [ Exp ]
           | Constant Int    | Abs String Exp
```

Suppose we have built a quasi-quotation mechanism that internally stores templates as `Exps` (`<4>` means (`Constant 4`), and `< ~f ~x >` means (`Apply f x`), and `<fn x => x>` means (`Abs "x" (Variable "x")` etc.). We could support an interface to this abstract type that did not reveal the details of the actual implementation type `Exp` by supplying constants with the following types, which we display below in a Haskell-style language.

```
isApp   :: <b> -> M(<a->b>,<a>)          gensym :: M (Sym a)
isAbs   :: <a->b> -> M(<a> -> <b>)       var :: Sym a -> <a>
isConst :: <Int> -> M Int                instance Eq (Sym a)
isVar   :: <a> -> M (Sym a)
```

Here M is a monad with failure (`fail`) and plus operation (`++`) such that (`++`) is associative and `fail` is its unit. It might help to think of M as the `Maybe` type constructor with additional structure. Under this interpretation, the expression `isConst <3>` evaluates to (`Just 3`), the expression `isApp < ~f ~x >` evaluates to (`Just (f,x)`), but `isApp <3>` evaluates to `fail`. In each case the operators either succeed, producing as result some sub-structure of the object-code matched against, or they fail. The operator (`++`) is used to try a sequence of potentially failing expressions one after another.

The operators `isAbs`, `isVar`, `gensym`, and `var` are used to deal with variables and binding operators such as lambda-abstraction. Because the actual name of a bound variable does not matter, we would like our implementation to respect this constraint.

The type constructor `Sym` is an abstract type which is a member of the `Eq` class. Its only operators (beside equality testing with (`==`)) are `gensym` and `var`. The operator `Abs` works in conjunction with the operators over `Symbols` to analyze the structure of lambda-abstractions and variables. The operator `isAbs`, when applied to a piece of code which is an object-level abstraction, returns a meta-level function. Given an "argument", this meta-level function re-produces the body of the abstraction with all occurrences of the bound variable replaced by the "argument". Under this scheme the user cannot observe the actual names of object-variables. The operator `gensym` produces new symbols that can only be observed through the `Sym` abstract type interface. This interface is designed to avoid harmful use of variables.

For example to test if some code term x matches the code value `< \f -> f 5 >` one writes as follows. We use a Haskell-like syntax because of its excellent support for monadic computation using the `do` and `return` operators.

```
test :: <(Int -> a) -> a> -> M Bool
test x =
  do { g <- isAbs x
     ; y <- gensym
     ; (fpart,arg) <- isApp (g (var y))
     ; n <- isConst arg
     ; z <- isVar fpart
     ; return ( n==5 && y==z )
     }
```

Using the do notation, a successful match binds the elements to the left of the arrow (<-), causing the evaluation to proceed to the next clause. A single failure causes the complete do expression to fail.

Not the use of gensym and var to generate new object-level variables. A key observation is that all production of variables happens within the monad M. One can write an equality function that compares two pieces of code for syntactic equality (modulo alpha-equivalence) as follows:

```
eq :: <a> -> <a> -> M Bool
eq x y =
  (do { n <- isConst x; m <- isConst y; return(n==m)) ++
  (do { (f,x) <- isApp x; (g,z) <- isApp y; b1 <- eq f g
      ; b2 <- eq x z; return (b1 && b2) }) ++
  (do { f <- isAbs x; g <- isAbs y; x' <- gensym
      ; eq (f (var x')) (g (var x')) }) ++
  (do { x' <- isVar x; y' <- isVar y; return(x'==y')}) ++
  (return False)
```

The purpose of the monad is to put structure on the possibility of failure, and to delimit the scope where object-bound variables may live. The problem is that the use of gensym may produce free variables which are never eliminated. For example:

```
do { x <- gensym
   ; return (var x)
   }
```

returns a variable which has no binding location. One saving grace here is that the expression above has type M <a>, not <a>. One purpose of the monad is to prevent the escape of such variables. Thus an important open question is "How do you get out of the monad?"

An operation with type M a -> a is clearly too general, since it might allow the abstract Sym values to escape the monadic computation. One solution might be to use a qualified type, qualifying a as follows:

```
run :: NotCode a => M a -> Maybe a
```

If a cannot contain code then things will be safe. But clearly one often wants to write code analyzers that return code. How to accomplish this is an interesting open question.

This approach can even be lifted to complex object-code expressions such as case-expressions. For example:

```
isCase :: <a> -> M([Exists x . (<x -> b>,<x> -> <a>)],<b>)
```

Applying isCase to an object-level case, if it succeeds returns a pair. The first part of the pair is a list corresponding to each arm of the case, and the second part of the pair corresponds to the argument of the case. For example:

```
test = <case g x of
          Cons (x,xs) => x + sum xs
        | Nil () => 0>
```

```
do { ([(c1,f),(c2,h)],arg)   <- isCase test
   ; ...
   }
```

Each item in the list, corresponding to the arms of the case, is a pair. The first element corresponds to the constructor function, and the second element (as in the isAbs example) is a meta-function that could be used to obtain the right-hand-side of the arm.

For example the binding of (isCase test) in the example above, binds the meta-variables whose types and bindings are indicated in the table below:

```
arg :: <[Int]>                          arg        --> <g x>
c1  :: <(Int,[Int]) -> Int>             c1         --> <Cons>
c2  :: <() -> Int>                      c2         --> <Nil>
f   :: <(Int,[Int])> -> <Int>           f <(a,b)> --> <a + sum b>
h   :: <()> -> <Int>                    g <()>     --> <0>
```

Clearly, there remains considerable work to extend and polish this proposal so that it would be robust, and apply to a realistic size object-language. In the case of MetaML one needs to deal with statically scoped variables like %length, and deal with typing issues for constructors like Tuple.

10   Higher Level Interfaces to Code Analysis

Quasi-quoted templates were introduced as an abstract way to construct code, but can also be used as patterns against which code can be matched. This supplies a more abstract interface to intensional analysis of code than the interface in the previous section. If a quasi-quoted template is used as a pattern, then the anti-quoted variables in the template are meta-variables which are bound to object-code fragments during pattern matching. We have built a simple prototype implementation of this into MetaML.

```
-| fun decompose <(~x,~y)> = (x,y)
   | decompose _ = error "bad"
val decompose = Fn  : <('b * 'a )> -> (<'b > * <'a >)

-| decompose <(3,5)>;
val it = (<3>,<5>) : (<int> * <int>)

-| decompose <(fn x => (x,x)) 5>;
Error: bad
```

Several engineering problems remain to be solved to fully use templates as patterns. Pattern templates use antiquotation to indicate the meta-variables destined to be bound when the pattern matches. Most templates include enough context (in the form of concrete-syntax) to disambiguate which kind of object-level term is being matched. Two cases remain problematic: constants and sequence-based constructs. If one wants to match a particular constant, it is straightforward to just wrap it in quoting brackets to make an object-language pattern that matches code containing that constant.

```
fun is_five < 5 > = true
  | is_five _     = false
```

But, how does one write a pattern that matches against all code constants, and when doing this binds a meta-variable to the value of the constant in the code matched against? This is easy to do using algebraic datatypes. Using the algebraic datatype `Exp` introduced in Section 5, we write:

```
fun  f2 (Constant n) = n
```

Using templates, there is not enough context inside the brackets to distinguish constants. For example < ~n > matches any code, not just constants.

A similar problem occurs when matching against language constructs which are sequence-based; i.e., consist of an unbounded number of similar sub-constructs. Examples include tuples and let-expressions with multiple bindings.

For example, the pattern below matches all tuples with three components.

```
fun g <(~x,~y,~z)> = 3
```

What pattern will match all tuples? Again this is easy using an algebraic datatype approach. The pattern (`Tuple xs`) matches all tuples, and the meta-variable `xs` is bound to a *list* of sub-expressions. Typing such an interface is also problematic. A robust template-based approach to pattern matching against code will need to address these issues.

To use quasi-quoted templates to match against binding constructs such as function abstraction and case-expressions requires solving the same problems of variable escape that we saw in Section 9.

11   Quasi-Quotes Distinguish Stages

A valuable property of quotes and anti-quotes is that they serve as staging annotations that distinguish the meta-program from the object-program. Such annotations are important because they remove ambiguity. Consider the program transformation that replaces exceptions with **Either** types[1] in a Haskell-like object-program. The meta-program below defines the *magic-brackets* ([| _ |]) which specify the transformation.

```
[| x |]              = Inl x
[| lambda x . e |]   = Inl (lambda x . [| e |])
[| e1 e2 |]          = match [| e1 |]
                             (lambda v1 . match [| e2 |] v1 Inr) Inr
[| raise |]          = Inl Inr
[| try e3 |]         = Inl (lambda h . match [| e3 |] Inl  h)
[| let x = e4 in e5 |] = match [| e4 |] (lambda x .[| e5 |]) Inr
```

This transformation is a meta-program. Meta-programs described in this format are typically found in research papers. It manipulates two separate object-languages. It does a case analysis over the structure of the *source object-language*,

---

[1] `data Either a b = Inl a | Inr b`

and builds an element of the *target object-language*. It contains both object-variables and meta-variables. Can you tell which variables are which? If you are a skilled programming language researcher you can probably use your past experience, and context to figure out which is which. But as an unambiguous algorithm it leaves much to be desired.

Staging annotations remove this ambiguity. Below we use MetaML-like staging annotations.

```
[| < %x > |]                  = <Inl ~x>
[| <lambda x . ~(e <x>)> |]   = <Inl (lambda y . ~[| e y |])>
[| < ~e1 ~e2 > |]             = <match ~[| e1 |]
                                    (lambda v1 . match ~[| e2 |] v1 Inr)
                                    Inr>
[| <raise> |]                 = <Inl Inr>
[| <try ~e3> |]               = <Inl (lambda h . match ~[| e3 |] Inl h)>
[| <let x = ~e4 in ~(e5 x)> |] = <match ~[| e4 |]
                                    (lambda y . ~[| e5 y |]) Inr>
```

Note how the quotations (< and >), delimit the object-code, and how the anti-quotations (~) indicate the meta-computations that compute object-code sub-terms. It is possible to distinguish object-variables from meta-variables by noting whether their binding occurrence is within quotations. Several unresolved problems remain. The percent (%) in front of x is an attempt to indicate that this pattern should match only variables, and that the meta-variable x should be bound to the object-variable the pattern matches. The other problem concerns manipulating binding occurrences of object-variables (like in lambda). In the example above we have used a solution which is similar in feel to the use of the function isAbs of Section 9. Patterns matching lambdas bind variables which are functions from terms to terms. This is discussed in further detail in Section 13.

12   Templates and Heterogeneous Meta-systems

In the MetaML implementation the object-language and the meta-language share the same fixed representation, the same parser, and the same type checker etc. The representation of both the meta and object languages was chosen *once* by the MetaML system's developers.

In a heterogeneous system, such templates become problematic. Instead of a single, fixed object-language, the user can define multiple object-languages. Thus neither a fixed strategy, nor shared representation is possible. In a heterogeneous system meta-programmers will have to develop their own representations.

A good step in this direction is addressed by the *conctypes* of Annika Aasa [1,2,3]. She describes how an algebraic datatype facility can be extended to one that allows concrete syntax descriptions. In her work a fixed parsing strategy is embedded into the extension, and the users write *conctype* specifications which behave like both a grammar specification, and an algebraic datatype definition.

Integrating this with a system that treats object-bound variables sensibly, handles the ambiguity problems of constants and sequence-based constructs, and that allows object-language typing as well remains an open problem.

13   Manipulating Binding Constructs

As we have seen, meta-programs are particularly difficult to write correctly if they must manipulate object-terms that have a notion of statically scoped variables. There are two related problems. The first occurs when generating programs that include new binding occurrences. When generating a new binding construct, some meta-systems use a *gensym* operator that produces a new unique name that will never be introduced again. This strategy is used to avoid inadvertent name capture of free variables in the scope of the binding construct.

Such a solution is awkward to use since it separates the introduction of the name from its binding, and prescribes a stateful implementation from which new names can be selected. In Section 7 we discussed how a quasi-quote template based interface can hide this gensym process from the programmer.

The second problem occurs when deconstructing programs that include binding occurrences. The exact representation of the bound variable is generally uninteresting, and the meta-program must make subtle "administrative changes" to the object-program so that it maintains its original "meaning". Such names also need special attention to prevent the escape of bound variables from their scope. In our discussion of intensional analysis of code, the handling of variables was a major complication.

A representation where the meta-program can be freed from the responsibility of concretely representing bound variables and their names, yet which facilitates correct program manipulations would be quite useful indeed!

An interesting representation technique based upon an idea that goes back, at least, to Alonzo Church [16] exploits the binding mechanism of the meta-language to implement the binding mechanism(s) of the object-language. We saw an inkling of this in the use of our function `isAbs`.

To illustrate the elegance of the approach contrast the definition of `Term` and `Term'` below. In `Term'` we represent the object-language lambda abstraction (`Abs'`) using the meta-language function abstraction. Note, in our examples, how the `id'` term and the `apply'` term are represented by applying the `Abs'` constructor to a meta-language function.

```
data Term = App Term Term              data Term' = App' Term' Term'
          | Abs String Term                       | Abs' (Term' -> Term')
          | Const Int                             | Const' Int
          | Var String                  -- \ x -> x
-- \ x -> x                             id' = Abs' (\ x -> x)
id = Abs "x" (Var "x")                  -- \f -> \ x -> f x
-- \f -> \ x -> f x                     apply' =
apply = Abs "f" (Abs "x"                  Abs' (\ f ->
          (App (Var "f") (Var "x")))              Abs' (\ x -> (App' f x)))
```

The higher-order abstract syntax representation (HOAS) Term' is elegant in that a concrete representation for variables is not needed, and that it is not necessary to invent unique, new names when constructing lambda-expressions which one can only hope do not clash with other names. Unfortunately, there are drawbacks as well. HOAS works fine for constructing statically known representations, but quickly breaks down when trying to construct or observe a representation in an algorithmic way. There are four problems that we illustrate in the examples below:

– **Opaqueness.** HOAS bindings are "opaque". We cannot pattern match or observe the structure of the body of an Abs', or any object-level binding, because they are represented as functions in the meta-language, and meta-level functions are extensional. We can observe this by casting our Term' example above into a simulated evaluation session in Haskell, and noticing that id' prints as Abs' fn.

```
id' = Abs'(\ x -> x);

Main> id
Abs' fn
```

– **Junk.** HOAS admits *junk* [13]. I.e. there are terms in the meta-language with type Term' that do not represent any legal object-program. Consider the example:

```
junk = Abs'(\ x -> case x of
                    App' f y -> y
                  ; Const' n -> x)
```

No legal object-abstraction behaves in this way, analyzing its bound variable.

– **Loss of expressivity.** Using HOAS, there exist meta-functions over object-terms that cannot be expressed. Consider writing a show function for Term' that turns a Term' into a string suitable for printing. What legal meta-program value do we use for ?v ?

```
show (App' f x) = (show f) ++ " " ++ (show x)
show (Const' n) = toString n
show (Abs' g) = "\\ "++ ?v ++ " -> " ++ (show (g ?v))
```

Since g is a Term' to Term' function, we need some sort of "variable" with type Term', to which we can apply g. Unfortunately, no such thing can be created (this was solved in Section 9 by the use of gensym and var). There are other "tricks" for solving this problem [26], but in the end, they only make matters worse.

– **Latent effects.** HOAS delays non-termination and other effects. This problem is especially obvious in a strict language. Computational effects of the meta-language are introduced into the purely syntactic representation of the object language. Even worse, the effects are only introduced when the object-term is observed. If a term is observed multiple times, it causes the effects to be introduced multiple times.

For example, because functions delay computation, a non-terminating computation producing a `Term'` may delay non-termination until the `Term'` object is observed. This may be arbitrarily far from its construction, and can make things very hard to debug. Consider the function `bad`.

```
bad (Const' n) = Const' (n+1)
bad (App' x y) = App'(bad x)(bad y)
bad (Abs' f) = Abs'(\ x -> diverge(bad (f x)))
```

`bad` walks over a `Term'` increasing every explicit constant by one. Suppose the programmer made a mistake and placed an erroneous divergent computation in the `Abs'` clause. Note that `bad` does not immediately diverge.

We believe the trick to representing object-level binding is to use a binding mechanism of the meta-language. I.e. higher-order abstract syntax. The catch 22 – the function (λ) abstraction mechanism is not the right binding mechanism. And, function abstraction is often the *only* binding mechanism the meta-language has. The solution is to introduce a *new* binding mechanism.

Ten years ago Dale Miller informally proposed a simple and elegant extension to SML for supporting higher-order abstract syntax [47] using a new kind of "variable binding" we call *object-level binding*. His proposal illustrated the simplicity and elegance of HOAS as a means for representing object-languages but left the formal semantics, the typing of such a system, and demonstration of its practical usefulness as open problems. We illustrate a variation of Miller's extension as a basis for representing object-languages with binders. We have presented a simple operational semantics for our variation of Miller's language [59,58], where we established that this operational semantics is sound and adequate with respect to a simple, natural reduction semantics. We outline here how object-level binding works.

Consider the lambda calculus example once again. We will use the infix operator (a => b) as both a meta-language term constructor (for our new binding mechanism) and as a type constructor. Using this we define the algebraic datatype `Term2` analogous to `Term'` but using the new object-level binding construct rather than function abstraction.

```
datatype Term2 = App2 Term2 Term2 | Abs2 (Term2 => Term2) | Const2 Int
```

Terms of type (a => b) are introduced using the meta-language construct for object-binding introduction. For example: (#x => App2(#x,Const2 0)) :: (Term2 => Term2). Here we use the convention that hashed variables (#x) denote object-level variables to distinguish them from meta-level variables. This new operator has the following properties:

- **Evaluation under binding.** Latent effects and junk arise because the body of an object-binding is a computation (i.e. a suspended function), rather than a constant piece of data. To solve both these problems, object-level binding evaluates under the binding operator =>. Below are two attempts to construct an object-language program:

```
Abs' (\x -> bottom)                    Abs2 (#x => bottom)
```

The expression on the left (in the `Term'` language) uses a meta-language binding mechanism (λ abstraction). It succeeds in representing an object-language program which obviously has no meaning. The expression on the right (in the `Term2` language), however, does not represent any object-language program, since by our semantics, evaluation proceeds "under" the object-level binding operator and thus never terminates. Note that the effect on the left has seeped into the object-language program representation (junk), while on the right non-termination occurs before the object-language program is constructed and thus is never present in the object-language program itself.

In a lazy setting, the similar problems occur, but they manifest themselves differently. Pattern matching repeatedly against `Abs'` `(\x-> e)` will cause `e` to be re-computed. But pattern matching against `Abs` `(#x => e)` will only evaluate `e` once.

An intuitive way to think about object-level binding, is to think of it having an underlying first order implementation supplied with a rich interface. Inside this first order implementation object-level bindings are represented by pairs. A construction like: `(Abs2 (#x => e))` `:: Term2` is translated into the underlying representation (e.g. `Term`) by using a *gensym* construct to provide a "fresh" name for the required object-bound variable:

```
let y = gensym () in Abs y ((\ #x -> e)(Var y))
```

It is important to emphasize that both the *gensym* and the underlying first-order implementation are hidden from the user. Earlier, we criticized the use of a *gensym* construct since such a construct is stateful, and hence forces our meta-language to be stateful, rather than purely functional. Fortunately, the statefulness of this use of gensym can only be observed if one can observe the value of the name produced by gensym. If the interface to the hidden underlying implementation allows access to variables only in restricted ways, it is possible to mask this statefulness.

- **Higher-order pattern matching.** To solve the problem of opaqueness the new binding mechanism should support higher-order pattern matching. We use a higher-order pattern when we pattern match against a constructor like `Abs` which takes an object-level binding as an argument. Like all patterns, a higher-order pattern "binds" a meta-variable, but the meta-variable bound by a higher-order pattern does not bind to an object-term, but instead binds to a meta-level function with type `Term2 -> Term2`.

  To illustrate this consider the rewrite rule **f** for object-terms `Term2`, which might be expressed as: $\mathbf{f} : \mathtt{Abs2(\#x => App2}\ e'\ \mathtt{(Const2\ 5))} \to (e'[0/\#x])$
  Here, the prime in e' indicates that e is a meta-variable of the rule, and $e'[0/\#x]$ indicates the capture free substitution of `(Const2 0)` for `#x` in e'. The subtlety that e' might have free occurrences of `#x` inside is what higher-order pattern matching makes precise. The bound meta-variable introduced by a higher-order pattern is a function from `Term2 -> Term2`, and this function behaves like the function $\lambda y.e'[y/\#x]$.

We make this idea concrete by extending the notion of pattern in our meta-language. Patterns can now have explicit object-level abstractions, but any pattern-variables inside the body of an object-level abstraction are higher-order pattern-variables, i.e. will bind to functions. Thus the rewrite rule **f** can be specified as follows:

```
f (Abs2(#x => App2(e' #x)(Const2 5))) = e'(Const2 0)
```

In this example the meta-function **f** matches its argument against an object-level abstraction. The body of this abstraction must be an application of a term to the constant 5. The function part of this object-application can be any term. This term may have free occurrences of the object-bound variable (which we write as **#x** in the pattern, but which can have any name in the object-term it matches against). Because of this we use a higher-order pattern (**e' #x**) composed of an application of a meta-variable to an object-bound variable. This application reminds the user that **e'** is a function whose formal parameter is the object-bound variable **#x**. If the underlying implementation is first order (like **Term**), patterns of this form (in **Term2**) have an efficient and decideable implementation, which one could visualize as follows:

```
f (Abs x e) = let e' y = subst [(x,y)] e  in  e' (Const 0)
```

- **Loss of expressivity.** Many simple programs can be expressed simply by using the meta-language construct for object-binding (x => e), to introduce object-variables. For example the identity function over **Term2** can be expressed as:

```
identity (App2 f x) = App2 (identity f) (identity y)
identity (Const2 n) = Const2 n
identity (Abs2(#x => e' #x)) = Abs2(#y => identity (e' #y))
identity (x @ #_) = x
```

The fourth clause of the **identity** function illustrates the pattern matching construct for object-level variables introduced by the x => e operator. Similar to the **isVar** function from Section 9, a pattern (x @ #_) matches against any object-level variable and binds the meta-variable x to the **Term** matched.

It is sometimes necessary to introduce a new object-variable simply as a place holder, and to then eliminate it completely from a computation. This was the problem with the **show** function from Section 13, and the reason for the **gensym** and **var** functions in Section 9. The solution to this problem is a new language construct *discharge*. The construct (**discharge #x => e1**) introduces a new object-level variable (**#x**), whose scope is the body e1. The value of the discharge construct is its body e1. The body e1 can have any type, unlike an object-level binding (**#x => e2**), where e2 must be an object term.

In addition, discharge incurs an obligation that the variable (**#x**) does not appear in the value of the body (**e1**). An implementation must raise an error if this occurs.

For example consider a function which counts the number of **Const2** sub-terms in a **Term2**.

```
count :: Term2 -> Int
count (Const2 _) = 1
count (App2 f x) = (count f) + (count x)
count (Abs2(#x => e' #x)) = discharge #y => count (e' #y)
count #_ = 0
```

Note how the fourth clause conveniently replaces all introduced object-bound variables with 0, thus guaranteeing that no object-variable appears in the result. The obligation that the variable does not escape the body of the discharge construct may require a run-time check (though in this example, since the result has type Int, no such occurrence can happen).

14   FreshML – An Alternative Approach to Binding

In contrast to higher-order abstract syntax approaches, which use the binding mechanisms of the meta-language to represent binding constructs in the object-language, an alternative approach has recently emerged in work of Andrew Pitts and Murdoch J. Gabbay [27,28,63].

Their work is based upon Frankel-Mostovsky set theory (which dates back to the 1930's). They use this theory to model and reason about datatypes that represent first order terms (with variable names) modulo α convertibility. FreshML [27] introduces several language constructs for correctly manipulating such terms, and a type system that ensures that one is indeed manipulating α equivalence classes. Intuitively, their approach resembles a *nameful* version of the well-known "nameless" de Bruijn style of representing binding constructs[21]. The main advantage for the programmer is that the burden of reasoning about (as well as complicated algorithmic interface to) nameless terms is cast into a more user-friendly setting.

We shall present an example of such a language (with slightly modified syntax from [63]), to demonstrate the concepts.

```
data LambdaTerm = Abs of [atm]LambdaTerm
                | App of LambdaTerm * LambdaTerm
                | Var of atm
```

The expression (a.Var a) of type [atm]LambdaTerm denotes an atom abstraction. One can think of an atom abstraction as consisting of a pair of an *atom* (representing an object-variable name) and a lambda term that may contain the name as a subterm.

The language also contains constructs for ensuring "freshness" of atoms with respect to bindings inside terms.

```
val Apply = Abs (x => (Abs (y => App (Var x, Var y))));
```

The term Apply :: LambdaTerm represents the well-known lambda calculus term $\lambda x.\lambda y.x\, y$. We use the a => e construct to build an atom abstraction. The construct introduces a *fresh* atom which is bound to the meta-variable a and the whole construct evaluates to an atom abstraction with type [atm]t if e :: t.

The freshness construct assures that the actual name of the atoms in atom abstractions are irrelevant and can be freely transposed to obtain equivalent values.

The language also supplies facilities for pattern-matching against atom abstractions. Consider the following two examples

```
fun right (Abs (a. App(x,y))) = Abs (a. App(y,x))
fun wrong (Abs (a. App(x,y))) = App(x,Abs (a . y))
```

The function right analyzes a LambdaTerm abstraction. The pattern matching is similar to taking apart a pair. However, the type system ensures that the result of the function is a lambda term which does not depend on the actual name of the object-variable a.

The second function, wrong, is rejected by the type checker because the resulting term may indeed result in terms belonging to different α equivalence classes under different transpositions of the atom a (this happens when the atom, denoted by a occurs as a subterm of x).

Both FreshML and HOAS seek to model classes of α equivalent terms. The FreshML approach has the advantage of a well-formalized set theoretical foundation as well as supporting first-order, datatype-style induction over its terms.

Both HOAS and the FreshML approach lack efficient and robust implementations in a programming language setting with which to experiment.

Open problems in this area include the further development of operational semantics and the development of a calculus for performing equational reasoning.

15   Manipulating Typed Object-Programs

If meta-programmed systems are to gain wider acceptability, especially run-time code generators, then systematic efforts to guarantee safety properties of the object-programs produced must be developed. One example of this is type-safety.

The key to tracking the type-safety of object-programs, by static analysis of the meta-programs that manipulate them, is the embedding of the type of the object-program in the type of object-terms. In MetaML this is straight forward to accomplish. As explained above, a new type constructor (< t >) is used to give every object-level term a *code* type. Because MetaML is a homogeneous system, the type of object-level terms (the t in < t >) can be captured by the same type system used to capture types in the meta-language. The quasi-quotation mechanism can can be exploited to infer the type of the object-language fragments within the meta-language, since both languages have the same structure, and are typed by the same type system. This is a principal design feature of MetaML.

```
-| val x = <3 + 2> ;
val x = <3 %+ 2> : <int>

-| val code = <show ~x> ;
val code = <%show (3 %+ 2)> : <string>
```

Note how x has type <int> (pronounced *code of int*), and code has type <string>. In MetaML the type correctness of a meta-program guarantees the type correctness (as well as the syntactic correctness) of the object-programs it manipulates [74].

16   Polymorphism and Staging

In this section we discuss the interaction of staging with polymorphism. In Hindley-Milner style type inference, let bound variables can be generalized to have polymorphic types. The introduction of staging introduces a new possibility for generalization. Should templates be a new generalization point? Should homogeneous meta-systems be designed such that:

```
< \ x -> x > :: all a . < a -> a>
```

or, should code templates be given rank-2 polymorphic types?

```
< \ x -> x > :: < all a . a -> a>
```

This question has been studied in the context of inferring static types for dynamic documents by Mark Shields in his Ph.D. thesis [71]

In his thesis Shields also studies the interaction of staging with implicit parameters [45]. This is interesting because implicit parameters in a staged context could be interpreted as parameters that will be supplied by the environment that the generated code will execute in. The interaction of staging, implicit parameters, and polymorphism that is discussed there is quite interesting. For example what type should be assigned to the template below:

```
<fn x => ?y x> :: ??
```

The design issues implicit in this problem are quite complex, and beyond the scope of this short synopsis. I refer you to the thesis for full details.

17   Dependently Typed Meta-programs

It is not unusual to have meta-programs which when given different inputs of the same type, produce object-programs with different types. This behavior is usually typed by a dependent type system. For example we might like to write the following meta-program using MetaML style quasi-quotations.

```
f 0 = < () >
f n = <(1, ~(f (n-1)) )>
```

The result of applying f to a few values is given below:

```
f 0 --> < () >
f 1 --> < (1, ()) >
f 2 --> < (1,(1,())) >
```

Each of which has a different type

```
f 0 :: < () >
f 1 :: <(Int,())>
f 2 :: <(Int,(Int,()))>
```

The type of f n depends upon the value of n. One normally indicates this using a Pi type ($\Pi x : t . s$). A Pi type is like a function arrow ($t \to s$), only the type to the right of the dot (s) can depend upon the value of the bound variable (x) to the left of the dot. We can give the function f the dependent type: $\Pi n : Int . <g\ n>$ where the function g is a function from Int to types.

```
g 0 = ()
g n = (Int,g (n-1))
```

In a language with dependent types, programs with dependent types must be given explicit type signatures. These signatures are notoriously difficult to discover and to reason about, so dependent types are not normally used in normal programming languages. Unfortunately, useful meta-programs with dependent types occur all the time. It is an open problem to discover how to mix dependent types and meta-programming in usable manner.

One approach to writing dependently typed meta-programs is to delay some typing till run-time [72]. In this approach the code type constructor (< _ >) is no longer a type constructor, but simply a type (<>). As in MetaML, code is constructed by templates, but the representation of code at run-time carries not only information about the structure of the code, but also information about its type. Each quasi-quoted template (without anti-quotations) can be statically typed, but is assigned the type <>.

```
-| val good = <length [1,2]>
good = <%length [1,2] > :: <>

-| val bad  = <5 0>
Error: The sub term: "5" is not a function.
```

Any use of code, either via run, or via splicing into another piece of code (via anti-quotation), must meet a run-time check that the code is used in a type meaningful context. Thus templates can be statically typed, but splicing and run must wait until run-time for type checking. For example consider an algebraic data type representing the syntax for a simple functional language:

```
data Term = Cnat Nat | Cbool Bool | Var String | Abs String Term
          | App Term Term | Cond Term Term Term | Eq | Plus
```

It is possible to write an interpreter interp :: Term -> Env -> <> where the code constructed is dynamically type checked as it is constructed.

```
interp (Cnat n) env = < n >
interp (Cbool b) env = if b then <True> else <False>
interp (Var s) env = env s
interp (Abs x e) env = <\ y -> ~(interp e (extend e x <y>))>
interp (App f x) env = < ~(interp f env) ~(interp x env) >
interp (Cond x y z) env =
   <if ~(interp x env) then ~(interp y env) else ~(interp z env) >
```

```
interp Eq env = <(==)>
interp Plus env = <(+)>
```

Thus (interp (App (Cnat 5) (Cnat 0)) env) causes a run-time type error, since the code fragment <5> is spliced into a context that requires a function. A similar kind of error can occur when running a piece of code. Thus, the term

```
(0 + (run (interp (Cbool True) env)))
```

causes a run-time error, even though the result of interp is a well typed program (of type Bool), because it is used in a context that requires an Int.

A rich dependent-type system could infer some kinds of errors like these statically. This remains an open problem.

18   Typing Heterogeneous Meta-programs

In heterogeneous systems, the introduction of a simple code type constructor is no longer possible, since the type system of the meta-language may be completely different from the type system needed to type the object-language. Nevertheless, the idea of typing every object-level term with a *type constructor* applied to an argument which encodes the type of the object-level term is a good one. We need to broaden the notion of a legal argument to a type constructor.

Kinds. Functional languages have used the notion of *kind* to make the same fine distinction on types, that types make on values.

type grammar	kind grammar	example types	example kinds

$t \rightarrow$ Int
  | t -> t
  | $[t]$
  | (t, t)
  | Tree t
	$k \rightarrow$ Star
	  | k -k-> k
		5 :: Int
		(5,2) :: (Int, Int)
		\x->x+1 :: Int->Int
		[1,2,3] :: [Int]
		Tip 4 :: Tree Int
			Int :k: Star
			(Int, Int) :k: Star
			Int -> Int :k: Star
			Tree :k: Star -k-> Star
			(->) :k:
			    Star -k->
			        (Star -k-> Star)

In a typed language, types partition the value space into sets of values with similar properties. Kinds partition the type space into sets of types with similar properties. All types that fall in the partition of values have (for historical reasons) kind Star. Example kinds are given in the table above. Because type constructors construct types from types, we give type constructors higher-order kinds. We use -k-> to distinguish the kind arrow from the type arrow, and we use :k: to distinguish the *has kind* relation from ::, the *has type* relation.

For 20 years functional languages have supported extensible type systems. The user can add to the well formed types by defining new types or type-constructors by using algebraic datatype definition facilities. For example, in Haskell, one can add the type constructor Tree by writing:

```
data Tree a = Tip a | Fork (Tree a) (Tree a)
```

Such definitions add the new type constructor (**Tree**) to the grammar of well formed types, and new values such as (**Tip 5**) and (**Fork (Tip 1) (Tip 5)**) to the well formed values.

The addition of extensible kinds as well as extensible types, is one way to attack the problem of object-code types. We will introduce a new kind, that will be an algebraic structure which models the type of object-terms. We will then use this new kind as an index to the object-term type constructor. By writing:

```
datakind T = TypConst | TypPair T T
            -- comment    TypConst :k: T,
            --            TypPair :k: T -k-> T -k-> T
```

We add the new kind **T** to the grammar of well formed kinds, and new types like **TypConst** and (**TypPair TypConst TypConst**) to the grammar of well formed types. But unlike types we are familiar with, types **TypConst** and (**TypPair TypConst TypConst**) have kind **T** rather than kind **Star**. Notice there are no program values with these types. Types with kind other than **Star** are used only to encode the object-level types of object programs.

Indexed Object Types. We have now enriched our type system with sufficient power to encode an object-language type constructor, which takes a T kind as a parameter, indicating the type of the object-term encoded. We call such a type an *indexed type*, where the index set is the set of well-formed type terms of some kind (like **T**).

In order to represent such types, we need to generalize our algebraic datatype definition facility. We do this by explicitly kinding the type (or type constructor) being defined, as well as the full type of each of the datatype's constructor functions. For example the familiar **Tree** definition: data Tree a = Tip a | Fork (Tree a) (Tree a) could be considered as a short hand for the the more verbose, and precise definition below:

```
data Tree :k: Star -k-> Star where
  Tip :: a -> Tree a
  Fork :: Tree a -> Tree a -> Tree a
```

Let's use this power to define an object-language for an expression language with products. Values of this algebraic datatype will have a type which is a type constructor applied to a kind **T**.

```
data Exp :: T -k-> Star where
  ExpConst :: Int -> Exp TypConst
  ExpPair :: Exp a->Exp b->Exp(TypPair a b)
  ExpPi1 :: Exp(TypPair a b) -> Exp a
  Pi2 :: Exp(TypPair a b) -> Exp b
```

$$\frac{x :: a \quad y :: b}{\text{ExpPair } x\, y \; :: \text{TypPair } a\, b}$$

$$\frac{x :: \text{TypPair } a\, b}{\text{ExpPi1 } x \; :: a}$$

Object-languages are usually specified by their syntax (which specifies their form) and by type judgments (which specifies the membership of the set of well formed object-terms). The enriched algebraic datatype definition mechanism in cooperation with the extensible kind mechanism is a very powerful mechanism since it allows us to do both within a single framework. Note how the meanings of the type judgments on the right are captured by the type system of the meta-language in the types of the value constructor functions of the object-type Exp.

It is an open problem to construct a system where any well typed meta-program of type Exp a, is not only a specification of the object-term described, but also a proof that it has object-type a.

Functions over indexed-typed terms. Object-language representations with indexed types can be manipulated with meta-programs in the normal way. The type system of the meta-language will maintain the well typedness of the object-language terms. A simple example is given below.

```
data Value :k: (T -k-> Star) where
  ValConst :: Int -> Value TypConst
  ValPair :: Value a -> Value b -> Value(TypPair a b)


eval :: Exp a -> Value a
eval (ExpConst n) = ValConst n
eval (ExpPair x y) = ValPair (eval x) (eval y)
eval (ExpPi1 x) = case eval x of ValPair a b -> a
eval (ExpPi2 x) = case eval x of ValPair a b -> b
```

Here, we have introduced a second object-language we call Value. A Value is an indexed type with the same index (T) as Exp. The Meta-program eval transforms an Exp a into a Value a.

Meta-programs which manipulate indexed object-level terms need a richer type checking system than those used to type more traditional programs. There are two problems here. First, the function eval can be type checked only if it is given a polymorphically recursive type. In the clause:

```
eval (ExpPair x y) = ValPair (eval x) (eval y)
```

there are 3 occurrences of eval. In the terms

```
eval (ExpPair x y)    eval has type Exp(TypPair a b) -> Value(TypPair a b)
eval x                eval has type Exp a -> Value a
eval y                eval has type Exp b -> Value b
```

Both the second and third instances cannot be reconciled with the first without giving eval a polymorphically recursive type. This has important considerations since type inference of polymorphically recursive functions is not, in general, possible. This means meta-programs which manipulate indexed object-level terms must be given explicit type signatures (like eval :: Exp a -> Value a).

The other problem concerns the way such functions are type checked. Usually, every clause in a multiple clause definition must have exactly the same type. With indexed object-level terms this rule must be relaxed. Study each of the clauses below on the left, and its type on the right.

```
eval (ExpConst n) = ValConst n                    -- eval :: Exp TypConst -> Value TypConst
eval (ExpPair x y) = ValPair (eval x) (eval y)    -- eval :: Exp(TypPair a b) ->
                                                  --             Value(TypPair a b)
eval (ExpPi1 x) = case eval x of ValPair a b -> a -- eval :: Exp c -> Value c
eval (Pi2 x) = case eval x of ValPair a b -> b    -- eval :: Exp d -> Value d
```

Note that the type of the first (`Exp TypConst -> Value TypConst`) and second (`Exp(TypPair a b) -> Value(TypPair a b)`) clause are incompatible and cannot be unified, because the indices (`TypConst` and `(TypPair a b)`) are incompatible. The indexed *type constructors*, are identical, and with out the indexing, each of the clause gives the typing `eval :: Exp -> Value`. Because each clause differs only in its indices, and each indices is instance of the declared indices, and because the clauses are mutually exclusive and exhaustive, typing each clause independently should be a sound mechanism. It is an open problem to find the right combination of type system and theory to prove such a soundness property.

19   Indexed Types and Dependently Typed Programs

In the world of indexed object-terms, there is a special class of programs with dependent types, that are easy to understand and which can be handled quite efficiently: those programs where the dependency is on the index of a type, and not on its value. Such programs can be handled quite easily using a constrained (or qualified) type system.

In a constrained type system, a function f can have a constrained type of the form $\forall a.Ca \Rightarrow a \rightarrow b$. Interpret this as: for all types a which meet the constraint Ca, the function f has type $a \rightarrow b$. The constraint *qualifies* the quantification. Such types are used in the type class system of Haskell [40,41].

A simliar mechanism can be used to track dependencies on indexes. For example, consider an alternative to the `eval` function above, which rather than returning another kind of object-term like `Value`, returns an actual tuple. Note the qualified type of `eval2` below:

```
eval2 :: Encodes a b => Exp a -> b
eval2 (ExpConst n) = n
eval2 (ExpPair x y) = (eval2 x,eval2 y)
eval2 (ExpPi1 x) = case eval2 x of (a,b) -> a
eval2 (ExpPi2 x) = case eval2 x of (a,b) -> b
```

The function `eval2` has a dependent type, since the type of the result depends upon the value of the `Exp` it consumes. This dependency is actually weaker than it seems at first. The type of `eval2` depends only on the index parameter (a in the type `Exp a`), and not on the value. We can express this in the type of `eval2`. Interpret `eval2`'s type as, if the constraint `Encodes a b` is met, then `eval2` takes an `Exp a` as input and produces a value of type `b`.

```
rule Encodes :: T -> Star -> Rule
Encodes TypConst Int
Encodes (TypPair a b) (x,y) <- Encodes a x,
                               Encodes b y
```

`Encodes` is a predicate on types that can be given a simple Prolog-like definition. The constraint `Encodes a b` can be used to track the type dependency of the result of `eval2` on its input.

Tracking dependencies. There is a well understood theory of constraint propagation and management that can be brought to bear on meta-programs such as `eval2` above [40,41]. Consider a defintion of a function `f`.

```
f x y = eval2 x + y
```

In a constrained type system, the constraint `Encodes a b` in the type of `eval2` is propagated by type inference into the type of `f`, which can be given by
`f :: Encodes a Int => Exp a -> Int -> Int`
Further more, using the Prolog-like rules for constraint resolution, we can solve the constraint `Encodes a Int` by unifying a and `TypConst`. Thus we infer the new type `f :: Exp TypConst -> Int -> Int`.
A sound system built upon these ideas would have to answer many questions, and remains an open problem. Recapping, we discussed 4 ways in which we might deal with dependently typed meta-programs:

- First, require full dependent type declarations on all meta-programs and use a language like Cayenne [5] to do the type checking.
- Second, punt. Put off some type checking to run-time [72]. Thus some program errors will only be caught at run-time.
- Third, use extensible kinds to implement indexed types. Use the index to track value information (like the length of a list) in the type of objects. Then the dependency can be on the index and not the value.
- Fourth, extend the third mechanism with qualified types to track more sophisticated dependencies.

20   The Theory of Meta-programs

The foundations for meta-programming systems were laid by the programming language community. Most theoretical so far work has concentrated on meta-programming systems for generating code. Both denotational, operational and type-theoretic treatments abound. In the area of code analyzers there has been considerably less work.

Flemming Nielson and Hanne Nielson [51,52,53,54] have thoroughly studied the denotational semantics and abstract interpretation of two-level languages in the context of compiler design and specification.

The area of partial evaluation has attacked the performance problems of interpreted solutions. Of particular interest to the meta-programming community is the work of of Robert Glück and Jesper Jørgensen [30,31,32]. They study untyped, multi-stage languages in the context of binding time analysis for offline partial evaluation.

Important, early formal investigations into lanuages for staging computation were carried out by Rowan Davies and Frank Pfenning. They studied the *typed multi-stage languages* MiniML$^\square$ [20] and MiniML$^\bigcirc$ [19]. These languages explore type systems (and find connections to intuitionistic modal logic, and linear-time constructive modal logic) for languages with type-constructors for code.

An important work relating these areas is the thesis of Walid Taha [74]. His thesis explains the utility of program generation in general and the importance of a type-safety guarantee in a generation paradigm. The thesis explains in detail, the difficulties that arise in specifying a mathematical semantics of staged programs, and then presents one along with two proofs.

The first proof justifies the claim that only type safe programs are ever generated. This proof is a "subject reduction" proof. A key technical contribution of the work provides a type system where the generated code can also be "run" or executed in the same framework where the code was constructed. Taha's thesis explains how MetaML [80] combines features of both MiniML$^{\Box}$ and MiniML$^{\bigcirc}$ together with other useful features. This is an important generalization from the work of Davies and Pfenning. Such a guarantee is highly desirable in a system with run-time code generation.

In addition to the type-saftey properties, Taha's work is the first to provide an equational theory for a staged programming language [76]. This theory can be used to prove equivalencies between two staged programs, or between a normal program and its staged (or partially evaluated) counterpart. Taha's equational theory is built upon an equivalence proof between a small-step reduction semantics, and operational big-step semantics.

Taha's reduction semantics relies only on the standard notion of substitution, and unlike much of the earlier work[2], does not need any additional machinery for performing renaming at "run-time". This insight is a major advance in the theory of program generators. It opens the way to using standard techniques for manipulating program generators as formal objects.

In addition to Taha's thesis much work was done in improving the preciseness of type systems for MetaML [79,80,81]. These type systems and are designed to prevent *phase errors*, i.e., situations when values are used at a stage prior to their definition (as illustrated in Section 7).

Other papers [49,75,77,78,79] develop reduction and natural semantics for MetaML and prove important properties about them. Denotational semantics of MetaML from the perspective of categorical analysis were studied by Eugenio Moggi, Tim Sheard, Walid Taha and Zine El-Abidine Benaissa [9,10,48] yielding a semantics and a class of categorical models for MetaML.

Motivated by the categorical analysis, the same group did a more rigorous formulation of MetaML, supporting both open and closed code [50]. A theoretical study of multi-stage imperative programming languages has been undertaken by Christiano Calgano, Eugenio Moggi and Walid Taha [14]. They study operational semantics and type systems for a language that safely combines imperative state with multi-stage programming.

Practical applications of these semantic approaches to meta-programming systems have yet to bear much fruit. They supply a firm foundation, but the engineering work necessary to realizing robust implementations for staged programming languages has yet to be done.

---

[2] Notable exceptions are MiniML$^{\Box}$ and MiniML$^{\bigcirc}$.

21   Building Good Implementations

Meta-programming in general, and staged programming in particular is an important way to think about computation. For a long time we have been hampered in our attempts to promote this view of computation because of a lack of vocabulary: we lack running systems that treat object-computations in a first class manner. The challenge of building robust implementations of program generation systems remains. A few attempts have been made, but none has really caught the attention of the community at large.

MetaML: A First Attempt. The MetaML interpreter is an attempt to provide a tool where representations of programs (called `code`) are first class objects. MetaML is an *excellent tool for demonstrating that meta-computation can be expressed at a high-level of abstraction in a type-safe manner*, but it is still an interpreter, the code it produces is too slow, and it cannot interact with other languages or systems.

From this exercise in staged language implementation, I have learned many valuable lessons. Not the least of those is that building any system, polishing it so that other people may use it, and supporting it, is a huge amount of work. MetaML is the largest system I have ever worked on, yet in many respects it is still a toy.

Despite these limitations building MetaML has been an extremely valuable experience which is worth sharing. Some of the important lessons learned while building the MetaML system are summarized below.

– **Homogeneous System.** MetaML is a homogeneous system because both the meta-language and the object-language are the same. Homogeneity plays an important role in many aspects of MetaML, but experience has shown that heterogeneous systems also have an important role to play. A heterogeneous system with a fixed meta-language, in which it is possible to build multiple systems each with a different object-language, or one system with multiple object-languages would be equally useful.
– **Template Based Presentation.** MetaML constructs object-code using pattern-based object-code templates. Templates "look like" the object language they represent. Program fragments are easy to combine into larger program fragments using templates with "holes". Templates make MetaML really easy to use to construct object-programs. Much remains to be done to use templates to pattern match against code when deconstructing object-programs.
– **Explicit Annotations.** Manually placing staging annotations is not a burden when supported by a quasi-quote presentation. Manually annotated programs are within a few percent of their non-staged versions. Annotations should me semantically meaningful, not just ad-hoc suggestions to the compiler or preprocessor. If you cannot define precisely what they mean, then their implementation will certainly be problematic.
– **Staged Generators.** MetaML is an N-stage meta-programming *generation* system. MetaML produces code generators. MetaML generators pro-

duce object-code as output, which itself can be another generator in a future stage. There is no limit to the number of stages in a MetaML program. This has been useful theoretically, but has found very little practical use. Programmers find it hard to write programs with more than a few stages.

- **Intensional analysis of code.** MetaML was *not* designed to produce code analyzers, but the ability to analyze the internal structure of code objects is an important capability that should be designed into any meta-programming system. Analysis of code is important even in the domain of program generation, since it allows generators to optimize code as it is generated.

- **Static Scoping.** MetaML handles free variables in object-code templates by building code where the *free* variables obey the rules of static scoping. Variables free in a template are bound in the scope where the template appears, not in the scope where the resulting code is executed. MetaML also handles *bound* variables in object-code templates in a way which guarantees no name clashes (inadvertent variable capture).

- **Type Safety.** In MetaML type-safe meta-programs are guaranteed to manipulate and produce only type-safe object-programs. This is the most important lesson learned. Writing meta-programs is hard. There are too many dimensions in which it is possible to introduce errors. Tools, such as object-level typing, which help the programmer in this task are worth their weight in gold.

- **Observability.** Object-programs can be observed and printed. This is essential for debugging of meta-programs. In MetaML object-programs are pretty-printed in the manner in which they are normally written by programmers. They are not represented by some abstract representation unfamiliar to the meta-programmer.

- **Reflection.** In MetaML object-programs can be constructed, typed, and run, all in a single system. This ability to test generated code without leaving the meta-system is a great boon to programmers. Such a facility ought to be made available in any meta-programming system, even a heterogeneous system. The meta-language ought to embed an interpreter for the object-language to facilitate object-language testing.

Other attempts have emphasized different aspects of the code generation paradigm. In particular speed is an important concern of most other run-time generation systems. There is a tradeoff in this dimension, one can either generate code quickly or generate code that runs fast. Techniques which support one of these strategies often get in the way of addressing the other.

There is basically two strategies to achieving run-time code generation. Either generate source code (or some abstraction of it) at run-time, or generate machine code directly at run-time.

The first can be implemented in a straightforward manner using a *run-time compiler*. This lends itself to post-processing phases such as code transformations and register allocation. Since such processing requires time, the goal of generating code quickly is thwarted. It also requires larger run-time systems as the whole compiler must always be available.

Generating machine code directly is more complex, but potentially quicker to perform, since an intermediate step is not required. Unfortunately important optimizations like register allocation are harder to perform under this scheme. Generating machine code is hard to make generic and cross platform compatible since the machine architecture is intimately involved in the code generation phase.

Other issues to be addressed include allocation and garbage collection for generated code (constructing generated code of an unknown and unbounded size, and collecting generated code when its no longer needed). Most garbage collection systems are designed to collect data only, not code, which are often resident in different portions of memory[3]. In a staged system the maxim that *code is data* was never more true.

One problem with run-time code generation is that different kinds of variables (let bound, lambda bound, global, external) often use different access methods depending on the kind of variable (they may reside on the stack, in the heap, or in a register). Keeping track of all this at run-time is difficult, and general purpose solutions that work for all kinds of variables often introduce inefficiencies.

In this light we discuss several dynamic code generation systems.

- **'C and tcc.** 'C (pronounced Tick C), and its compiler tcc [25,64] were designed to generate C code at run-time. 'C is a two-stage language with no type system at the object-level. It uses a template based approach to construct object-level C code in an implementation independent manner. A goal of 'C is to generate code quickly, yet still generate code that runs fast. They claim that tcc "generates code at a rate on the order of 60-600 instructions per generated instruction, depending on the level of dynamic optimization employed." A sophisticated run-time register allocation scheme is used [65] to increase the performance of the generated code.
- **Tempo.** Tempo [17] is a large project investigating the use of partial evaluation strategies on C code. One aspect of the Tempo is dynamic code generation via specialization [18,55]. This capability is relies on the binding time analysis of the C partial evaluator. Given the static parameters as input, the dynamic code generation partitions the C code into two stages. The static stages are compiled in the normal fashion, and the dynamic stages are reduced to code templates. Each template is compiled to a sequence of instructions that generates code at run-time.

  In Tempo the staging is performed in a semiautomatic manner by the BTA. The Tempo implementation is strongly tied to the code generation capabilities of the Gnu C Compiler, and is not very portable. A strong advantage of the Tempo system is its ability to be applied to an existing code base.
- **The Dynamo Project.** The Dynamo [11,12] project works on implementing an infrastructure for building programs with *dynamic optimizations* which use run-time information unavailable to static optimizers, to perform further optimizations on a program as it is executing.

---

[3] An exception to this is: SML/NJ, that collects code since code is allocated in the heap.

The *Dynamo* compiler is broken down into a number of stages. User annotations determine which stages are run statically (at compile-time) or dynamically (at run-time) for each annotated code fragment. Thus the user can make specific tradeoffs of speed vs. time, or space vs. time depending upon which stages of the compiler are delayed until run-time.

Each stage uses a different run-time representations of code, each of which is better suited to certain kinds of optimizations. Annotations (somewhat ad-hoc in nature) are placed by the programmer. These annotations, together (potentially) with profiling information, are used to decide which representation of code should be used for what particular piece of source program, and when it will (finally) be fully compiled.

- **Fabius.** Fabius [42,43,44] is a compiler for a staged language. Fabius uses explicit annotations to stage a program in an ML-like language. The staging annotations of Fabius are based upon the type systems devised by Frank Pfenning and Rowan Davies [20,19]. Other than MetaML, Fabius is the only dynamic code generator that types object-level code.
- **The UW Dynamic Compilation Project.** DyC [34,6,35] is a C based dynamic compilation system. In DyC regions of code are marked for specialization, and variables in those regions are declared either dynamic or static. An analysis then determines which code can be compiled at compile-time, and which code must be deferred for run-time compilation. Regions can be nested or even overlap.

Annotations can be provided by the programmer to control a number of tradeoffs in both space and time. Implementations have been generated for a number of different architectures

22   Applications of Meta-programming

Recently I have worked on, or read about several interesting applications of meta-programming techniques which I think are worth mentioning.

- **Macro design.** Macros are an application of staged programming, because macros define computation intended to run at compile-time. Most macro systems have been string based (except for the LISP and Scheme macro systems) and have been designed to run before type checking. Macros have also traditionally been used to define *new* binding constructs. This use is beyond the scope of the meta-systems discussed in this note. Recently, Steven Ganz, Amr Sabry, and Walid Taha have designed a macro system that is both strongly typed, and capable of introducing new binding constructs [29]. They do this by providing a translation of their macro language into a two stage MetaML program.
- **Language implementation.** Staged programming, combined with monads, can be used to implement Domain Specific Languages [70]. Staging a semantics-based interpreter produces a compiler for the language interpreted. Monads complement staging by describing control structure and effects in a manner that is orthogonal to the staging issues present in compiler

implementation. The equational logic of MetaML can be used to prove that the compiled code produces the same outputs as the non-staged reference interpreter.

- **Dynamically adaptable software.** Staged programming has recently used to specify adaptive systems that, based on profiling information gathered at run-time, can recompile themselves to adapt better to their current running environment [37]. MetaML's staging annotation allow the programmer to express this rather difficult concept at a very high-level of abstraction that frees the user completely from the minutiae of runtime code generation.

- **Interacting with other systems.**
  Generators are often designed to generate code for a single environment. How do we build meta-systems with the ability to produce object-programs that interact with differing environments? The environment of a program generator is often a fixed, legacy system, and beyond the clients control. Wouldn't it be nice to construct a generator that could be configured to generate code for multiple environments? Norman Ramsey has recently written a clear exposition of the many interesting issues that need to be addressed when building such a system [68].

23   Conclusion

I hope that these notes inspire discussion, research, and implementation efforts in the field of meta-programming.

References

1. A. Aasa. *User Defined Syntax.* PhD thesis, Chalmers University, Dept of Computer Science, Chalmers University, Sweden, 1992.
2. A. Aasa. Precedence for conc types. In *FPCA'93: Conference on Functional Programming Languages and Computer Architecture, Copenhagen, Denmark,* pages 83–91, New York, June 1993. ACM Press.
3. A. Aasa, K. Petersson, and D. Synek. Concrete syntax for data objects in functional languages. In *Proceedings of the 1988 ACM Conference on LISP and Functional Programming,* pages 96–105. ACM, ACM, July 1988.
4. M. Abadi and L. Cardelli. An imperative object calculus (invited paper). *Theory and Practice of Object Sytems,* 1(3):151–166, 1995.
5. L. Augustsson. Cayenne — a language with dependent types. *ACM SIGPLAN Notices,* 34(1):239–250, Jan. 1999.
6. J. Auslander, M. Philipose, C. Chambers, S. J. Eggers, and B. N. Bershad. Fast, effective dynamic compilation. In *Proceedings of the ACM SIGPLAN '96 Conference on Programming Language Design and Implementation,* pages 149–159, Philadelphia, Pennsylvania, May 1996.
7. B. Barras, S. Boutin, C. Cornes, J. Courant, J. Filliatre, E. Giménez, H. Herbelin, G. Huet, C. M. noz, C. Murthy, C. Parent, C. Paulin, A. Saïbi, and B. Werner. The Coq Proof Assistant Reference Manual – Version V6.1. Technical Report 0203, INRIA, August 1997.

8. A. Bawden. Quasiquotation in LISP (invited talk). In *ACM SIGPLAN Workshop on Partial Evaluation and Semantics-Based Program Manipulation*, pages 4–12. ACM, BRICS Notes Series, january 1999.

9. Z. E.-A. Benaissa, E. Moggi, W. Taha, and T. Sheard. A categorical analysis of multi-level languages (extended abstract). Technical Report CSE-98-018, Department of Computer Science, Oregon Graduate Institute, Dec. 1998. Available from [56].

10. Z. E.-A. Benaissa, E. Moggi, W. Taha, and T. Sheard. Logical modalities and multi-stage programming. In *Federated Logic Conference (FLoC) Satellite Workshop on Intuitionistic Modal Logics and Applications (IMLA)*, July 1999. To appear.

11. R. G. Burger. *Efficient Compilation and Profile-Driven Dynamic Recompilation in Scheme*. PhD thesis, Indiana University Computer Science Department, March 1997.

12. R. G. Burger and R. K. Dybvig. An infrastructure for profile-driven dynamic recompilation. In *Proceedings of the 1998 International Conference on Computer Languages*, pages 240–249. IEEE Computer Society Press, 1998.

13. R. Burstall and J. Goguen. An informal introduction to specifications using Clear. In R. Boyer and J. Moore, editors, *The Correctness Problem in Computer Science*, pages 185–213. Academic, 1981. Reprinted in *Software Specification Techniques*, Narain Gehani and Andrew McGettrick, editors, Addison-Wesley, 1985, pages 363–390.

14. C. Calcagno, E. Moggi, and W. Taha. Closed types as a simple approach to safe imperative multi-stage programming. In *Automata, Languages and Programming*, pages 25–36, 2000.

15. R. Carnap. *The Logical Syntax of Language*. Kegan Paul, Trench and Trubner, 1937.

16. A. Church. A formulation of the simple theory of types. *Journal of Symbolic Logic*, 5:56–68, 1940.

17. Consel, Hornof, Marlet, Muller, Thibault, and Volanschi. Tempo: specializing systems applications and beyond. *CSURVES: Computing Surveys Electronic Section*, 30, 1998.

18. C. Consel and F. Noël. A general approach for run-time specialization and its application to C. In *Conference Record of POPL '96: The 23rd ACM SIGPLAN-SIGACT Symposium on Principles of Programming Languages*, pages 145–156, St. Petersburg Beach, Florida, 21–24 Jan. 1996.

19. R. Davies. A temporal-logic approach to binding-time analysis. In *Proceedings, 11th Annual IEEE Symposium on Logic in Computer Science*, pages 184–195, New Brunswick, July 1996. IEEE Computer Society Press.

20. R. Davies and F. Pfenning. A modal analysis of staged computation. In *23rd Annual ACM Symposium on Principles of Programming Languages (POPL'96)*, pages 258–270, St. Petersburg Beach, Jan. 1996.

21. N. G. de Bruijn. Lambda-calculus notation with nameless dummies: a tool for automatic formula manipulation with application to the Church-Rosser theorem. *Indag. Math.*, 34(5):381–392, 1972.

22. R. K. Dybvig. From macrogeneration to syntactic abstraction. *Higher-Order and Symbolic Computation*, 13(1–2):57–63, Apr. 2000.

23. R. K. Dybvig, R. Hieb, and C. Bruggeman. Syntactic abstraction in Scheme. *LISP and Symbolic Computation*, 5(4):295–326, Dec. 1992.

24. C. M. Elliott. *Extensions and Applications of Higher-Order Unification*. PhD thesis, School of Computer Science, Carnegie Mellon University, May 1990. Available as Technical Report CMU-CS-90-134.

25. D. R. Engler, W. C. Hsieh, and M. F. Kaashoek. 'C: A language for efficient, machine-independent dynamic code generation. In *Proceedings of the 23rd ACM SIGPLAN-SIGACT Symposium on Principles of Programming Languages (POPL '96)*, pages 131–144, St. Petersburg Beach, Florida, January 1996. An earlier version is available as MIT-LCS-TM-526.

26. L. Fegaras and T. Sheard. Revisiting catamorphisms over datatypes with embedded functions (or, programs from outer space). In *Conf. Record 23rd ACM SIGPLAN/SIGACT Symp. on Principles of Programming Languages, POPL'96, St. Petersburg Beach, FL, USA, 21–24 Jan 1996*, pages 284–294. ACM Press, New York, 1996.

27. M. Gabbay and A. Pitts. A new approach to abstract syntax involving binders. In G. Longo, editor, *Proceedings of the 14th Annual Symposium on Logic in Computer Science (LICS'99)*, pages 214–224, Trento, Italy, July 1999. IEEE Computer Society Press.

28. M. J. Gabbay. *Theory of Inductive Definitions With α-equivalence: Semantics, Implementation, Programming Language*. PhD thesis, Cambridge University, 2000.

29. S. E. Ganz, A. Sabry, and W. Taha. Macros as multi-stage computations: Type-safe, generative, binding macros in macroml. In *Proceedings of the ACM SIGPLAN International Conference on Functional Programming (ICFP-2001)*, New York, September 2001. ACM Press.

30. R. Glück and J. Jørgensen. Efficient multi-level generating extensions for program specialization. In S. D. Swierstra and M. Hermenegildo, editors, *Programming Languages: Implementations, Logics and Programs (PLILP'95)*, volume 982 of *Lecture Notes in Computer Science*, pages 259–278. Springer-Verlag, 1995.

31. R. Glück and J. Jørgensen. Fast binding-time analysis for multi-level specialization. In D. Bjørner, M. Broy, and I. V. Pottosin, editors, *Perspectives of System Informatics*, volume 1181 of *Lecture Notes in Computer Science*, pages 261–272. Springer-Verlag, 1996.

32. R. Glück and J. Jørgensen. An automatic program generator for multi-level specialization. *LISP and Symbolic Computation*, 10(2):113–158, 1997.

33. M. J. C. Gordon and T. F. Melham. *Introduction to HOL: A theorem proving environment for higher order logic*. Cambridge University Press, 1993.

34. Grant, Mock, Philipose, Chambers, and Eggers. DyC: An expressive annotation-directed dynamic compiler for C. *TCS: Theoretical Computer Science*, 248, 2000.

35. B. Grant, M. Philipose, M. Mock, C. Chambers, and S. J. Eggers. An evaluation of staged run-time optimizations in DyC. In *Proceedings of the ACM SIGPLAN '99 Conference on Programming Language Design and Implementation*, pages 293–304, Atlanta, Georgia, May 1–4, 1999.

36. R. Harper, F. Honsell, and G. Plotkin. A framework for defining logics. In *Proceedings Symposium on Logic in Computer Science*, pages 194–204, Washington, June 1987. IEEE Computer Society Press. The conference was held at Cornell University, Ithaca, New York.

37. B. Harrison and T. Sheard. Dynamically adaptable software with metacomputations in a staged language. In *Proceedings of the Workshop on Semantics, Applications and Implementation of Program Generation (SAIG'01)*, September 2001. Appearing in this proceedings.

38. L. Hornof and T. Jim. Certifying compilation and run-time code generation. *Higher-Order and Symbolic Computation*, 12(4):337–375, Dec. 1999.

39. S. Johnson. Yacc – yet another compiler compiler. Technical Report 32, Bell Labs, 1975.

40. M. P. Jones. *Qualified Types: Theory and Practice*. Programming Research Group, Oxford University, July 1992.
41. M. P. Jones. A theory of qualified types. In B. Krieg-Bruckner, editor, *ESOP '92, 4th European Symposium on Programming, Rennes, France, February 1992, Proceedings*, volume 582 of *Lecture Notes in Computer Science*, pages 287–306. Springer-Verlag, New York, NY, 1992.
42. P. Lee and M. Leone. Optimizing ML with run-time code generation. In *SIGPLAN '96 Conference on Programming Language Design and Implementation*, pages 137–148, 1996.
43. M. Leone and P. Lee. Lightweight run-time code generation. In *Partial Evaluation and Semantics-Based Program Manipulation, Orlando, Florida, June 1994 (Technical Report 94/9, Department of Computer Science, University of Melbourne)*, pages 97–106, 1994.
44. M. Leone and P. Lee. Dynamic specialization in the Fabius system. *ACM Computing Surveys*, 30(3es):??–??, Sept. 1998. Article 23.
45. J. R. Lewis, J. Launchbury, E. Meijer, and M. Shields. Implicit parameters: Dynamic scoping with static types. In *Proceedings of the 27th ACM SIGPLAN-SIGACT Symposium on Principles of Programming Languages (POLP-00)*, pages 108–118, N.Y., Jan. 19–21 2000. ACM Press.
46. H. Massalin. *Synthesis: An Efficient Implementation of Fundamental Operating System Services*. PhD thesis, Columbia University, 1992.
47. D. Miller. An extension to ML to handle bound variables in data structures: Preliminary report. In *Informal Proceedings of the Logical Frameworks BRA Workshop*, June 1990. Available as UPenn CIS technical report MS-CIS-90-59.
48. E. Moggi. Functor categories and two-level languages. In *FoSSaCS '98*, volume 1378 of *Lecture Notes in Computer Science*. Springer Verlag, 1998.
49. E. Moggi, W. Taha, Z. Benaissa, and T. Sheard. An idealized MetaML: Simpler, and more expressive. In *European Symposium on Programming (ESOP)*, volume 1576 of *Lecture Notes in Computer Science*, pages 193–207. Springer-Verlag, 1999.
50. E. Moggi, W. Taha, Z. El-Abidine Benaissa, and T. Sheard. An idealized MetaML: Simpler, and more expressive. *Lecture Notes in Computer Science*, 1576:193–207, 1999.
51. F. Nielson. Program transformations in a denotational setting. *ACM Trans. Prog. Lang. Syst.*, 7(3):359–379, July 1985.
52. F. Nielson. Correctness of code generation from a two-level meta-language. In B. Robinet and R. Wilhelm, editors, *Proceedings of the European Symposium on Programming (ESOP 86)*, volume 213 of *Lecture Notes in Computer Science*, pages 30–40, Saarbrücken, Mar. 1986. Springer.
53. F. Nielson. Two-level semantics and abstract interpretation. *Theoretical Computer Science*, 69(2):117–242, Dec. 1989.
54. F. Nielson and H. R. Nielson. Two-level semantics and code generation. *Theoretical Computer Science*, 56(1):59–133, Jan. 1988.
55. F. Noël, L. Hornof, C. Consel, and J. L. Lawall. Automatic, template-based runtime specialization: Implementation and experimental study. In *Proceedings of the 1998 International Conference on Computer Languages*, pages 132–142. IEEE Computer Society Press, 1998.
56. Oregon Graduate Institute Technical Reports. P.O. Box 91000, Portland, OR 97291-1000,USA. Available online from ftp://cse.ogi.edu/pub/tech-reports/README.html. Last viewed August 1999.
57. L. C. Paulson. Isabelle: The next 700 theorem provers. In P. Odifreddi, editor, *Logic and Computer Science*, pages 361–386. Academic Press, 1990.

58. E. Pašalić, T. Sheard, and W. Taha. DALI: An untyped, CBV functional language supporting first-order datatypes with binders (technical development). Submitted to ICFP2000.

59. E. Pašalić, T. Sheard, and W. Taha. DALI: An untyped, CBV functional language supporting first-order datatypes with binders (technical development). Technical Report CSE-00-007, OGI, 2000. Available from [56].

60. F. Pfenning. Elf: A language for logic definition and verified meta-programming. In *Fourth Annual Symposium on Logic in Computer Science*, pages 313–322, Pacific Grove, California, June 1989. IEEE Computer Society Press.

61. F. Pfenning. Logic programming in the LF logical framework. In G. Huet and G. Plotkin, editors, *Logical Frameworks*, pages 149–181. Cambridge University Press, 1991.

62. F. Pfenning and C. Schürmann. System description: Twelf — A meta-logical framework for deductive systems. In H. Ganzinger, editor, *Proceedings of the 16th International Conference on Automated Deduction (CADE-16)*, volume 1632 of *LNAI*, pages 202–206, Berlin, July 7–10, 1999. Springer-Verlag.

63. A. M. Pitts and M. J. Gabbay. A metalanguage for programming with bound names modulo renaming. In R. Backhouse and J. N. Oliveira, editors, *Mathematics of Program Construction. 5th International Conference, MPC2000, Ponte de Lima, Portugal, July 2000. Proceedings*, volume 1837 of *Lecture Notes in Computer Science*, pages 230–255. Springer-Verlag, Heidelberg, 2000.

64. M. Poletto, W. C. Hsieh, D. R. Engler, and M. F. Kaashoek. 'C and tcc: A language and compiler for dynamic code generation. *ACM Transactions on Programming Languages and Systems*, 21(2):324–369, March 1999.

65. M. Poletto and V. Sarkar. Linear scan register allocation. *ACM Transactions on Programming Languages and Systems*, 21(5):895–913, September 1999.

66. R. Pollack. *The Theory of LEGO: A Proof Checker for the Extended Calculus of Constructions*. PhD thesis, University of Edinburgh, 1994.

67. C. Pu, H. Massalin, and J. Ioannidis. The synthesis kernel. *Usenix Journal, Computing Systems*, 1(1):11, Winter 1988.

68. N. Ramsey. Pragmatic aspects of reusable software generators. In *Proceedings of the Workshop on Semantics, Applications and Implementation of Program Generation (SAIG)*, pages 149–171, September 2000. Workshop held in collaboration with the International Conference on Functional Programming (ICFP).

69. T. Sheard. Using MetaML: A staged programming language. *Lecture Notes in Computer Science*, 1608:207–??, 1999.

70. T. Sheard, Z. Benaissa, and E. Pasalic. Dsl implementation using staging and monads. In *Second Conference on Domain-Specific Languages (DSL'99)*, Austin, Texas, October 1999. USEUNIX.

71. M. Shields. *Static Types for Dynamic Documents*. PhD thesis, Department of Computer Science, Oregon Graduate Institute, Feb. 2001. Available at http://www.cse.ogi.edu/~mbs/pub/thesis/thesis.ps.

72. M. Shields, T. Sheard, and S. P. Jones. Dynamic typing through staged type inference. In *Proceedings of the 25th ACM SIGPLAN-SIGACT Symposium on Principles of Programming Languages*, pages 289–302, Jan. 1998.

73. G. L. Steele, Jr. and R. P. Gabriel. The evolution of LISP. *ACM SIGPLAN Notices*, 28(3):231–270, 1993.

74. W. Taha. *Multi-Stage Programming: Its Theory and Applications*. PhD thesis, Oregon Graduate Institute of Science and Technology, July 1999. Revised October 99. Available from author (taha@cs.chalmers.se).

75. W. Taha. A sound reduction semantics for untyped CBN multi-stage computation: Or, the theory of MetaML is non-trivial. In *Proceedings of the 2000 ACM SIGPLAN Workshop on Evaluation and Semantics-Based Program Manipulation (PEPM-00)*, pages 34–43, N.Y., Jan. 22–23 2000. ACM Press.

76. W. Taha. A sound reduction semantics for untyped CBN mutli-stage computation. Or, the theory of MetaML is non-trivial. In *2000 SIGPLAN Workshop on Partial Evaluation and Semantics-Based Program Maniplation (PEPM'00)*, Jan. 2000.

77. W. Taha, Z.-E.-A. Benaissa, and T. Sheard. Multi-stage programming: Axiomatization and type-safety. In *25th International Colloquium on Automata, Languages, and Programming*, volume 1443 of *Lecture Notes in Computer Science*, pages 918–929, Aalborg, July 1998.

78. W. Taha, Z.-E.-A. Benaissa, and T. Sheard. Multi-stage programming: Axiomatization and type safety. Technical Report CSE-98-002, Oregon Graduate Institute, 1998. Available from [56].

79. W. Taha and T. Sheard. Multi-stage programming with explicit annotations. In *Proceedings of the ACM-SIGPLAN Symposium on Partial Evaluation and semantic based program manipulations PEPM'97, Amsterdam*, pages 203–217. ACM, 1997. An extended and revised version appears in [81].

80. W. Taha and T. Sheard. MetaML and multi-stage programming with explicit annotations. Technical Report CSE-99-007, Department of Computer Science, Oregon Graduate Institute, Jan. 1999. Extended version of [79]. Available from [56].

81. W. Taha and T. Sheard. MetaML: Multi-stage programming with explicit annotations. *Theoretical Computer Science*, 248(1-2), 2000. Revised version of [80].

82. S. Thibault, C. Consel, and G. Muller. Safe and efficient active network programming. In *Seventeenth IEEE Symposium on Reliable Distributed Systems (SRDS '98)*, pages 135–143, Washington - Brussels - Tokyo, Oct. 1998. IEEE.

83. W. van Orman Quine. *Mathematical Logic*. Harvard University Press, Cambridge, 2 edition, 1974.

A Semantics for Advice and Dynamic Join Points in Aspect-Oriented Programming
Abstract of Invited Talk

Mitchell Wand*

College of Computer Science
Northeastern University
360 Huntington Avenue, 161CN
Boston, MA 02115, USA
wand@ccs.neu.edu
http://www.ccs.neu.edu/home/wand

A characteristic of aspect-oriented programming [KLM+97], as embodied in AspectJ [KHH+01], is the use of *advice* to incrementally modify the behavior of a base program. An advice expression specifies an action to be taken whenever some condition arises during the course of execution of the base program. A typical condition might be

```
pcalls(f) && pwithin(g) && cflow(pcalls(h)).
```

This indicates that the piece of advice is to be executed at every call to procedure f from within the text of procedure g, but only when that call occurs dynamically within a call to procedure h. Such a condition is *dynamic* in that it is in general not statically determinable.

We present a model of dynamic join points, pointcut designators, and advice. We introduce a tractable minilanguage embodying these features and give it a denotational semantics.

This work is part of the Aspect Sandbox (ASB) project. The goal of ASB to produce an experimental workbench for aspect-oriented programming removed from the complications of Java. ASB includes a small base language and will include a set of exemplars of different approaches to AOP. The work reported here is a model of one of those exemplars, namely dynamic join points and advice with dynamic weaving. We hope to extend this work to other AOP models, including static join points, Demeter [Lie96], and Hyper/J [OT00], and to other models of weaving.

This work is joint with Gregor Kiczales, Christopher Dutchyn, and Benjamin Leperchey.

References

KHH+01. Gregor Kiczales, Erik Hilsdale, Jim Hugunin, Mik Kersen, Jeffrey Palm, and William G. Griswold. An overview of AspectJ. In *ECOOP '01*, 2001. to appear.

* Work supported by the National Science Foundation under grant number CCR-9804115.

© Springer-Verlag Berlin Heidelberg 2001

KLM⁺97. Gregor Kiczales, John Lamping, Anurag Menhdhekar, Chris Maeda, Cristina Lopes, Jean-Marc Loingtier, and John Irwin. Aspect-oriented programming. In Mehmet Akşit and Satoshi Matsuoka, editors, *ECOOP '97 — Object-Oriented Programming 11th European Conference, Jyväskylä, Finland*, volume 1241, pages 220–242. Springer-Verlag, Berlin, Heidelberg, and New York, 1997.

Lie96.   Karl J. Lieberherr. *Adaptive Object-Oriented Software: The Demeter Method with Propagation Patterns.* PWS Publishing Company, 1996.

OT00.   Harold Ossher and Peri Tarr. Hyper/J: multi-dimensional separation of concerns for Java. In *Proceedings of the 22nd International Conference on Software Engineering, June 4-11, 2000, Limerick, Ireland*, pages 734–737, 2000.

Short Cut Fusion: Proved and Improved

Patricia Johann

Department of Mathematics and Computer Science
Dickinson College, Carlisle, PA 17013 USA
johannp@dickinson.edu

Abstract. *Short cut fusion* is a particular program transformation technique which uses a single, local transformation — called the `foldr-build` rule — to remove certain intermediate lists from modularly constructed functional programs. Arguments that short cut fusion is correct typically appeal either to intuition or to "free theorems" — even though the latter have not been known to hold for the languages supporting higher-order polymorphic functions and fixed point recursion in which short cut fusion is usually applied. In this paper we use Pitts' recent demonstration that contextual equivalence in such languages is relationally parametric to prove that programs in them which have undergone short cut fusion are contextually equivalent to their unfused counterparts. The same techniques in fact yield a much more general result. For each algebraic data type we define a generalization `augment` of `build` which constructs substitution instances of its associated data structures. Together with the well-known generalization `cata` of `foldr` to arbitrary algebraic data types, this allows us to formulate and prove correct for each a contextual equivalence-preserving `cata-augment` fusion rule. These rules optimize compositions of functions that uniformly consume algebraic data structures with functions that uniformly produce substitution instances of them.

1 Introduction

Fusion [4,5,6,17,15] is the process of removing certain intermediate data structures from modularly constructed functional programs. *Short cut fusion* [4,5] is a particular fusion technique which uses a single, local transformation rule — called the `foldr-build` rule — to fuse compositions of list-processing functions. The `foldr-build` rule is so named because it requires list-consuming and -producing functions to be written in terms of the program constructs `foldr` and `build`, respectively.

Short cut fusion successfully fuses a wide variety of list-processing programs, but its applicability is limited because list-producing functions cannot always be usefully expressed in terms of `build`. This observation led Gill [4] to introduce another construct, called `augment`, which generalizes `build` to efficiently handle more general list production. Gill also formulated a `foldr-augment` rule, similar to the `foldr-build` rule, for lists.

W. Taha (Ed.): SAIG 2001, LNCS 2196, pp. 47–71, 2001.
© Springer-Verlag Berlin Heidelberg 2001

Like other fusion techniques, short cut fusion was first investigated for lists. This quickly gave rise to generalizations of short cut fusion for non-list algebraic data types, as well as to their incorporation into a number of automatic fusion tools (*e.g.*, [3,4,7,8,9,10]. Generalizations of `augment` and the `foldr-augment` rule for lists to non-list algebraic data types, on the other hand, have remained virtually unstudied.

In this paper we generalize Gill's `augment` for lists to non-list algebraic data types. Together with the well-known generalization `cata` of `foldr` to arbitrary algebraic data types, this allows us to formulate and prove correct for each a corresponding `cata-augment` fusion rule which generalizes the `foldr-augment` rule for lists. We interpret `augment` as constructing substitution instances of algebraic data structures, and view generalized `cata-augment` fusion as optimizing compositions of functions that uniformly consume algebraic data structures with functions that uniformly produce substitution instances of them.

1.1   The Problem of Correctness

Short cut fusion and its generalizations have successfully been used to improve programs in modern functional languages. They have even been used to transform modular programs into monolithic counterparts exhibiting order-of-magnitude efficiency increases over those from which they are derived. Nevertheless, there remain difficulties associated with their use. One of the most substantial is that these fusion techniques have not been proved correct for the languages in which they are typically applied.

Short cut fusion and its generalizations have traditionally been treated purely syntactically, with little consideration given to the underlying semantics of the languages in which they are applied. In particular, the fact that these fusion techniques are valid only for languages admitting parametric models has been downplayed in the literature. Instead, their application to functional programs has been justified by appealing either to intuition about the operational behavior of `cata`, `build`, and `augment`, or else to Wadler's "free theorems" [18].[1] But intuition is unsuitable as a basis for proofs, and the correctness of the "free theorems" itself relies on the existence of relationally parametric models. Since no relationally parametric models for modern functional languages are known to exist, these justifications of short cut fusion and its generalizations are unsatisfactory.

Simply put, parametricity is the requirement that all polymorphic functions definable in a language operate uniformly over all types. This requirement gives rise to corresponding uniformity conditions on models, and these uniformity conditions are satisfied by models supporting a relationally parametric structure. Relationally parametric models are known to exist for some higher-order polymorphic languages [2], but because these fail to model fixed point recursion they

---

[1] In fact, the only proof of correctness of short cut fusion for a modern functional language on record [4] appeals to Wadler's "free theorems". Correctness proofs for generalizations of short cut fusion do not appear in the literature at present.

do not adequately accommodate short cut fusion and its generalizations. While it may be possible to extend these models to encompass fixed point recursion, this has not been reported in the literature. In fact, until recently the existence of relationally parametric models for languages supporting both higher-order polymorphic functions and fixed point recursion had not been demonstrated. Like their counterparts for the modern functional languages which extend them, short cut fusion and its generalizations for even the most streamlined of higher-order polymorphic languages with fixed point recursion have therefore enjoyed no proof of correctness.

1.2   Proving Correctness

In Section 5 of this paper we prove the correctness of generalized **cata-augment** fusion for algebraic data types in calculi supporting both higher-order polymorphic functions and fixed point recursion. Correctness for these calculi of short cut fusion for lists, the **foldr-augment** rule for lists, and generalizations of short cut fusion for lists to **cata-build** fusion for arbitrary algebraic data types, all are immediate consequences of this result. But because functional languages typically support features that cannot be modeled in the calculi considered here, our results do not apply to them directly. Nevertheless, our results do make some progress toward bridging the gap between the theory of parametricity and the practice of program fusion.

Our proof of the correctness of short cut fusion relies on Pitts' recent demonstration of the existence of relationally parametric models for a class of polymorphic lambda calculi supporting fixed point recursion at the level of terms and recursion via data types with non-strict constructors at the level of types [13,14]. Pitts uses logical relations to characterize contextual equivalence in these calculi, and this characterization enables him to show that identifying contextually equivalent terms gives rise to relationally parametric models for them. Our main result (Theorem 1) employs Pitts' characterization of contextual equivalence to demonstrate that programs in these calculi which have undergone generalized **cata-augment** fusion are contextually equivalent to their unfused counterparts. The semantic correctness of **cata-augment** fusion for them follows immediately.

Our proof techniques, like those of Pitts on which they are based, are operational in nature. Denotational approaches to proving the correctness of short cut fusion — e.g., fixed point induction — have thus far been unsuccessful. While it may be possible to construct a proof directly using the denotational notions that Pitts captures syntactically, to our knowledge this has not yet been accomplished. Similar remarks apply to directly constructing relationally parametric models of rank-2 fragments of suitable polymorphic calculi. It is worth noting that Pitts' relationally parametric characterization of contextual equivalence holds even in the presence of fully impredicative polymorphism. Characterization of contextual equivalence for predicative calculi — i.e., for calculi in which types are quantified only at the outermost level — can be achieved by appropriately restricting the characterizations for the corresponding impredicative ones.

```
foldr :: forall a. forall b.
            (a -> b -> b) -> b -> List a -> b
foldr = /\a b. \c n xs. case xs of
                          Nil -> n
                          Cons z zs -> c z (foldr a b c n zs)
map :: forall a. forall b. (a -> b) -> List a -> List b
map = /\a b. \f l. case l of
                          Nil -> Nil
                          Cons z zs -> Cons (f z) (map a b f zs)
append :: forall a. List a -> List a -> List a
append = /\a. \xs ys. case xs of
                          Nil -> ys
                          Cons z zs -> Cons z (append a zs ys)
```

Fig. 1. Recursive functions on lists

The remainder of this paper is organized as follows. Section 2 informally introduces short cut fusion and `foldr-augment` fusion for lists. In Section 3 the polymorphic lambda calculus PolyFix for which we will formulate and prove the correctness of generalized `cata-augment` fusion is introduced; the notion of Poly-Fix contextual equivalence on which this relies is also formulated in Section 3. In Section 4, `cata-augment` fusion for arbitrary algebraic data types is formalized, and its correctness is proved in Section 5. Section 6 concludes.

2   Fusion

In functional programming, large programs are often constructed as compositions of small, generally applicable components. Each component in such a composition produces a data structure as its output, and this data structure is immediately consumed by the next component in the composition. Intermediate data structures thus serve as a kind of "glue" allowing components to be combined in a mix-and-match fashion.

The components comprising modular programs are typically defined as recursive functions. The definitions in Figure 1 are common examples of such functions: `foldr` consumes lists, while `map` and `append` both consume and produce lists. Using these functions we can define, for example, the function `mappend` which maps a function over the result of appending two lists:

```
mappend :: forall a. forall b.
              (a -> b) -> List a -> List a -> List b
mappend = /\a b. \f xs ys. map a b f (append a xs ys)
```

In the informal discussion in this section we will express program fragments in a Haskell-like notation with explicit type quantification, abstraction, and application. Quantification of the type t over the type variable a is denoted `forall a.t`, abstraction of the term M over the type variable a is denoted `/\a.M`, and application of the term M to the type t is denoted `M[t]`.

Unfortunately, modularly constructed programs like `mappend` tend to be less efficient than their non-modular counterparts. The main difficulty is that the direct implementation of compositional programs *literally* constructs, traverses, and discards intermediate data structures — even when they play no essential role in a computation. The above implementation of `mappend`, for instance, unnecessarily constructs and then traverses the intermediate list resulting from appending `xs` and `ys`. This requires processing the list `xs` twice. Even in lazy languages this is expensive, both slowing execution time and increasing heap space requirements.

It is often possible to avoid manipulating intermediate data structures by using a more elaborate style of programming in which the computations performed by component functions in a composition are intermingled. In this monolithic style of programming the function `mappend` is defined as

```
mappend' :: forall a. forall b.
                 (a -> b) -> List a -> List a -> List b
mappend' = /\a b. \f xs ys.
               case xs of
                 Nil -> map a b f ys
                 Cons z zs -> Cons (f z) (mappend' a b f zs ys)
```

The list `xs` is only processed once by `mappend'`.

Experienced programmers writing a function to map over the result of appending two lists would instinctively produce `mappend'` rather than `mappend`; small functions like `mappend` are easily optimized at the keyboard. But because they are used very often, it is essential that small functions are optimized whenever possible. Automatic fusion tools ensure that they are.

On the other hand, when programs are either very large or very complex, even experienced programmers may find that eliminating intermediate data structures by hand is not a very attractive alternative to the modular style of programming. Methods for automatically eliminating intermediate data structures are needed in this situation as well.

2.1   Short Cut Fusion

Automatic elimination of intermediate data structures combines the clarity and maintainability of the modular style of programming with the efficiency of the monolithic style. Use of short cut fusion to eliminate intermediate lists is based on the observation that many list-manipulating functions can be written in terms of the list-consuming function `foldr` and the list-producing function `build`, and then fused via the `foldr-build` rule. Since `foldr` is another name for the standard catamorphism for lists, we denote it by `cata-list` in the rest of this paper. And since the `build` function of Gill *et al.* is the instantiation to lists of a `build` function applying to more general algebraic data types, we denote it by `build-list` below.

Operationally, `cata-list` takes as input types `t` and `t'`, a replacement term `c :: t -> t' -> t'` for `Cons`, a replacement term `n::t'` for `Nil`, and a list `xs`

```
map :: forall a. forall b. (a -> b) -> List a -> List b
map = /\a b. \f l. build-list b
                    (/\t. \(c :: b -> t -> t) (n::t).
                     cata-list a t
                         (\(y::a) (l'::t). c (f y) l') n l)
append :: forall a. List a -> List a -> List a
append = /\a. \xs ys. build-list a
                    (/\t. \(c::a -> t -> t) (n::t).
                     cata-list a t c
                        (cata-list a t c n ys) xs)
```

Fig. 2. Functions in build-cata form

of type List t. It replaces all (fully-applied) occurrences of Cons in xs by c, and the single occurrence of Nil in xs by n. The result is a value of type t'. The definition of cata-list — *i.e.*, of foldr — appears in Figure 1.

The function build-list, on the other hand, takes as input a type t and a term M providing a type-independent template for constructing "abstract" lists with "elements" of type t. It instantiates all occurrences of the "abstract" list constructors which appear in the result list specified by M with the "concrete" list constructors Cons and Nil. The result is a list of elements of type t. That is, if t is a type and M is any term with type forall a. (t -> a -> a) -> a -> a, then

build-list t M = M (List t) Cons Nil

Compositions of list-consuming and -producing functions defined in terms of cata-list and build-list can be fused via *short cut fusion* for lists:

> Let M be a term of type forall a. (t -> a -> a) -> a -> a. Then any occurrence of cata-list t t' c n (build-list t M) in a program can be replaced by M t' c n.

Short cut fusion makes sense intuitively: the result of a computation is the same regardless of whether the function M is first applied to List t, Cons, and Nil and then these are replaced in the resulting list by c and n, respectively, or the abstract constructors in (an appropriate instance of) M are replaced by c and n, respectively, directly.

Figure 2 shows the build-cata forms of the functions in Figure 1. The fused function mappend' can be derived from mappend by inlining these definitions and applying short cut fusion in conjunction with standard program simplifications.

2.2   The Cata-Augment Rule for Lists

Although short cut fusion successfully fuses many compositions of list-processing functions, some compositions involving common functions remain problematic. This is because the argument M to build-list must abstract *all* of the Cons and

Nil cells which appear in the list it produces — not just the "top-level" ones contributed by M itself.

To see why, suppose that we want to express the function append for lists of elements of an arbitrary type t in terms of build-list and cata-list. This would make it possible to fuse append with list-producers on the right and list-consumers on the left. It is tempting to write

```
append = /\a. \xs ys. build-list a
                    (/\t. \c n. cata-list a t c ys xs)
```

but the expression on the right hand side is ill-typed: ys is of type List a, but cata-list's replacement for Nil needs to be of the more general type t. The problem here is that, although the constructors in ys are part of the result of append, they are not properly abstracted by build-list.

One solution to this problem is to use cata-list to prepare the constructors in ys for abstraction via build-list. This entails replacing the occurrence of ys in the body of the definition of append by cata a t c ys. The result is the build-cata form

```
append = /\a. \xs ys. build-list a (/\t. \c n.
                    cata-list a t c (cata-list a t c ys) xs)
```

for append. Although this solution does indeed provide a replacement of type t for Nil, it does so by introducing an extra list consumption into the computation. Unfortunately, subsequent removal of this consumption via fusion cannot be guaranteed.

An alternative solution is to generalize build-list to abstract the "base list" ys of append. Gill *et al.* [5] adopt this approach, defining a new construct augment-list to perform this task. Its definition is

```
augment-list t M ys = M (List t) Cons ys
```

Appending one list onto another is now easily expressed by passing ys as the second argument to augment-list:

```
append = /\a. \xs ys. augment-list t
                    (/\t. \c n. cata-list a t c n xs) ys
```

This definition of augment-list also gives

```
build-list t M = augment-list t M Nil
```

and is the basis for *the* cata-augment *rule* for lists from Gill [4] for fusing compositions of functions written in terms of cata-list and augment-list:

> Let t be a type, let M :: forall a. (t -> a -> a) -> a -> a be a closed term, and let ys :: List t. Then any occurrence of
>
> cata-list t t' c n (augment-list t M ys)
>
> in a program can be replaced by

M t' c (cata-list t t' c n ys).

The short cut for lists is just the special case of the cata-augment rule for lists in which ys has been specialized to Nil, augment-list has been replaced by build-list, and cata-list t t' c n has been applied to Nil to yield n. Although the cata-augment rule for lists does not eliminate the entire intermediate list produced by the left-hand side of the equation, it does avoid production and subsequent consumption of the base list ys. Passing ys to augment-list has the effect of specifying a particular list to be substituted for the occurrence of Nil in the list produced by M. This interpretation of augment as constructing substitution instances of data structures will lead to generalizations of augment-list and the cata-augment rule for lists to algebraic data types in Section 4.

3   PolyFix and Contextual Equivalence

Extrapolating from the situation for lists, we formulate in Section 4 a suitable generalization of the cata-augment rule for lists to one for non-list algebraic data types. In Section 5 we demonstrate that these generalizations describe optimizations for the uniform consumption of uniformly produced substitution instances of non-list algebraic data structures. In doing so, we work in the same setting as Pitts [13], and our presentation is heavily influenced by that paper. In this section we introduce Pitts' PolyFix, the polymorphic lambda calculus for which we state, and prove the correctness of, the generalized cata-augment rule. We also outline the elements of Pitts' development of contextual equivalence for terms of PolyFix which are needed in this endeavor.

3.1   PolyFix: The Fixed Point Calculus

The *Polymorphic Fixed Point Calculus* PolyFix combines the Girard-Reynolds polymorphic lambda calculus with fixed point recursion at the level of expressions and (positive) recursion via non-strict constructors at the level of types. Since the treatment of ground types (*e.g.*, natural numbers and booleans) in the theory developed here is precisely the same as the treatment of algebraic data types, for notational convenience we assume that PolyFix supports only the latter.

The syntax of PolyFix types and terms is given in Figure 3, in which the Haskell-like syntax

$$\mathbf{data}(\alpha \ = \ c_1^\delta \tau_{11}...\tau_{1k_1} \mid ... \mid c_m^\delta \tau_{m1}...\tau_{mk_m}) \tag{1}$$

is used for recursive data types. The syntax in (1) provides an anonymous notation for a data type δ satisfying the fixed point equation

$$\delta = (\tau_{11}[\delta/\alpha] \times ... \times \tau_{1k_1}[\delta/\alpha]) + ... + (\tau_{m1}[\delta/\alpha] \times ... \times \tau_{mk_m}[\delta/\alpha])$$

The injections into the m-fold sum are named explicitly by δ's constructors $c_1^\delta,...,c_m^\delta$. Terms of type δ are introduced using these constructors and eliminated

Types	$\tau := \alpha$	type variable
	$\mid \tau \rightarrow \tau$	function type
	$\mid \forall \alpha.\tau$	$\forall$-type
	$\mid \delta$	algebraic data type

Data types $\delta := \mathtt{data}(\alpha = \mathtt{c}_1^\delta \overline{\tau_{k_1}} \mid \dots \mid \mathtt{c}_m^\delta \overline{\tau_{k_m}})$

Terms	$M := x$	variable
	$\mid \lambda x : \tau.\,M$	function abstraction
	$\mid MM$	function application
	$\mid \Lambda \alpha.\,M$	type abstraction
	$\mid M\tau$	type application
	$\mid \mathtt{fix}(M)$	fixpoint recursion
	$\mid \mathtt{c}_i^\delta \overline{M_{k_i}}$	data value
	$\mid \mathtt{case}\ M\ \mathtt{of}$	
	$\qquad \{\mathtt{c}_1^\delta \overline{x_{k_1}} \Rightarrow M \mid$	
	$\qquad \dots$	
	$\qquad \mid \mathtt{c}_m^\delta \overline{x_{k_m}} \Rightarrow M\}$	case expression

Fig. 3. Syntax of PolyFix

using case expressions. The types τ_{ij}, for $i = 1, ..., m$ and $j = 1, ..., k_i$, appearing in (1) can be built up from type variables using function types, $\forall$-types, and data types, provided the defined type α occurs only positively in the τ_{ij} (see Definition 1 below).

Example 1. The following are PolyFix data types:

$$Bool = \mathtt{data}(\alpha = \mathtt{True} \mid \mathtt{False})$$
$$Nat = \mathtt{data}(\alpha = \mathtt{Succ}\ \alpha \mid \mathtt{Zero})$$
$$List\,\tau = \mathtt{data}(\alpha = \mathtt{Cons}\ \tau\,\alpha \mid \mathtt{Nil})$$

A number of remarks concerning the definitions of Figure 3 are in order. Type variables, variables, and constructors range over disjoint countably infinite sets. If s ranges over a set S, then for each n, $\overline{s_n}$ ranges over n-element sequences of elements of S. If M is a term and $\overline{s_n}$ is a sequence of n types or terms, we write $M\overline{s_n}$ to indicate the n-fold application $Ms_1...s_n$. Similarly, we write $\lambda \overline{x_n} : \overline{\tau_n}.\,M$ to indicate the n-fold abstraction $\lambda x_1 : \tau_1.\ ...\lambda x_n : \tau_n.\,M$. Finally, to be well-formed, we require a data type as in (1) to have distinct data constructors $\mathtt{c}_i^\delta$, $i = 1, ..., m$, and to be algebraic in the sense of Definition 1.

Definition 1. *The sets* $ftv^+(\tau)$ *and* $ftv^-(\tau)$ *of free type variables occurring positively and occurring negatively in the type τ partition* $ftv(\tau)$ *into two disjoint subsets. These are defined by*

$$ftv^+(\alpha) \quad\ = \{\alpha\}$$
$$ftv^-(\alpha) \quad\ = \emptyset$$
$$ftv^\pm(\tau \to \tau') = ftv^\mp(\tau) \cup ftv^\pm(\tau')$$
$$ftv^\pm(\forall \alpha. \tau) = ftv^\pm(\tau) \setminus \{\alpha\}$$
$$ftv^\pm(\delta) \quad\ = \bigcup_{i=1}^{m} \bigcup_{j=1}^{k_m} ftv^\pm(\tau_{ij}) \setminus \{\alpha\} \ \textit{if } \delta \textit{ is as in (1)}.$$

A data type (1) is algebraic *if there are only positive free occurrences of its bound variable α in the types τ_{ij}, i.e., if $\alpha \notin ftv^-(\tau_{ij})$ for all $i = 1, ..., m$ and $j = 1, ..., k_i$.*

The constructions $\forall\alpha(-)$, $\mathtt{data}(\alpha = -)$, $\mathtt{case}\ M\ \mathtt{of}\ \{... \mid c_i^\delta \overline{x_{k_i}} \Rightarrow M_i \mid ...\}$, $\lambda x : \tau.-$, and $\Lambda\alpha.-$ are binders, and free occurrences of the variables $x_1, ..., x_{k_i}$ become bound in the case expression $\mathtt{case}\ D\ \mathtt{of}\ \{... \mid c_i^\delta \overline{x_{k_i}} \Rightarrow M_i \mid ...\}$. As is customary, we identify types and terms which differ only by renamings of their bound variables. We write $ftv(e)$ for the (finite) set of free type variables of a type or term e, and $fv(M)$ for the (finite) set of free variables of a term M. The result of substituting the type τ for all free occurrences of the type variable α in a type or term e is denoted $e[\tau/\alpha]$. The result of substituting the term M' for all free occurrences of the variable x in the term M is denoted $M[M'/x]$.

We will be concerned only with PolyFix terms which are typeable. The type assignment relation for PolyFix is completely standard; it is given in Figure 4. In the last two clauses of Figure 4, δ is assumed to be $\mathtt{data}(\alpha = c_1 \overline{\tau_{1k_1}} \mid ... \mid c_m \overline{\tau_{mk_m}})$. A *typing environment* Γ is a pair A, Δ with A a finite set of type variables and Δ a function defined on a finite set $dom(\Delta)$ of variables which maps each $x \in dom(\Delta)$ to a type with free type variables in A. We write $\Gamma \vdash M : \tau$ to indicate that term M has type τ in the type environment Γ. Implicit in this notation are four assumptions, namely that $\Gamma = A, \Delta$, that $ftv(M) \subseteq A$, that $ftv(\tau) \subseteq A$, and that $fv(M) \subseteq dom(\Delta)$. The notation $\Gamma, x : \tau$ indicates the typing environment obtained from $\Gamma = A, \Delta$ by extending the function Δ to map $x \notin dom(\Delta)$ to τ. Similarly, the notation Γ, α denotes the extension of A with a type variable $\alpha \notin A$.

The explicit type annotations on lambda-bound term variables and constructors c_i^δ in data values $c_i^\delta \overline{M_{k_i}}$ ensure that well-formed PolyFix terms have unique types. More specifically, given Γ and M, there is at most one type τ for which $\Gamma \vdash M : \tau$ holds. For convenience we may suppress type information below.

A type τ is *closed* if $ftv(\tau) = \emptyset$. A term M is *closed* if $fv(M) = \emptyset$, regardless of whether or not M contains free type variables. The set of closed PolyFix types is denoted Typ. For $\tau \in Typ$ the set of closed PolyFix terms M for which $\emptyset, \emptyset \vdash M : \tau$ is denoted $Term(\tau)$.

Given δ as in (1), let Rec_δ comprise the elements i of $\{1, ..., m\}$ for which $\alpha_{ij} \in fv(\tau_{ij})$ for some $j \in \{1, ..., k_i\}$, and let $NonRec_\delta$ be the set $\{1, ..., m\} - Rec_\delta$. We say that the data constructors c_i, $i \in Rec_\delta$, are *recursive constructors* of δ and that c_i, $i \in NonRec_\delta$, are *nonrecursive constructors* of δ. In addition, given a constructor c_i, let $RecPos_{c_i}$ comprise those elements $j \in \{1, ..., k_i\}$ for which $\alpha \in fv(\tau_{ij})$, and let $NonRecPos_{c_i}$ be the set $\{1, ..., k_i\} - RecPos_{c_i}$. We say that the indices in $RecPos_{c_i}$ indicate the *recursive positions* of c_i and

$$\Gamma, x : \tau \vdash x : \tau$$

$$\frac{\Gamma \vdash F : \tau \to \tau}{\Gamma \vdash \mathtt{fix}(F) : \tau}$$

$$\frac{\Gamma, x : \tau_1 \vdash M : \tau_2}{\Gamma \vdash \lambda x : \tau_1. \, M : \tau_1 \to \tau_2}$$

$$\frac{\Gamma \vdash F : \tau_1 \to \tau_2 \qquad \Gamma \vdash A : \tau_1}{\Gamma \vdash F A : \tau_2}$$

$$\frac{\Gamma, \alpha \vdash M : \tau}{\Gamma \vdash \Lambda \alpha. \, M : \forall \alpha. \tau}$$

$$\frac{\Gamma \vdash G : \forall \alpha. \tau_1}{\Gamma \vdash G \, \tau_2 : \tau_1[\tau_2/\alpha]}$$

$$\frac{\Gamma \vdash \mathsf{M}_j : \tau_j[\delta/\alpha] \qquad j = 1, .., k_i}{\Gamma \vdash \mathsf{c}_i M_1 ... M_{k_i} : \delta}$$

$$\frac{\Gamma \vdash D : \delta \qquad \Gamma, \overline{x_{k_i}} : \overline{\tau_{k_i}[\delta/\alpha]} \vdash M_i : \tau \qquad i = 1, .., m}{\Gamma \vdash \mathsf{case} \; D \; \mathsf{of} \; \{\mathsf{c}_1 \overline{x_{k_1}} \Rightarrow M_1 \mid ... \mid \mathsf{c}_m \overline{x_{k_m}} \Rightarrow M_m\} : \tau}$$

Fig. 4. PolyFix type assignment

that the indices in $NonRecPos_{\mathsf{c}_i}$ indicate the *nonrecursive positions* of c_i. The distinction between recursive and nonrecursive constructors and positions will be useful to us in stating our main result in Section 4.

The notation of the next definition allows us to order, and to project onto the resulting sequence of, arguments to function abstractions. We will use it to express `cata`, `build`, and `augment` in PolyFix.

Definition 2. *Let δ be as in (1), τ be a closed type, $Rec_\delta = \{u_1, ..., u_p\}$, and $NonRec_\delta = \{v_1, ..., v_q\}$. For all $\rho_i : \tau_{i1}[\tau/\alpha] \to ... \to \tau_{ik_i}[\tau/\alpha] \to \tau$, for all $i = 1, ..., m$, define*

$$\phi_i(\rho_{u_1}, ..., \rho_{u_p}, \rho_{v_1}, ..., \rho_{v_q}) = \rho_i.$$

Further, if $RecPos_{\mathsf{c}_i} = \{z_1, ..., z_p\}$ and $NonRecPos_{\mathsf{c}_i} = \{y_1, ..., y_q\}$ for all $i = 1, ..., m$, define

$$\phi_{ij}(\rho_{z_1}, ..., \rho_{z_p}, \rho_{y_1}, ..., \rho_{y_q}) = \rho_j.$$

For each data type δ as in (1) we can also define a corresponding pure polymorphic type τ_δ by

$$\tau_\delta = \forall \alpha. (\tau_{11} \to ... \to \tau_{1k_1} \to \alpha) \to ... \to (\tau_{m1} \to ... \to \tau_{mk_m} \to \alpha) \to \alpha.$$

Using these types, we have

$$V \Downarrow V \ (V \text{ is a value}) \qquad \frac{F \Downarrow \lambda x : \tau. M \qquad M[A/x] \Downarrow V}{F A \Downarrow V}$$

$$\frac{G \Downarrow \Lambda\alpha. M \qquad M[\tau/\alpha] \Downarrow V}{G\tau \Downarrow V} \qquad \frac{F \ (\text{fix } F) \Downarrow V}{\text{fix } F \Downarrow V}$$

$$\frac{D \Downarrow c_i \overline{M_{k_i}} \qquad M[\overline{M_{k_i}}/\overline{x_{k_i}}] \Downarrow V}{\text{case } D \text{ of } \{... \mid c_i \overline{x_{k_i}} \Rightarrow M \mid ...\} \Downarrow V}$$

Fig. 5. PolyFix evaluation relation

Definition 3. *For each data type δ define*

$$
\begin{aligned}
\text{build}^\delta \quad &= \lambda M : \tau_\delta. \, M \, \delta \, \overline{c_m} \\
&\text{where for each } c_i, \text{ we define } c_i = \lambda \overline{p_{k_i}} : \overline{\tau_{k_i}[\delta/\alpha]}. \, c_i \overline{p_{k_i}} \\
\text{unbuild}^\delta &= \text{fix}(\lambda h : \delta \to \tau_\delta. \, \lambda d : \delta. \, \Lambda\alpha. \, \lambda \overline{f_m} : \overline{\tau_{m1} \to ... \to \tau_{mk_m} \to \alpha}. \\
&\quad \text{case } d \text{ of} \\
&\qquad \{... \mid c_i \overline{x_{k_i}} \Rightarrow f_i \phi_{ik_i}(\overline{hx_{z_1} \alpha \overline{f_m}, ...hx_{z_p} \alpha \overline{f_m}}, x_{y_1}, ..., x_{y_q}) \mid ...\}) \\
&\quad \text{where } RecPos_{c_i} = \{z_1, ..., z_p\} \text{ and } NonRecPos_{c_i} = \{y_1, ..., y_q\} \\
\text{cata}^\delta \quad &= \Lambda\alpha. \, \lambda \overline{f_m}. \, \lambda d. \, \text{unbuild}^\delta \, d \, \alpha \, \overline{f_m}
\end{aligned}
$$

If δ is closed then each of build^δ, unbuild^δ, and cata^δ is a closed PolyFix term. In the notation of Definition 3, we have that $\text{cata-list } \tau = \text{cata}^{List \, \tau}$ and $\text{build-list } \tau = \text{build}^{List \, \tau}$. Note that data type constructors must be fully applied in well-formed PolyFix terms.

3.2 Operational Semantics

The operational semantics of PolyFix is given by the *evaluation relation* in Figure 5. There, δ is assumed to be $\text{data}(\alpha = ... \mid c_i \overline{\tau_{ik_i}} \mid ...))$ It relates a closed term M to a value V of the same closed type; this is denoted $M \Downarrow V$. The set of PolyFix *values* is given by

$$V ::= \lambda x : \tau.M \mid \Lambda\alpha.M \mid c_i \overline{M_{k_i}}$$

Note that function application is given a call-by-name semantics, constructors are non-strict, and type applications are not evaluated "under the Λ." In addition, PolyFix evaluation is deterministic, although the rule for fix entails the existence of terms whose evaluation does not terminate.

3.3 Contextual Equivalence

With the operational semantics of PolyFix in place, we can now make precise the notion of contextual equivalence for its terms. Informally, two terms in a programming language are contextually equivalent if they are interchangeable in any program with no change in observable behavior when the resulting programs are executed. In order to formalize this notion for PolyFix we must specify what a PolyFix program is, as well as the PolyFix program behavior we are interested in observing.

We define a PolyFix *program* to be a closed term of some data type, and the *observable behavior* of a PolyFix program to be the outermost constructor in the data value, if any, to which the program evaluates. (Recall that ground types have been replaced by algebraic data types in PolyFix.) Since merely observing termination of PolyFix evaluation (or lack thereof) at data types gives rise to the same notion of contextual equivalence, we define two PolyFix terms M_1 and M_2 such that $\Gamma \vdash M_1 : \tau$ and $\Gamma \vdash M_2 : \tau$ to be *contextually equivalent with respect to* Γ if for any context $\mathcal{M}[-]$ for which $\mathcal{M}[M_1], \mathcal{M}[M_2] \in Term(\delta)$ for some closed data type δ, we have

$$\mathcal{M}[M_1] \Downarrow \Leftrightarrow \mathcal{M}[M_2] \Downarrow .$$

As usual, a *context* $\mathcal{M}[-]$ is a PolyFix term with a subterm replaced by the placeholder '$-$', and $\mathcal{M}[M]$ denotes the term which results from replacing the placeholder by the term M. Note that replacement may involve variable capture. We write $\Gamma \vdash M_1 =_{ctx} M_2 : \tau$ to indicate that M_1 and M_2 are contextually equivalent with respect to Γ. If M_1 and M_2 are closed terms of closed type, we write $M_1 =_{ctx} M_2 : \tau$ instead of $\emptyset, \emptyset \vdash M_1 =_{ctx} M_2 : \tau$, and we say simply that M_1 and M_2 are *contextually equivalent*.

For all terms M and M' of type τ_1, A of type τ_2, and F of type τ, the following contextual equivalences are shown to hold in Pitts [13]:

$$(\lambda x : \tau_2. M)A =_{ctx} M[A/x] : \tau_1 \tag{2}$$
$$(\Lambda \alpha. M)\tau_2 =_{ctx} M[\tau_2/\alpha] : \tau_1[\tau_2/\alpha] \tag{3}$$
$$\texttt{case } c_i^\delta \overline{M_{k_i}} \texttt{ of } \{... \mid c_i^\delta \overline{x_{k_i}} \Rightarrow M' \mid ...\} =_{ctx} M'[\overline{M_{k_i}}/\overline{x_{k_i}}] : \tau_1 \tag{4}$$
$$\texttt{fix}(F) =_{ctx} F\texttt{fix}(F) : \tau \tag{5}$$

4   A Generalized Cata-Augment Rule

In this section we state our main result, the Substitution Theorem. This theorem allows us to generalize Gill's `cata-augment` rule for lists to arbitrary algebraic data types. It also allows us to make precise the sense in which the generalized `cata-augment` rule and its specializations preserve the meanings of fused PolyFix programs. Proof of the Substitution Theorem appears in Section 5.3.

We will consider only closed types and terms in the remainder of this paper. This restriction is reasonable because contextual equivalence for open terms is reducible to contextual equivalence for closed terms, as shown in Pitts [13].

Theorem 1. (Substitution Theorem) *Let δ be a closed data type as in (1), and let $u_1, ..., u_p, v_1, ..., v_q$, and $\phi_1, ..., \phi_m$ be as in Definition 2. In addition, let*

$$M : \forall \alpha.(\tau_{11} \to ... \to \tau_{1k_1} \to \alpha) \to ... \to (\tau_{m1} \to ... \to \tau_{mk_m} \to \alpha) \to \alpha$$

be a closed term, let τ, $\tau'_{ij} = \tau_{ij}[\tau/\alpha]$, and $\tau''_{ij} = \tau_{ij}[\delta/\alpha]$ for $i = 1, ..., m$ and $j = 1, ..., k_i$ be closed types, and, for $i = 1, ..., m$ and $v \in NonRec_\delta$, let

$$c_i = \lambda \overline{p_{k_i}} : \overline{\tau''_{k_i}}. c_i \, \overline{p_{k_i}},$$

$$n_i : \tau'_{i1} \to ... \to \tau'_{ik_i} \to \tau,$$

and

$$\mu_v : \tau''_{v1} \to ... \to \tau''_{vk_v} \to \delta$$

be closed terms. Then

$$\mathsf{cata}^\delta \, \tau \, \overline{\phi_m(n_{u_1}, ..., n_{u_p}, n_{v_1}, ..., n_{v_q})} \, (M \, \delta \, \overline{\phi_m(c_{u_1}, ...c_{u_q}, \mu_{v_1}, ..., \mu_{v_q})})$$

$$=_{ctx} M \, \tau \, \overline{\phi_m(n_{u_1}, ..., n_{u_p}, \mu'_{v_1}, ..., \mu'_{v_q})} \; : \; \tau$$

where, for each $v \in NonRec_\delta$, the closed term $\mu'_v : \tau'_{v1} \to ... \to \tau'_{vk_v} \to \tau$ is given by

$$\mu'_v x_1 ... x_{k_v} = \mathsf{cata}^\delta \, \tau \, \overline{\phi_m(n_{u_1}, ..., n_{u_p}, n_{v_1}, ..., n_{v_q})} \, (\mu_v x_1 ... x_{k_v}).$$

The functions μ_v for $v \in NonRec_\delta$ can be thought of as substitutions mapping appropriate combinations of arguments of types τ''_{vj}, $j = 1, ..., k_v$, to terms of type δ; they determine the portion of the intermediate data structure not produced by M itself, *i.e.*, the non-initial segment of the intermediate data structure. The Substitution Theorem describes one way to optimize uniform consumption of substitution instances of algebraic data structures: it says that the result of using μ_v to substitute terms of data type δ for applications of the nonrecursive data constructors in a uniformly produced element of type δ, and then consuming the data structure resulting from that substitution with a catamorphism, is the same as simply producing the "abstract" data structure in which applications of recursive data constructors are replaced by their corresponding arguments to the catamorphism, and nonrecursive data constructors are replaced by the results of applying the catamorphism to their substitution values.

Just as the `cata-augment` rule for lists avoids production and then consumption of the portion of the intermediate list constructed by `augment`'s polymorphic function argument, so the Substitution Theorem indicates how to avoid production and subsequent consumption of the initial segments of more general algebraic data structures. Additional efficiency gains may be achieved in situations in which the representations of the substitutions μ_v allow us to carry out each application $\mathsf{cata}^\delta \, \overline{\phi_m(n_{u_1}, ..., n_{u_p}, n_{v_1}, ..., n_{v_q})} \, (\mu_v x_1 ... x_{k_v})$ exactly once.

If we generalize the definition of `augment-list` to a non-list data type δ by

$$\mathsf{augment}^\delta = \lambda M. \, \lambda \overline{\mu_{v_q}}. \, M \, \delta \, \overline{\phi_m(c_{u_1}, ..., c_{u_p}, \mu_{v_1}, ..., \mu_{v_q})}$$

then we can use this notation to rephrase the conclusion of Theorem 1 in a manner reminiscent of the `cata-augment` rule for lists:

Definition 4. *Suppose the conditions of Theorem 1 hold. The* generalized cata-augment rule *is given by*

$$\mathsf{cata}^\delta \ \tau \ \overline{\phi_m(n_{u_1}, ..., n_{u_p}, n_{v_1}, ..., n_{v_q})} \ (\mathsf{augment}^\delta \ M \ \overline{\mu_{v_q}})$$

$$=_{ctx} M \tau \overline{\phi_m(n_{u_1}, ..., n_{u_p}, \mu'_{v_1}, ..., \mu'_{v_q})} \ : \ \tau$$

Note that the generalized `cata-augment` rule allows the replacement terms for the nonrecursive data constructors to be specified by any appropriately typed substitutions $\mu_{v_1}, ..., \mu_{v_q}$. In this notation, the `cata-augment` rule for lists requires exactly one such term, corresponding to the nonrecursive constructor `Nil`. Since `Nil` takes no term arguments we see that, for each type τ, each term $M : \tau_\delta$, and each $\mu : List \, \tau$, `augment-list` $\tau \, M \, \mu$ from Section 2.2 is precisely $\mathsf{augment}^{List \, \tau} \, M \, \mu$.

For any data type δ, specializing μ_v to c_v for $v \in NonRec_\delta$ in $\mathsf{augment}^\delta \, M \, \overline{\mu_{v_q}}$ gives $\mathsf{build}^\delta \, M$, just as for lists. With this specialization, the Substitution Theorem yields the usual `cata-build` rule for algebraic data types. The Substitution Theorem thus makes precise the sense in which short cut fusion for these data types preserves the meanings of programs.

Note that the term arguments to `build` and `augment` need not be closed in function definitions; in fact, none of the term arguments to `build-list` in the definitions of Figure 2 are closed terms. While this observation may at first glance suggest that the generalized `cata-augment` rule and its specializations cannot be applied to them, in all situations in which these rules are used to fuse programs the free variables in the term arguments to `build` and `augment` will already have been instantiated with closed terms.

The following example illustrates the use of the generalized `cata-augment` rule to remove a non-list intermediate data structure from a program.

Example 2. Let $Expr \, \tau$, a data type of expressions, be given by

$$Expr \, \tau \ = \ \mathsf{data}(\alpha = \mathsf{Var} \, \tau \mid \mathsf{Lit} \, Nat \mid \mathsf{Op} \, Ops \, \alpha \, \alpha),$$

where

$$Ops \ = \ \mathsf{data}(\alpha = \mathsf{Add} \mid \mathsf{Sub} \mid \mathsf{Mul} \mid \mathsf{Div}).$$

Also let $env : \tau \to Expr \, \tau$ be an expression environment, let $\mu_{\mathsf{Var}} = env$, $\mu_{\mathsf{Lit}} = \lambda i : Nat. \mathsf{Lit} \, i$, and $c_{\mathsf{Op}} = \lambda o : Ops. \lambda v_1 : Expr \, \tau. \lambda v_2 : Expr \, \tau. \mathsf{Op} \, o \, v_1 \, v_2$. Finally, for each $e : Expr \, \tau$, let

$$M_e : \forall \alpha. (\tau \to \alpha) \to (Nat \to \alpha) \to (\mathsf{Ops} \to \alpha \to \alpha \to \alpha) \to \alpha$$

be the polymorphic function associated with e; for example,

$$M_{\mathsf{Var} \, n} = \forall \alpha. \, \lambda v. \, \lambda l. \, \lambda o. \, v \, n,$$
$$M_{\mathsf{Lit} \, 9} = \forall \alpha. \, \lambda v. \, \lambda l. \, \lambda o. \, l \, 9,$$

and

$$M_{\mathsf{Op} \, \mathsf{Add} \, (\mathsf{Lit} \, 7)(\mathsf{Op} \, \mathsf{Sub} \, (\mathsf{Lit} \, 4) \, (\mathsf{Var} \, m))}$$
$$= \forall \alpha. \, \lambda v. \, \lambda l. \, \lambda o. \, o(\mathsf{Add}, l \, 7, o(\mathsf{Sub}, l \, 4, v \, m)).$$

Then

$$subst\ env\ e = \mathbf{augment}^{Expr\ \tau}\ M_e\ \mu_{\mathtt{Var}}\ \mu_{\mathtt{Lit}}$$

defines a substitution function over $Expr\ \tau$, and

$$eval = \mathbf{cata}^{Expr\ \tau}\ Nat\ error\ (\lambda i : Nat.\ i)\ (\lambda o.\lambda v_1.\ \lambda v_2.\ o\ v_1\ v_2)$$

defines an evaluation function $eval : Expr\ \tau \to Nat$. Here, $error$ indicates a failed computation.

We can use the generalized `cata-augment` rule to optimize the evaluation of a substitution instance of an expression:

$$eval\ (subst\ env\ e) = M_e\ Nat\ \mu'_{\mathtt{Var}}\ \mu'_{\mathtt{Lit}}\ (\lambda o.\lambda v_1.\ \lambda v_2.\ o\ v_1\ v_2)$$

Here, $\mu'_{\mathtt{Var}} = \lambda n.\ eval\ (env\ n)$ and $\mu_{\mathtt{Lit}} = \lambda i : Nat.\ eval\ (\mathtt{Lit}\ i)$. The fusion performed gives a more efficient, yet functionally equivalent, implementation of evaluation of substitution instances of expressions in which substitution and evaluation are interleaved.

5   Correctness of Cata-Augment Fusion

To prove the Substitution Theorem we would like to define a logical relation which coincides with PolyFix contextual equivalence, while at the same time incorporating a notion of relational parametricity analogous to that introduced by Reynolds for the pure polymorphic lambda calculus [16]. Unfortunately, a naive approach to defining such a logical relation — i.e., one which quantifies over *all* appropriately typed relations in the defining clause for ∀-types — is not sufficiently restrictive to give good parametricity behavior. What is needed is some criterion for identifying precisely those relations which are "admissible for fixpoint induction," in the sense that they syntactically capture to domain-theoretic notion of admissibility. (In domain theory, a subset of a domain is said to be *admissible* if it contains the least element of the domain and is closed under taking least upper bounds of chains in the domain.) The notion of ⊤⊤-closure defined below, taken from Pitts [13], provides a criterion sufficient to guarantee this kind of admissibility [1].

The notion of ⊤⊤-closure is induced by a Galois connection between term relations and evaluation contexts, i.e., contexts $\mathcal{M}[-]$ which have a single occurrence of the placeholder '−' in the position at which the next subexpression will be evaluated. In Pitts [13], analysis of evaluation contexts is aided by recasting them in terms of the notion of frame stack given in Definition 5 below; indeed, this frame stack realization of evaluation contexts gives rise to Pitts' syntactic characterization of the PolyFix termination properties entailed by contextual equivalence. The resulting PolyFix *structural termination relation* provides the key to appropriately specifying the clause for ∀-types in the logical relation which coincides with contextual equivalence.

After sketching Pitts' characterization of contextual equivalence in terms of logical relations in Sections 4.1 and 4.2, we use it in Section 5 to prove the Substitution Theorem.

$$\Gamma \vdash Id : \tau \hookrightarrow \tau$$

$$\frac{\Gamma \vdash S : \tau' \hookrightarrow \tau'' \qquad \Gamma \vdash A : \tau}{\Gamma \vdash S \circ (- M) : (\tau \hookrightarrow \tau') \hookrightarrow \tau''}$$

$$\frac{\Gamma \vdash S : \tau'[\tau/\alpha] \hookrightarrow \tau'' \qquad \alpha \text{ not free in } \Gamma}{\Gamma \vdash S \circ (-\tau) : (\forall \alpha.\tau) \hookrightarrow \tau''}$$

$$\frac{\Gamma \vdash S : \tau \hookrightarrow \tau' \qquad \Gamma, \overline{x_{k_i}} : \overline{\tau_{ik_i}} \vdash M_i : \tau \qquad i = 1,.., m}{\Gamma \vdash S \circ (\textbf{case} - \textbf{of} \{c_1 \overline{x_{1k_1}} \Rightarrow M_1 \mid ... \mid ...c_m \overline{x_{mk_m}} \Rightarrow M_m\}) : \delta \hookrightarrow \tau'}$$

Fig. 6. Frame stack type judgements

5.1 ⊤⊤-closed Relations

Definition 5. *The grammar for PolyFix frame stacks is*

$$S ::= Id \mid S \circ F$$

where F ranges over frames:

$$F ::= (-M) \mid (-\tau) \mid \textbf{case} - \textbf{of} \{...\}.$$

Frame stacks have types and typing derivations, although explicit type information is not included in their syntax. The type judgement $\Gamma \vdash S : \tau \hookrightarrow \tau'$ for a frame stack S indicates the argument type τ and the result type τ' of S. As usual, Γ is a typing environment and certain well-formedness conditions of judgements hold; in particular, Γ is assumed to contain all free variables and free type variables of all expressions occurring in the judgement. The axioms and rules inductively defining this judgement are given in Figure 6. We will only be concerned with stacks which are typeable. Although well-formed frame stacks do not have unique types, they do satisfy the following property: Given Γ, S, and τ, there is at most one τ' such that $\Gamma \vdash S : \tau \hookrightarrow \tau'$ holds. In this paper, the argument types of frame stacks will always be known at the time of use.

Given closed types τ and τ', we write $Stack(\tau, \tau')$ for the set of frame stacks for which $\emptyset, \emptyset \vdash S : \tau \hookrightarrow \tau'$. We are particularly interested in the case when τ' is a data type, and so write

$$Stack(\tau) = \bigcup \{Stack(\tau, \delta) \mid \delta \text{ is a data type}\}$$

The operation $S, M \mapsto SM$ of *applying a stack to a term* is the analogue for frame stacks of the operation of filling the hole in an evaluation context with a term. It is defined by induction on the number of frames in the stack as follows:

$$\begin{aligned} Id \, M \quad &= M \\ (S \circ F) \, M &= S(F[M]) \end{aligned}$$

$$\frac{S = S' \circ (-A) \qquad S' \top M[A/x]}{S \top \lambda x : \tau.\, M} \qquad\qquad \frac{S \circ (-A) \top F}{S \top F A}$$

$$\frac{S = S' \circ (-\tau) \qquad S' \top M[\tau/\alpha]}{S \top \varLambda\alpha.M} \qquad\qquad \frac{S \circ (-\tau) \top G}{S \top G\tau}$$

$$\frac{S \circ (-\mathtt{fix}\,F) \top F}{S' \top \mathtt{fix}\,F} \qquad\qquad \frac{S = Id}{S \top \mathtt{c}_i \overline{M_{k_i}}}$$

$$\frac{S = S' \circ \mathsf{case} - \mathsf{of}\ \{... \mid \mathtt{c}_i \overline{M_{k_i}} \Rightarrow M' \mid ...\} \qquad S' \top M'[\overline{M_{k_i}}/\overline{x_{k_i}}]}{S \top \mathtt{c}_i \overline{M_{k_i}}}$$

$$\frac{S \circ \mathsf{case} - \mathsf{of}\ \{...\} \top M}{S \top \mathsf{case}\ M\ \mathsf{of}\ \{...\}}$$

Fig. 7. PolyFix structural termination relation

Here, $F[M]$ is the term that results from replacing '$-$' by M in the frame F. If $S \in Stack(\tau, \tau')$ and $M \in Term(\tau)$, then $SM \in Term(\tau')$. Unlike PolyFix evaluation, stack application is strict in its second argument. This follows from the fact that

$$S M \Downarrow V \text{ iff there exists a value } V' \text{ such that } M \Downarrow V' \text{ and } S V' \Downarrow V,$$

which can be proved by induction on the number of frames in the frame stack S. The corresponding property

$$F[M] \Downarrow V \text{ iff there exists a value } V' \text{ such that } M \Downarrow V' \text{ and } F[V'] \Downarrow V$$

for frames, needed for the base case of the induction, follows directly from the inductive definition of the PolyFix evaluation relation in Figure 5.

PolyFix termination is captured by the termination relation $(-)\top(-)$ defined in Figure 7. More precisely, for all closed types τ, all closed data types δ, all frame stacks $S \in Stack(\tau, \delta)$, and all $M \in Term(\tau)$,

$$S M \Downarrow \text{ iff } S \top M.$$

Pitts uses this characterization of PolyFix termination to prove that, in any context, evaluation of a fixed point terminates iff some finite unwinding of it does. This, in turn, allows him to make precise the sense in which $\top\top$-closed relations — defined below — are admissible for fixed point induction.

Definition 6. *A PolyFix term relation is a binary relation between (typeable) closed terms. Given closed types* τ *and* τ' *we write* $Rel(\tau, \tau')$ *for the set of term relations which are subsets of* $Term(\tau) \times Term(\tau')$. *A PolyFix stack relation is a binary relation between (typeable) frame stacks whose result types are data types. We write* $Rel^\top(\tau, \tau')$ *for the set of relations which are subsets of* $Stack(\tau) \times Stack(\tau')$.

The relation $(-)^\top$ transforms stack relations into term relations and vice versa:

Definition 7. *Given any closed types* τ *and* τ', *and any* $r \in Rel(\tau, \tau')$, *define* $r^\top \in Rel^\top(\tau, \tau')$ *by*

$$(S, S') \in r^\top \Leftrightarrow \forall (M, M') \in r.\, S \top M \Leftrightarrow S' \top M'$$

Similarly, given any $s \in Rel^\top(\tau, \tau')$, *define* $s^\top \in Rel(\tau, \tau')$ *by*

$$(M, M') \in s^\top \Leftrightarrow \forall (S, S') \in s.\, S \top M \Leftrightarrow S' \top M'$$

The relation $(-)^\top$ gives rise to the notion of $\top\top$-closure which characterizes those relations which are suitable for consideration in the clause for $\forall$-types in the definition of the logical relation which coincides with contextual equivalence.

Definition 8. *A term relation* r *is said to be* $\top\top$-closed *if* $r = r^{\top\top}$.

Since $r \subseteq r^{\top\top}$ always holds, this is equivalent to requiring that $r^{\top\top} \subseteq r$. Expanding the definitions of $r^\top$ and $s^\top$ above gives $(M, M') \in r^{\top\top}$ iff

for each pair (S, S') of (appropriately typed) stacks,

$$\text{if } \forall (N, N') \in r.\, S \top N \Leftrightarrow S' \top N',$$

$$\text{then } S \top M \Leftrightarrow S' \top M'. \tag{6}$$

This characterization of $\top\top$-closedness will be used in Section 5.3.

5.2   Characterizing Contextual Equivalence

We are now in a position to describe PolyFix contextual equivalence in terms of parametric logical relations. The following constructions on term relations describe the ways in which the various PolyFix constructors act on term relations.

Definition 9. Action of $\to$ **on term relations:** *Given* $r_1 \in Rel(\tau_1, \tau'_1)$ *and* $r_2 \in Rel(\tau_2, \tau'_2)$, *define* $r_1 \to r_2 \in Rel(\tau_1 \to \tau_2, \tau'_1 \to \tau'_2)$ *by*

$$(F, F') \in r_1 \to r_2 \Leftrightarrow \forall (A, A') \in r_1.\, (FA, F'A') \in r_2$$

Action of $\forall$ **on term relations:** *Let* τ_1 *and* τ'_1 *be types with at most one free type variable* α *and let* R *be a function mapping term relations* $r \in Rel(\tau_2, \tau'_2)$

for any closed types τ_2 and τ_2' to term relations $R(r) \in Rel(\tau_1[\tau_2/\alpha], \tau_1'[\tau_2'/\alpha])$. Define the term relation $\forall r. R(r) \in Rel(\forall \alpha.\tau_1, \forall \alpha.\tau_1')$ by

$$(G, G') \in \forall r. R(r) \iff \forall \tau_2, \tau_2' \in Typ. \forall r \in Rel(\tau_2, \tau_2'). (G\tau_2, G'\tau_2') \in R(r)$$

Action of data constructors on term relations: *Let δ and δ' be the closed data types*

$$\delta = \mathsf{data}(\alpha = c_1 \tau_{11}...\tau_{1k_1} \mid ... \mid c_m \tau_{m1}...\tau_{mk_m})$$

and

$$\delta' = \mathsf{data}(\alpha = c_1 \tau_{11}'...\tau_{1k_1}' \mid ... \mid c_m \tau_{m1}'...\tau_{mk_m}').$$

For each $i = 1,...,m$, given term relations $r_{ij} \in Rel(\tau_{ij}[\delta/\alpha], \tau_{ij}'[\delta'/\alpha])$ for $j = 1,...,k_i$, we can form a term relation

$$c_i r_{i1}...r_{ik_1} = \{(c_i \overline{M_{k_i}}, c_i \overline{M_{k_i}'}) \mid \forall j = 1,...,k_i. (M_j, M_j') \in r_{ij}\}.$$

Using these notions of actions we can define the logical relations in which we are interested.

Definition 10. *A relational action Δ comprises a family of mappings*

$$r_1 \in Rel(\tau_1, \tau_1'),...,r_n \in Rel(\tau_n, \tau_n') \Delta_\tau(\overline{r_n}/\overline{\alpha_n}) \in Rel(\tau[\overline{\tau_n}/\overline{\alpha_n}], \tau[\overline{\tau_n'}/\overline{\alpha_n}])$$

from tuples of term relations to term relations, one for each type τ and each list $\overline{\alpha_n}$ of distinct variables containing the free variables of τ. These mappings must satisfy the five conditions given below.

1. $\Delta_\alpha(r/\alpha, \overline{r_n}/\overline{\alpha_n}) = r$
2. $\Delta_{\tau_1 \to \tau_2}(\overline{r_n}/\overline{\alpha_n}) = \Delta_{\tau_1}(\overline{r_n}/\overline{\alpha_n}) \to \Delta_{\tau_2}(\overline{r_n}/\overline{\alpha_n})$
3. $\Delta_{\forall \alpha.\tau}(\overline{r_n}/\overline{\alpha_n}) = \forall r. \Delta_\tau(r^{\top\top}/\alpha, \overline{r_n}/\overline{\alpha_n})$
4. *If δ is as in (1), then $\Delta_\delta(\overline{r_n}/\overline{\alpha_n})$ is a fixed point of the mapping*

$$r \mapsto \left(\bigcup_{i=1}^n c_i (\Delta_{\tau_{i1}}(r/\alpha, \overline{r_n}/\overline{\alpha_n})) ... (\Delta_{\tau_{ik_i}}(r/\alpha, \overline{r_n}/\overline{\alpha_n})) \right)^{\top\top}$$

5. *Assuming $ftv(\tau) \subseteq \{\overline{\alpha_n}, \overline{\alpha_m'}\}$ and $ftv(\overline{\tau_m'}) \subseteq \{\overline{\alpha_n}\}$,*

$$\Delta_{\tau[\overline{\tau_m'}/\overline{\alpha_m'}]}(\overline{r_n}/\overline{\alpha_n}) = \Delta_\tau(\overline{r_n}/\overline{\alpha_n}, (\Delta_{\overline{\tau_m'}}(\overline{r_n}/\overline{\alpha_n}))/\overline{\alpha_m'})$$

To see that the third clause above is sensible, note that $\tau[\overline{\tau_n}/\overline{\alpha_n}]$ and $\tau[\overline{\tau_n'}/\overline{\alpha_n}]$ are types containing at most one free variable, namely α, and that Δ_τ maps any term relation $r \in Rel(\sigma, \sigma')$ for closed types σ, σ' to the term relation $\Delta_\tau(r^{\top\top}/\alpha, \overline{r_n}/\overline{\alpha_n}) \in Rel(\tau[\overline{\tau_n}/\overline{\alpha_n}][\sigma/\alpha], \tau[\overline{\tau_n'}/\overline{\alpha_n}][\sigma'/\alpha])$. According to Definition 9, we thus have $\forall r. \Delta_\tau(r^{\top\top}/\alpha, \overline{r_n}/\overline{\alpha_n}) \in Rel(\forall \alpha.\tau[\overline{\tau_n}/\overline{\alpha_n}], \forall \alpha.\tau[\overline{\tau_n'}/\overline{\alpha_n}])$, as required by Definition 10.

We now define the relational actions μ and ν. Our focus on contextual equivalence — which identifies programs as much as possible unless there are observable reasons for not doing so — will mean that we are concerned primarily with ν in this paper. But since the results below hold equally well for μ and ν, we follow Pitts' lead and state results in the neutral notation of an arbitrary relational action Δ.

Definition 11. *The relational action μ is given as in Definition 10, where the least fixed point is taken when defining the relational action at a data type δ in the fourth clause above. The relational action ν is defined similarly, except that the greatest, rather than the least, fixed point is taken in the fourth clause. The action μ gives an inductive character to the action at data types, while ν gives a coinductive character at data types.*

Taking $n = 0$ in Definition 10, we see that for each closed type τ we can apply Δ_τ to the empty tuple of term relations to obtain the term relation $\Delta_\tau() \in Rel(\tau, \tau)$. Pitts has shown that this relation coincides with the relation of contextual equivalence of closed PolyFix terms at the closed type τ. In fact, Pitts shows a stronger correspondence between Δ and contextual equivalence: using an appropriate notion of closing substitution to extend Δ to a logical relation $\Gamma \vdash M \Delta M' : \tau$ between open terms, he shows that

$$\Gamma \vdash M =_{ctx} M' : \tau \quad \Leftrightarrow \quad \Gamma \vdash M \Delta M' : \tau. \tag{7}$$

The observation (7) guarantees that the logical relation Δ corresponds to the operational semantics of PolyFix. In particular, the definition of $\Delta_{\tau_1 \to \tau_2}$ in the second clause of Definition 10 reflects the fact that termination at function types is not observable in PolyFix. This is as expected: for types τ_1 and τ_2, the relation $\Delta_{\tau_1}(\overline{r_n}/\overline{\alpha_n}) \to \Delta_{\tau_2}(\overline{r_n}/\overline{\alpha_n})$ may not be $\top\top$-closed, and so may not capture PolyFix contextual equivalence.

As suggested by Pitts, it is possible to define call-by-value and call-by-name [11] versions of PolyFix. In each case, the definition of the relation $(-)\top(-)$ and the action of arrow types on term relations must be modified to reflect the appropriate operational semantics and notion of observability. Defining a call-by-name PolyFix also requires a slightly different notion of frame stack. The full development of these ideas for a call-by-value version of a subset of PolyFix is given in Pitts [12]; the details for a full call-by-value PolyFix and a call-by-name PolyFix remain unpublished. Laziness is necessary, for example, to capture the semantics of languages such as Haskell, whose termination at function types is observable. (Existence of the function **seq** guarantees that termination at function types is observable in Haskell. This function takes two arguments and reduces the first to weak head normal form before returning the second.)

For our purposes we need only the following two corollaries of (7). Proposition 1 guarantees that Δ is reflexive.

Proposition 1. *If Δ is a relational action, then for each closed type τ and each closed term M, $(M, M) \in \Delta_\tau()$.*

Proposition 2. *For all closed types τ and closed terms M and M' of type τ,*

$$M =_{ctx} M' : \tau \quad \Leftrightarrow \quad \forall S \in Stack(\tau). \, S \top M \Leftrightarrow S \top M'$$

5.3   Proof of the Substitution Theorem

Proof of Theorem 1: Let Δ be a relational action and suppose the hypotheses of the Substitution Theorem hold. Since M and its type are closed, Proposition 1 ensures that

$$(M, M) \in \Delta_{\forall \alpha.(\tau_{11} \to ... \to \tau_{1k_1} \to \alpha) \to ... \to (\tau_{m1} \to ... \to \tau_{mk_m} \to \alpha) \to \alpha}() \tag{8}$$

Applying the definition of Δ for $\forall$-types shows that (8) holds iff for all closed types τ' and τ and for all $r \in Rel(\tau', \tau)$,

$$(M\tau', M\tau) \in \Delta_{(\tau_{11} \to ... \to \tau_{1k_1} \to \alpha) \to ... \to (\tau_{m1} \to ... \to \tau_{mk_m} \to \alpha) \to \alpha}(r^{\top\top}/\alpha)$$

An m-fold application of the definition of Δ for arrow types ensures that for all closed types τ' and τ, for all $r \in Rel(\tau', \tau)$, for all $i \in \{1, ..., m\}$, and for all pairs of closed terms $(\oplus_i', \oplus_i) \in \Delta_{\tau_{i1} \to ... \to \tau_{ik_i} \to \alpha}(r^{\top\top}/\alpha)$, (8) holds iff $(M\tau'\overline{\oplus_m'}, M\tau\overline{\oplus_m}) \in \Delta_\alpha(r^{\top\top}/\alpha)$, i.e., iff $(M\tau'\overline{\oplus_m'}, M\tau\overline{\oplus_m}) \in r^{\top\top}$. Expanding the condition on $(\oplus_i', \oplus_i)$ for each $i = 1, ..., m$ shows it equivalent to the assertion that if $(a_{ij}', a_{ij}) \in \Delta_{\tau_{ij}}(r^{\top\top}/\alpha)$ for each $j = 1, ..., k_i$, then $(\oplus_i'\overline{a_{ik_i}'}, \oplus_i\overline{a_{ik_i}}) \in r^{\top\top}$. Since (8) holds, we conclude that for all closed types τ' and τ and for all $r \in Rel(\tau', \tau)$,

if, for all $i = 1, ..., m$,
$$(a_{ij}', a_{ij}) \in \Delta_{\tau_{ij}}(r^{\top\top}/\alpha) \text{ for all } j = 1, ..., k_i \text{ implies } (\oplus_i'\overline{a_{ik_i}'}, \oplus_i\overline{a_{ik_i}}) \in r^{\top\top},$$
$$\text{then } (M\tau'\overline{\oplus_m'}, M\tau\overline{\oplus_m}) \in r^{\top\top} \tag{9}$$

Note that all of the terms appearing in (9) are closed.

Now consider the instantiation

$$\tau' = \delta$$
$$r = \{(M, M') \mid \mathbf{cata}^\delta \, \tau \, \overline{\phi_m(n_{u_1}, ..., n_{u_p}, n_{v_1}, ..., n_{v_q})} \, M =_{ctx} M' : \tau\}$$
$$\oplus_i' = \phi_i(c_{u_1}, ..., c_{u_p}, \mu_{v_1}, ..., \mu_{v_q})$$
$$\oplus_i = \phi_i(n_{u_1}, ..., n_{u_p}, \mu_{v_1}', ..., \mu_{v_q}')$$

If we can verify that the hypotheses of (9) hold, then we may conclude that

$$\mathbf{cata}^\delta \, \tau \, \overline{\phi_m(n_{u_1}, ..., n_{u_p}, n_{v_1}, ..., n_{v_q})} \, (M \, \delta \, \overline{\phi_m(c_{u_1}, ..., c_{u_p}, \mu_{v_1}, ..., \mu_{v_q})})$$
$$=_{ctx} M \, \tau \, \overline{\phi_m(n_{u_1}, ..., n_{u_p}, \mu_{v_1}', ..., \mu_{v_q}')} : \tau$$

Then since $\mathbf{augment}^\delta \, M \, \overline{\mu_{v_q}} =_{ctx} M \, \delta \, \overline{\phi_m(c_{u_1}, ..., c_{u_p}, \mu_{v_1}, ..., \mu_{v_q})} : \delta$, we will have proved Theorem 1.

To verify that (9) holds, we first prove that r is $\top\top$-closed, and thus that r coincides with the PolyFix contextual equivalence relation. To see this let $(M, M') \in r^{\top\top}$. We show that $\mathbf{cata}^\delta \, \tau \, \overline{\phi_m(n_{u_1}, ..., n_{u_p}, n_{v_1}, ..., n_{v_q})} \, M =_{ctx} M' : \tau$. Let S be the "stack equivalent"

$$Id \circ \mathbf{case} - \mathbf{of} \, \{...\}$$

of the evaluation context $\mathtt{cata}^\delta \, \tau \, \overline{\phi_m(n_{u_1}, ..., n_{u_p}, n_{v_1}, ..., n_{v_q})}$. Then S is such that for all $N : \delta$,

$$S\,N \ =_{ctx} \ \mathtt{cata}^\delta \, \tau \, \overline{\phi_m(n_{u_1}, ..., n_{u_p}, n_{v_1}, ..., n_{v_q})} \, N \ : \ \tau \tag{10}$$

since

$$\mathtt{cata}^\delta \, \tau \, \overline{\phi_m(n_{u_1}, ..., n_{u_p}, n_{v_1}, ..., n_{v_q})} \, N$$
$$=_{ctx} (\lambda d. \Lambda \alpha. \lambda \overline{f_m}.\mathtt{case} \ d \ \mathtt{of}$$
$$\{... \mid c_i \overline{x_{k_i}} \Rightarrow$$
$$f_i \phi_{ik_i} (\mathtt{cata}^\delta ... x_{z_1} \alpha \overline{f_m}, ..., \mathtt{cata}^\delta ... x_{z_p} \alpha \overline{f_m}, x_{y_1}, ..., x_{y_q}) \mid ...\})$$
$$N \ \tau \ \overline{\phi_m(n_{u_1}, ..., n_{u_p}, n_{v_1}, ..., n_{v_q})}$$
$$=_{ctx} \mathtt{case} \ N \ \mathtt{of} \ \{...\}$$
$$=_{ctx} (Id \circ \mathtt{case} \ - \ \mathtt{of} \ \{...\}) \, N$$
$$=_{ctx} S\,N$$

The first equivalence is by (5) and the definition of $\mathtt{cata}$, the second is by repeated application of (2) and (3), the third is by the definition of frame stack application, and the fourth is by the definition of S.

Observe that if we define the append operation of frame stacks by

$$S @ Id = S$$

and

$$S' @ (S \circ F) = (S' @ S) \circ F$$

then

$$(S' @ S) \top M \ \Leftrightarrow \ S' \top (S M) \tag{11}$$

Moreover, for any $S' \in Stack(\tau)$, $(S' @ S, S')$ has the property that for all (N, N') with $\mathtt{cata}^\delta \, \tau \, \overline{\phi_m(n_{u_1}, ..., n_{u_p}, n_{v_1}, ..., n_{v_q})} \, N =_{ctx} N' : \tau$,

$$(S' @ S) \top N \ \Leftrightarrow \ S' \top S\,N \ \Leftrightarrow \ S' \top N'$$

The first equivalence by (11), and the second is by Proposition 2 and (10) and the fact that $=_{ctx}$ is transitive. Together with (9), the fact that $(M, M') \in r^{\top\top}$ implies that

$$(S' @ S) \top M \ \Leftrightarrow \ S' \top M' \tag{12}$$

But then

$$S' \top M' \Leftrightarrow (S' @ S) \top M$$
$$\Leftrightarrow S' \top S\,M$$
$$\Leftrightarrow S \top \mathtt{cata}^\delta \, \tau \, \overline{\phi_m(n_{u_1}, ..., n_{u_p}, n_{v_1}, ..., n_{v_q})} \, M$$

Here, the first equivalence is by (12), the second is by (11), and the third is by the definition of S. Since S' was arbitrary we have shown that

$$\forall S' \in Stack(\tau). \ S' \top M \ \Leftrightarrow \ S' \top \mathtt{cata}^\delta \, \tau \, \overline{\phi_m(n_{u_1}, ..., n_{u_p}, n_{v_1}, ..., n_{v_q})} \, M$$

By Proposition 2, we therefore have

$$M' =_{ctx} \mathsf{cata}^\delta \, \tau \, \overline{\phi_m(n_{u_1}, ..., n_{u_p}, n_{v_1}, ..., n_{v_q})} \, M \; : \; \tau$$

as desired.

To verify the hypotheses of (9), observe that since the type of M is closed, each τ_{ij} is either a closed type or is precisely α. In the first case, $\Delta_{\tau_{ij}}(r^{\top\top}/\alpha)$ is precisely $\Delta_{\tau_{ij}}()$. Thus, if $(a'_{ij}, a_{ij}) \in \Delta_{\tau_{ij}}(r^{\top\top}/\alpha)$, then by Proposition 1 then $a'_{ij} =_{ctx} a_{ij} : \tau_{ij}$. In the second case, we have $\Delta_{\tau_{ij}}(r^{\top\top}/\alpha) = r^{\top\top} = r$, i.e., $\mathsf{cata}^\delta \, \tau \, \overline{\phi_m(n_{u_1}, ..., n_{u_p}, n_{v_1}, ..., n_{v_q})} \, a'_{ij} =_{ctx} a_{ij} : \tau$. Since $=_{ctx}$ is a congruence, equivalences (2) through (5) guarantee that

$$\mathsf{cata}^\delta \, \tau \, \overline{\phi_m(n_{u_1}, ..., n_{u_p}, n_{v_1}, ..., n_{v_q})} (\oplus'_i \overline{a'_{ik_i}}) =_{ctx} \oplus_i \overline{a_{ik_i}} \; : \; \tau$$

i.e., that $(\oplus'_i \overline{a'_{ik_i}}, \oplus_i \overline{a_{ik_i}}) \in r$. By (9) we conclude that $(M\tau'\overline{\oplus'_m}, M\tau\overline{\oplus_m}) \in r$, i.e., that

$$\mathsf{cata}^\delta \, \tau \, \overline{\phi_m(n_{u_1}, ..., n_{u_p}, n_{v_1}, ..., n_{v_q})} \, (\mathsf{augment}^\delta M \, \overline{\mu_{v_q}})$$
$$=_{ctx} \, M \, \tau \, \overline{\phi_m(n_{u_1}, ..., n_{u_p}, \mu'_{v_1}, ..., \mu'_{v_q})} \; : \; \tau$$

It is also possible to derive $\top\top$-closedness of r as a consequence of (the analogue for non-list algebraic data types of) Lemma 6.1 of Pitts [14], but in the interest of keeping this paper as self-contained as possible, we choose to prove it directly.

6   Conclusion

In this paper we have defined a generalization of **augment** for lists for every algebraic data type, and used Pitts' characterization of contextual equivalence for PolyFix to prove the correctness of the corresponding **cata-augment** fusion rules for polymorphic lambda calculi supporting fixed point recursion at the level of terms and recursion via data types with non-strict constructors at the level of types. More specifically, we have shown that programs in such calculi which have undergone generalized **cata-augment** fusion are contextually equivalent to their unfused counterparts. The correctness of short cut fusion for algebraic data types, as well as of **cata-augment** fusion for lists, are special cases of this result.

The construct **augment** can be interpreted as constructing substitution instances of algebraic data structures. The generalized **cata-augment** rule can be seen as a means of optimizing compositions of functions that uniformly consume algebraic data structures with functions that uniformly produce substitution instances of them.

Acknowledgments. I am grateful to Olaf Chitil, Graham Hutton, and Andrew Pitts for helpful discussions on the topic of this paper. I also thank the volume editor and the anonymous referees for their comments. This work was completed while visiting the Foundations of Programming group at the University of Nottingham. It was supported, in part, by the National Science Foundation under grant CCR-9900510.

References

1. Abadi, M. ⊤⊤-closed relations and admissibility. *Mathematical Structures in Computer Science* 10, pp. 313 – 320, 2000.
2. Bainbridge, E., Freyd, P., Scedrov, A., and Scott, P.J. Functorial polymorphism. *Theoretical Computer Science* 70, pp. 35 – 64, 1990. Corrigendum in *Theoretical Computer Science* 71, p. 431, 1990.
3. Chitil, O. Type inference builds a short cut to deforestation. In *Proceedings, International Conference on Functional Programming*, pp. 249 – 260, 1999.
4. Gill, A. *Cheap Deforetation for Non-strict Functional Languages.* PhD thesis, Glasgow University, 1996.
5. Gill, A., Launchbury, J., and Peyton Jones, S. L. A short cut to deforestation. In *Proceedings, Conference on Functional Languages and Computer Architecture*, pp. 223 – 232, 1993.
6. Hu, Z., Iwasaki, H., and Takeichi, M. Deriving structural hylomorphisms from recursive definitions. in *Proceedings, International Conference in Functional Programming*, pp. 73 – 82, 1996.
7. Johann, P. An implementation of warm fusion. Available at `ftp://ftp.cse.ogi.edu/pub/pacsoft/wf/`, 1997.
8. Johann, P. and Visser, E. Warm fusion in Stratego: A case study in generation of program transformation systems. *Annals of Mathematics and Artifical Intelligence* 29(1-4), pp. 1 – 34, 2000.
9. Németh, L. *Catamorphism Based Program Transformations for Non-strict Functional Languages.* Draft, PhD thesis, Glasgow University, 2000.
10. Onoue, Y., Hu, Z., Iwasaki, H., and Takeichi, M. A calculational system HYLO. In *Proceedings, IFIP TC 2 Working Conference on Algorithmic Languages and Calculi*, pp. 76 – 106, 1997.
11. Plotkin, G. Call-by-name, call-by-value, and the lambda calculus. *Theoretical Computer Science* 1, pp. 125 – 159, 1975.
12. Pitts, A. Existential types: Logical relations and operational equivalence. In *Proceedings, International Colloquium on Automata, Languages, and Programming*, LNCS vol. 1443, pp. 309 – 326, 1998.
13. Pitts, A. Parametric Polymorphism, Recursive Types, and Operational Equivalence. Unpublished Manuscript.
14. Pitts, A. Parametric Polymorphism and Operational Equivalence. *Mathematical Structures in Computer Science* 10, pp. 1 – 39, 2000.
15. Takano, A. and Meijer, E. Short cut deforetation in calculational form. In *Proceedings, Conference on Functional Programming and Computer Architecture*, pp. 324 – 333, 1995.
16. Reynolds, J. C. Types, abstraction, and parametric polymorphism. *Information Processing* 83, pp. 513 – 523, 1983.
17. Sheard, T. and Fegaras, L. A fold for all seasons. In *Proceedings, Conference on Functional Programming and Computer Architecture*, pp. 233 – 242, 1993.
18. Wadler, P. Theorems for Free! In *Proceedings, Conference on Functional Programming and Computer Architecture*, pp. 347 – 359, 1989.

Generation of Efficient Programs for Solving Maximum Multi-marking Problems

Isao Sasano*, Zhenjiang Hu, and Masato Takeichi

Department of Information Engineering, University of Tokyo
7-3-1 Hongo, Bunkyo-ku, Tokyo 113-8656, JAPAN
{sasano,hu,takeichi}@ipl.t.u-tokyo.ac.jp
http://www.ipl.t.u-tokyo.ac.jp/~{sasano,hu,takeichi}

Abstract. Program generation has seen an important role in a wide range of software development processes, where effective calculation rules are critical. In this paper, we propose a more general calculation rule for generation of efficient programs for solving maximum marking problems. Easy to use and implement, our new rule gives a significant extension of the rule proposed by Sasano *et al.*, allowing multiple kinds of marks as well as more general description of the property of acceptable markings. We illustrate its effectiveness using several interesting problems.

Keywords: Program Generation Rule, Optimization Problem, Maximum Marking Problem, Functional Programming, Algorithm Synthesis.

1 Introduction

Program generation has seen an important role in a wide range of software development processes. A successful program generation system requires not only a powerful language supporting coding of program generation, but also a set of effective transformation rules for the generation of programs. An example, which convincingly shows the importance of the design of effective transformation rules, is the well-known *fold-build* rule [1] for fusing composition of functions in Glasgow Haskell Compiler (GHC). It is this general, concise and cheap calculation rule that makes it possible for GHC to *practically* generate from *large-scale* programs efficient programs without unnecessary intermediate data structures. Generally, the effective rules for program generation should meet several requirements.

- First, they should be general enough to be applied to a program pattern, by which a useful class of problems can be concisely specified.
- Second, they should be abstract enough to capture a big step of the program generating process rather than being a set of small rewriting rules.
- Third, they can be efficiently implemented by program generation systems.

---

* Isao Sasano is supported by JSPS Research Fellowships for Young Scientists.

W. Taha (Ed.): SAIG 2001, LNCS 2196, pp. 72–91, 2001.
© Springer-Verlag Berlin Heidelberg 2001

In this paper, we shall propose such a rule for generating efficient programs from the following program pattern

$$mmm\ p\ wf\ k\ =\ \uparrow_{wf}/\ \circ\ filter\ p\ \circ\ gen\ k,$$

with which one can straightforwardly specify solutions for the *maximum marking problems* [2] (sometimes also called *maximum weightsum problems* [3]): from the elements of a data structure, find a subset which satisfies a certain property p and whose weightsum is maximum. Informally speaking, this program pattern generates all the possible ways of marking the elements in the input data using the generation function *gen*, keeps those markings satisfying the property p, and finally selects one which has the maximum value with respect to the weight function *wf*. More formal explanation can be found in Section 3.

The maximum marking problems are interesting because they encompass a very large class of optimization problems [4,5], and they have attracted many researchers. Based on the algebraic laws of programs [6,7], Bird successfully derived a linear algorithm to solve the maximum segment sum problem [6], which is a maximum weightsum problem on lists. Bird *et al.* [7] demonstrated the derivation of many kinds of maximum marking problems. However, the success of derivation not only depends on a powerful calculation theorem but also involves careful and insightful justification to meet the conditions of the theorem, which makes it difficult for the theorem to be used for mechanical program generation. On the other hand, it has been shown for decades [4,5], that if specified by so-called *regular predicates* [5], the maximum marking problems are linear time solvable and such linear time programs can be automatically generated. Though being systematic and constructive, the generated linear time programs suffer from an impractically large table [5], which actually prevents them from practical use. To resolve this problem, Sasano *et al.* gave a new approach [3] to generating practical linear time algorithms for the maximum marking problems over data structures such as lists, trees, and decomposable graphs. The key point there is to express the property p by a *recursive* function of certain form, and to apply program transformation techniques for program optimization.

However, there still remain several limitations. First, the number of kinds of marks are basically restricted to two. Although by using two marks (marking an element or not) one can describe many combinatorial optimization problems such as the 0-1 knapsack problem, it is difficult to handle the optimization problems where more states on elements are required, as will be seen later. Second, the property p is restrictive in the sense it must be a function without the use of accumulating parameters, which makes it hard to specify history-sensitive properties. Third, the weight function *wf* is restricted to only the sum of marked elements.

To remedy this situation, we extend the work in Sasano *et al.* [3], giving a calculation rule for generating efficient programs for solving *maximum multi-marking problems*. Our main contributions can be summarized as follows:

- We propose a new calculation rule (Section 4) for generating efficient algorithms for solving maximum multi-marking problems. It can efficiently handle multi-marking, general weight functions, and property description with an accumulating parameter, leading to a more *general* framework for solving a wider class of combinatorial optimization problems, covering those in the previous work [3,2,4,5].

- We demonstrate, with several non-trivial example problems, that our calculation rule provides a practical and friendly interface for people both to specify those problems and to generate efficient programs automatically. Surprisingly, as partly shown in Section 5, our approach can deal with many optimization problems in Bird *et al.* [7]. By contrast, the derivation process in Bird *et al.* [7] is difficult to be mechanized.
- We show that our calculation rule can be easily implemented by using the existing transformation systems like MAG [8], and efficient programs can be obtained in a fully automatic way.

The organization of this paper is as follows: In Section 2, we briefly review the previous work on the maximum marking problems and explain limitations. In Section 3, we give a formal definition of the maximum multi-marking problems. In Section 4, we propose our optimization theorem which gives the rule for generation of efficient programs for maximum multi-marking problems. In Section 5, we show the effectiveness of our approach by deriving efficient algorithms for solving several interesting problems. Related work is discussed in Section 6, and the conclusion is made in Section 7.

2   Maximum Marking Problems

In this section, we briefly review the previous work on maximum marking problems and the results obtained in Sasano *et al.* [3]. The maximum marking problems are a special and simpler case of the maximum multi-marking problems.

We assume that the readers are familiar with the functional language Haskell [9], whose notation will be used throughout this paper.

2.1   Overview

Given a data structure xs (of type $D\ \alpha$), a *maximum marking problem* is to find a marking of xs's elements such that the marked data structure xs^* (of type $D\ \alpha^*$) satisfies a certain property p, and that the sum of the marked elements in xs^* is maximum. Here the "maximum" means that no other marking of xs satisfying p can produce a larger weightsum.

As an example, consider the maximum independent sublist sum problem (*mis* for short) [3], which is to compute a way of marking of the elements in a list xs, such that no two marked elements are adjacent and the sum of the marked elements are maximum. For instance, for

$$xs = [1, 2, 3, 4, 5]$$

the result is the marking of

$$[1^*, 2, 3^*, 4, 5^*],$$

which gives the maximum sum of 9 among all the feasible marking of xs. One can check that any other way of feasible marking cannot give a larger sum.

A straightforward solution for the general maximum marking problem, whose complexity is exponential to the number of elements in xs, can be defined precisely as follows:

$$mws \ : \ (D \ \alpha^* \to Bool) \to D \ \alpha \to D \ \alpha^*$$
$$mws \ p \ = \ \uparrow\!wsum \ / \ \circ \ filter \ p \ \circ \ gen.$$

The function gen generates all the possible markings of input data, and from those which satisfy the property p the function $\uparrow\!wsum$ / selects one whose weightsum of marked elements is maximum. The operator / is called *reduce* [10] and is defined as follows:

$$\oplus/[x_1, x_2, \ldots, x_n] = x_1 \oplus x_2 \oplus \cdots \oplus x_n$$

where $\oplus$ is an associative operator. The operator $\uparrow_f$ is called *selection* [10] and is defined as follows:
$$x \uparrow_f y = x, \quad \textbf{if } f \ x \geq f \ y$$
$$= y, \quad \textbf{otherwise.}$$

Using mws, one can specify many interesting optimization problems by giving different definition for the property p [3]. For example, the property p for the above mis problem can be naturally defined as follows:

$$p \ [] \qquad = True$$
$$p \ (x : xs) \ = \textbf{if } marked \ x \textbf{ then } p_1 \ xs \textbf{ else } p \ xs$$

$$p_1 \ [] \qquad = True$$
$$p_1 \ (x : xs) = not \ (marked \ x) \ \wedge \ p \ xs.$$

Here, the function *marked* takes as its argument an element x and returns *True* when x is marked and returns *False* otherwise. The calculation rule already proposed in Sasano *et al.* [3] says that if the property is described in a *mutumorphic* form (which can be considered as a mutually recursive version of *fold*), then a linear program can be automatically generated. So for the mis problem, since the property p is already described in a mutumorphic form, we can conclude that a linear program can be obtained.

2.2   Limitations

To see the limitations of the existing approach, consider the following coloring problem, a simple extension of the mis problem. Suppose there are three marks: red, blue, and yellow. The problem is to find a way of marking all the elements such that each sort of mark does not appear continuously, and that the sum of the elements marked in red minus the sum of the elements marked in blue is maximum. To obtain an efficient algorithm for this problem by using the existing approach [3], we intend to specify this coloring problem using the following program pattern:

$$mws\ p\ =\ \uparrow wsum\ /\ \circ\ filter\ p\ \circ\ gen.$$

Unfortunately, there are several problems preventing us from doing so. First, the existing generation function gen generates all the possible markings with just a single kind of mark, but a single kind of mark is not enough for this problem. That means we need to extend the generation function gen so that it can generate all the possible markings with multiple kinds of marks. A generation function for the coloring problem may be written as follows:

$$gen\ []\qquad =\ [[]]$$
$$gen\ (x:xs) = [(x,m):ys\ |\ m\leftarrow[Red,Blue,Yellow],ys\leftarrow gen\ xs].$$

Second, the property description p for the coloring problem can be naturally specified as follows:

$$indep\ xs\qquad\qquad = indep'\ xs\ Neutral$$
$$indep'\ []\ color\qquad = True$$
$$indep'\ (x:xs)\ color = markKind\ x\neq color\wedge indep'\ xs\ (markKind\ x).$$

But this is not in a required mutumorphic form such that the rule in Sasano *et al.* [3] can be applied, because $indep'$ has an additional accumulating parameter $color$. Here, $Neutral$ is used as the initial value of the accumulating parameter, which is different from all the colors used for coloring the elements. The function $markKind$ takes as its argument a marked element and returns the kind of mark of the element. If we insist on specifying $indep$ in a mutumorphic form, we would have to instantiate all the possible values of $color$ used by $indep'$, and could reach the following complicated definition:

$$indep\ []\qquad = True$$
$$indep\ (x:xs) = \textbf{case}\ markKind\ x\ \textbf{of}$$
$$Red\rightarrow indep_R\ xs$$
$$Blue\rightarrow indep_B\ xs$$
$$Yellow\rightarrow indep_Y\ xs$$

$$indep_R\ []\qquad = True$$
$$indep_R\ (x:xs) = \textbf{case}\ markKind\ x\ \textbf{of}$$
$$Red\rightarrow False$$
$$Blue\rightarrow indep_B\ xs$$
$$Yellow\rightarrow indep_Y\ xs$$

$$indep_B\ []\qquad = True$$
$$indep_B\ (x:xs) = \textbf{case}\ markKind\ x\ \textbf{of}$$
$$Red\rightarrow indep_R\ xs$$
$$Blue\rightarrow False$$
$$Yellow\rightarrow indep_Y\ xs$$

$$indep_Y \; [\,] \qquad = \; True$$
$$indep_Y \; (x : xs) = \textbf{case} \; markKind \; x \; \textbf{of}$$
$$Red \rightarrow indep_R \; xs$$
$$Blue \rightarrow indep_B \; xs$$
$$Yellow \rightarrow False.$$

In fact, this instantiation not only leads to a complicated definition, but also makes the generated program less efficient than that generated in Section 4.

Finally, the weight function $wsum$ fixed in the program pattern $mws \; p$ is rather restrictive. For the coloring problem, we may hope to use the following weight function:

$$wf = +/ \; \circ \; map \; f$$
$$\textbf{where} \; f \; x = \textbf{case} \; markKind \; x \; \textbf{of}$$
$$Red \rightarrow weight \; x$$
$$Blue \rightarrow -(weight \; x)$$
$$Yellow \rightarrow 0,$$

which is clearly not a simple $wsum$.

To overcome these limitations, in this paper we will give a more general program pattern for specifying the maximum marking problems with multiple marks, while guaranteeing that an efficient program can be automatically generated from this program pattern.

3 Maximum Multi-marking Problems

In this section, we give a formal definition of the maximum multi-marking problems. To simplify our presentation, we focus on the problems on lists in this paper.

A maximum multi-marking problem can be specified as follows: Given a list xs, the task is to find a way to mark each element in xs such that the marked data structure xs, say xs^*, satisfies a certain property p, and the value of weight function wf of marked list xs^* is maximum. A straightforward program mmm to solve this problem is

$$mmm \qquad : \; ([\alpha^*] \rightarrow Bool) \rightarrow ([\alpha^*] \rightarrow Weight) \rightarrow Int \rightarrow [\alpha] \rightarrow [\alpha^*]$$
$$mmm \; p \; wf \; k = \uparrow_{wf} / \; \circ \; filter \; p \; \circ \; gen \; k.$$

We use $gen \; k$, which is different from that in Section 2, to generate all the possible markings of an input list with k kinds of marks, and from those which satisfy the property p we use $\uparrow_{wf} /$ to select one with maximum value of the weight function wf. Many optimization problems, including the coloring problem in Section 2, can be expressed using mmm by giving a suitable property p and weight function wf.

Before defining gen and wf, we explain some of our notation for marking. For a data type of α, we use α^* to extend α with marking information. It can be defined more precisely as follows:

$$\alpha^* = (\alpha, Mark)$$

where *Mark* is the type of marks. We use integers from 1 to k as marks where k is the integer which is given as the third argument of *mmm*. Of course it is possible to use any set holding k elements for *Mark*. Accordingly, we use a^*, b^*, ..., x^* to denote variables of the type α^* and use $xs^*, ys^*, \ldots$ to denote variables of the type $[\alpha^*]$.

The function *gen*, exhaustively enumerating all the possible ways of marking elements using marks from 1 to k, can be recursively defined as follows:

$$
\begin{aligned}
gen &\quad : \quad Int \to [\alpha] \to [\alpha^*] \\
gen\ k\ [] &\ = [[]] \\
gen\ k\ (x : xs) &\ = [\,x^* : xs^* \mid x^* \leftarrow mark\ x, xs^* \leftarrow gen\ k\ xs\,]
\end{aligned}
$$

where *mark* is a function for marking which is defined as follows:

$$
mark\ x = [\,(x, m) \mid m \leftarrow [1 \mathinner{..} k]\,].
$$

In addition, in order to get the mark from a marked element, we define the function *markKind* as follows:

$$
markKind\ (x, m) = m.
$$

Using *mmm* we can express various kinds of problems. For example, the coloring problem in Section 2 can be specified as follows:

$$coloring\ =\ mmm\ indep\ wf\ 3$$

$$
\begin{aligned}
indep\ xs\ &=\ indep'\ xs\ 0 \\
indep'\ []\ color\ &=\ True \\
indep'\ (x : xs)\ color\ &=\ markKind\ x \neq color \land indep'\ xs\ (markKind\ x)
\end{aligned}
$$

$$
\begin{aligned}
wf\ =\ &+/\ \circ\ map\ f \\
&\textbf{where}\ f\ e^*\ =\ \textbf{case}\ markKind\ e^*\ \textbf{of} \\
&\qquad\qquad\qquad 1 \to weight\ e^* \\
&\qquad\qquad\qquad 2 \to -(weight\ e^*) \\
&\qquad\qquad\qquad 3 \to 0.
\end{aligned}
$$

Of course, this definition of *mmm* is terribly inefficient, though it is straightforward. In the next section, we would like to show that they can be automatically transformed to an efficient linear one.

4   Program Generation

In this section, we propose a theorem for generating efficient algorithms for solving maximum multi-marking problems, and highlight how this theorem can be easily implemented for automatic generation of efficient executable programs.

4.1   Generation Rule

We shall propose a theorem for generating efficient algorithms for solving maximum multi-marking problems. The theorem gives a significant extension of the theorem proposed in Sasano *et al.* [3]. It can efficiently handle multi-marking, general weight functions, and property description with an accumulating parameter. Before giving the theorem, we should be more precise about the requirement of the weight function *wf* and the property *p* used for specifying a maximum multi-marking problem *mmm* in Section 3.

The previous work, including ours, restricted the weight function *wf* to be just the sum of weight of marked elements [3,2,4,5]. As seen in the coloring problem in Section 2, we often need to use a more general weight function. For this purpose, we define the following general form, a kind of list homomorphism [10], which we call *homomorphic weight function*.

Definition 1 (Homomorphic Weight Function). *A function wf is a homomorphic weight function if it is defined as follows:*

$$
\begin{aligned}
wf &: \quad [\alpha^*] \rightarrow \textit{Weight} \\
wf &= \quad \oplus/ \circ \textit{ map } f
\end{aligned}
$$

where $\oplus$ is an associative binary operator which can be computed in $O(1)$ time, which has an identity element $\iota_\oplus$, and which satisfies the condition called distributivity over $\uparrow_{id}$:

$$
(\uparrow_{id} / \; xs) \; \oplus \; (\uparrow_{id} / \; ys) \quad = \quad \uparrow_{id} /[\; x \oplus y \mid x \in xs \wedge y \in ys \;].
$$

A homomorphic weight function allows any $O(1)$ computation f over each marked element and a more general operation $\oplus$ rather than just $+$ for "summing up". This enables us to deal with the weight function for the coloring problem in Section 3.

For the property p which is to specify the feasible markings with multiple kinds of marks, the existing approach [3] (as seen in the definition of *indep* in Section 2) only allows p to be defined in a *mutumorphic* form with several other functions, say $p_1, \ldots, p_n$, whose ranges are finite.

$$
\begin{aligned}
p \;[] &= e \\
p \;(x : xs) &= \phi \; x \; (p \; xs, p_1 \; xs, \ldots, p_n \; xs)
\end{aligned}
$$
$$
\vdots
$$
$$
\begin{aligned}
p_i \;[] &= e_i \\
p_i \;(x : xs) &= \phi_i \; x \; (p \; xs, p_1 \; xs, \ldots, p_n \; xs)
\end{aligned}
$$
$$
\vdots
$$

If p is defined in the mutumorphic form, by applying the tupling transformation [11,12], we can always come up with the following definition for p, a composition of a project function with a *foldr*:

$$
\begin{aligned}
p = \textit{fst} \; &\circ \; \textit{foldr } \psi \; e' \\
\textbf{where} \; &\psi \; x \; es = (\phi \; x \; es, \phi_1 \; x \; es, \ldots, \phi_n \; x \; es) \\
&e' = (e, e_1, \ldots, e_n).
\end{aligned}
$$

To specify a history-sensitive property, we often want to use an accumulating parameter. So we extend the above p to a composition of a function with a $foldr_h$, a higher order version of $foldr$, which is defined as follows:

$$foldr_h \ (\phi_1, \phi_2) \ \delta \ [] \ e \qquad = \phi_1 \ e$$
$$foldr_h \ (\phi_1, \phi_2) \ \delta \ (x : xs) \ e = \phi_2 \ x \ e \ (foldr_h \ (\phi_1, \phi_2) \ \delta \ xs \ (\delta \ x \ e)).$$

Using this function $foldr_h$, we define the following form, which we call *finite accumulative property*.

Definition 2 (Finite Accumulative Property). *A property p is a finite accumulative property if it is defined as follows:*

$$p : [\alpha^*] \to Bool$$
$$p \ xs = g \ (foldr_h \ (\phi_1, \phi_2) \ \delta \ xs \ e_0)$$

where the domain of g and range of δ is finite.

Now we propose our main theorem.

Theorem 1 (Generation Rule). *Suppose a specification of a maximum multi-marking problem is given as*

$$mmm \ p \ wf \ k \ = \ \uparrow_{wf} / \ \circ \ filter \ p \ \circ \ gen \ k.$$

If wf is a homomorphic weight function

$$wf \ = \ \oplus / \ \circ \ map \ f$$

and p is a finite accumulative property

$$p \ xs \ = \ g \ (foldr_h \ (\phi_1, \phi_2) \ \delta \ xs \ e_0),$$

then the maximum multi-marking problem ($mmm \ p \ wf \ k$) can be solved by

$$opt \ k \ (\lambda(c, e) \ . \ g \ c \ \wedge \ e == e_0) \ (f, \oplus, \iota_\oplus) \ \phi_1 \ \phi_2 \ \delta.$$

The definition of opt is given in Figure 1.

This theorem has a form similar to that in Sasano et al. [3] except for using array in the definition of *opt* for efficiency, and it can be proved by induction on the input list. We omit the detailed proof in this paper, due to the space limitation. One remark worth making is about the cost of the derived program. Assuming that δ and g have the types

$$\delta : \alpha^* \to Acc \to Acc$$
$$g : Class \to Bool,$$

we can conclude that the generated program using *opt* can be computed in $O(|Acc| \cdot |Class| \cdot k \cdot n)$ time, where n is the length of input list, k is the number of marks, and $|Acc|$ and $|Class|$ denote the size of the type Acc and the type $Class$ respectively. That means that our approach is applicable only when the domain of g and the range of δ is finite. If our approach is applicable, our generated program is much more efficient than the initial specification program $mmm \ p \ wf \ k$, which is exponential.

$opt\ k\ accept\ (f, \oplus, \iota_\oplus)\ \phi_1\ \phi_2\ \delta\ xs =$
  let $opts = foldr\ \psi_2\ \psi_1\ xs$
  in $snd\ (\uparrow_{fst}\ /\ [\,(w, r^*)\ |\ Just\ (w, r^*) \leftarrow [\,opts!i\ |\ i \leftarrow range\ bnds,$
                                             $opts!i \neq Nothing, accept\ i\,]\,])$
    where $\psi_1 = array\ bnds\ [\,(i, g\ i)\ |\ i \leftarrow range\ bnds]$
         $\psi_2\ x\ cand = accumArray\ h\ Nothing\ bnds$
                   $[\,((\phi_2\ x^*\ e\ c, e),\ (f\ x^* \oplus w,\ x^* : r^*))$
                   $|\ x^* \leftarrow [\,(x, 1), (x, 2), \ldots, (x, k)\,],$
                   $e \leftarrow acclist,$
                   $((c, \_), Just\ (w, r^*)) \leftarrow$
                       $[\,(i, cand!i)\ |\ i \leftarrow [\,(c', \delta\ x^*\ e)\ |\ c' \leftarrow classlist],$
                                   $inRange\ bnds\ i,$
                                   $cand!i \neq Nothing\,]\,]$
      $g\ (c, e) = $ **if** $(c == phi_1\ e)$ **then** $Just\ (\iota_\oplus, [])$ **else** $Nothing$
      $h\ (Just\ (w_1, x_1))\ (w_2, x_2) = $ **if** $w_1 > w_2$ **then** $Just\ (w_1, x_1)$
                                      else $Just\ (w_2, x_2)$
      $h\ Nothing\ (w, x) = Just\ (w, x)$
      $bnds = ((head\ classlist, head\ acclist), (last\ classlist, last\ acclist))$
  $acclist = $ list of all the values in Acc
  $classlist = $ list of all the values in $Class$

Fig. 1. Optimization function opt.

An Example. To see how the theorem works, we demonstrate how to derive a linear algorithm for the coloring problem in Section 2. Recall that the specification for the coloring problem has been given in Section 3. The weight function has been written in our required form, and the property $indep$ can be easily rewritten using $foldr_h$ as follows:

$$indep\ xs = id\ (foldr_h\ (\phi_1, \phi_2)\ \delta\ xs\ 0)$$
$$\textbf{where}\ \phi_1\ e = True$$
$$\phi_2\ x\ e\ r = markKind\ x \neq e \wedge r$$
$$\delta\ x\ e = markKind\ x.$$

Now applying the theorem quickly yields a linear time algorithm, whose program coded in Haskell is given in Figure 2. Notice that in this example, $k = 3$, $|Acc| = 4$, and $|Class| = 2$. Evaluating the expression

```
> coloring [1,2,3,4,5]
```

gives the result of
$$[(1, 1), (2, 3), (3, 1), (4, 3), (5, 1)].$$

It is worth while to compare the generated algorithms from the two property description with and without an accumulating parameter. Consider the coloring problem with k colors and with certain homomorphic weight function wf. By using property description with an accumulating parameter, $O(k^2 n)$ algorithm is obtained because $|Acc| = k + 1$ and $|Class| = 2$. On the contrary, by using property description in mutumorphic form without accumulating parameters as described in Section 2, $O(2^k n)$ algorithm would be obtained by applying the previous method [3], if it could deal with multiple kinds of marks.

4.2 Implementation

Our generation rule can be implemented, so that efficient programs can be generated automatically. In this section, we highlight[1] how we can do so using MAG system [8], a transformation system with a powerful *higher order pattern matching*.

As seen in Figure 2, our obtained program can be divided into two parts: the dynamic and static parts. The dynamic part changes from problems to problems, while the static part remains the same. In Figure 2, the upper part is dynamic and the lower is static. We show how to generate the dynamic part from the specification *mmm p wf k*.

Using MAG, we may code the generation of the dynamic part from specification *mmm p wf k* as a rule called `mmmRule` as follows.

```
mmmRule: mmm p wf k
          = opt k accept (f,oplus,e) phi1 phi2 delta,
      if {
          wf = foldr (oplus) e . map f;
          p xs = g (h xs e0);
          h [] = phi1;
          h (x:xs) y = phi2 x y (h xs (delta x y));
          \(c,e) -> g c && e==e0 = accept
      };
```

Now for the coloring problem, we can apply this rule to the following specification and obtain a linear time program as in Figure 2 automatically.

```
coloring: coloring = mmm indep wf 3;
wf: wf = foldr (+) 0 . map f;
f: f = \x -> case markKind x of
                1 -> weight x
                2 -> - (weight x)
                3 -> 0;
p: p xs = p' xs 0;
p1: p' [] color = True;
p2: p' (x:xs) color = markKind x /= color && p' xs (markKind x);
classlist: classlist = [False,True];
acclist: acclist = [0..3]
```

---

[1] Although actually we cannot do it because of several restrictions of the MAG system, we are only showing the flavor of the implementation.

```
coloring = opt 3 accept (f, (+), 0) phi1 phi2 delta
acclist = [0..3]
classlist = [False, True]
accept (c,e) = c && e==0
f = \x -> case markKind x of
                1 -> weight x
                2 -> - (weight x)
                3 -> 0
phi1 e = True
phi2 x e c = markKind x /= e && c
delta x e = markKind x
markKind (_,m) = m
weight (x,_) = x
-------------------------------------------------------------------
opt k accept (f, oplus, id_oplus) phi1 phi2 delta xs =
  let opts = foldr psi2 psi1 xs
  in snd (getmax [(w,r) | Just (w,r) <- [ opts!i
                                        | i <- range bnds,
                                          opts!i /= Nothing,
                                          accept i]])
    where psi1 = array bnds [(i, g i) | i <- range bnds]
          psi2 x cand = accumArray h Nothing bnds
                          [((phi2 xm e c, e),
                            (f xm 'oplus' w, xm:r))
                           | xm <- [(x,m) | m <- [1..k]],
                             e <- acclist,
                             ((c,_),Just (w,r)) <-
                               [ (i,cand!i)
                                | i <- [ (c',delta xm e)
                                        | c' <- classlist],
                                  inRange bnds i,
                                  cand!i /= Nothing]]
          g (c,e) = if (c == phi1 e) then Just (id_oplus, [])
                    else Nothing
          h (Just (w1,x1)) (w2,x2) = if w1 > w2 then Just (w1,x1)
                                     else Just (w2,x2)
          h Nothing (w,x) = Just (w,x)
          bnds = ((head classlist,head acclist),
                  (last classlist,last acclist))
getmax [] = error "No solution."
getmax xs = foldr1 f xs
              where f (w1,cand1) (w2,cand2)
                      = if w1>w2 then (w1,cand1) else (w2,cand2)
```

Fig. 2. A linear-time Haskell program for the coloring problem.

With these, the MAG system can produce the linear time program as given in Figure 2. Note that the current version of MAG system has several restrictions such as not allowing **case** expression, so MAG system needs extension for our purpose.

5   More Examples

In this section, we give more examples, showing that our proposed gerneration rule is quite general and powerful.

5.1   Paragraph Formatting Problem

The paragraph formatting problem is the problem of breaking a sequence of words into lines to form a paragraph. At least one blank space must exist between any adjacent two words in the same line. Line length, *i.e.*, the number of characters each line holds, is fixed as m. We want to minimize the sum of the number of blank spaces in all the lines excluding the last line. We assume that the input sequence of words is given by a list of words and that a word is expressed by its length since the spelling of words is not needed. For example, the sequence of words "This is a dog. They are cats." is expressed as the list $[4, 2, 1, 4, 4, 3, 5]$.

We would like to treat this problem as a multi-marking problem, that is, to describe this problem in the form

$$mmm \ p \ wf \ k.$$

We use three kinds of marks, 1, 2, and 3. So, $k = 3$. If a word is marked 2, then it indicates that the word is the last word of the line it belongs to. If a word is marked 3, then it indicates that the word belongs to the last line. The other words are marked 1. We make special treatment of the last line in order to exclude the blank spaces when computing the sum of the number of blank spaces. The property p checks whether a marking represents a valid breaking or not. We describe the property p by using an accumulating parameter. The accumulating parameter holds the pair of position pos and mark mk, where pos represents the last position filled by the previous words in the current line, and mk represents the kind of mark of the previous word. We define the property p as follows:

$$
\begin{aligned}
&p \ xs = p' \ xs \ (0, 2) \\
&p' \ [] \ (pos, mk) = mk \neq 1 \\
&p' \ (x : xs) \ (pos, mk) = \\
&\quad \textbf{case } mk \textbf{ of} \\
&\quad\quad 1 \rightarrow \textbf{case } markKind \ x \textbf{ of} \\
&\quad\quad\quad 1 \rightarrow pos + l \ x + 1 \leq m \ \wedge \ p' \ xs \ (pos + l \ x + 1, 1) \\
&\quad\quad\quad 2 \rightarrow pos + l \ x + 1 \leq m \ \wedge \ p' \ xs \ (0, 2) \\
&\quad\quad\quad 3 \rightarrow False
\end{aligned}
$$

$$2 \rightarrow \textbf{case } markKind \; x \textbf{ of}$$
$$1 \rightarrow pos + l \; x \leq m \;\wedge\; p' \; xs \; (pos + l \; x, 1)$$
$$2 \rightarrow pos + l \; x \leq m \;\wedge\; p' \; xs \; (0, 2)$$
$$3 \rightarrow pos + l \; x \leq m \;\wedge\; p' \; xs \; (pos + l \; x, 3)$$
$$3 \rightarrow \textbf{case } markKind \; x \textbf{ of}$$
$$1 \rightarrow False$$
$$2 \rightarrow False$$
$$3 \rightarrow pos + l \; x + 1 \leq m \;\wedge\; p' \; xs \; (pos + l \; x + 1, 1),$$

where we use the function l to compute the length of a word.

Next, we have to describe the weight function wf. We want to minimize the sum of the number of blanks except for the last line. The function $white$ which returns the sum can be written as follows:

$$white = +/ \circ map \; f$$
$$\textbf{where } f \; x = \textbf{case } markKind \; x \textbf{ of}$$
$$1 \rightarrow -l \; x$$
$$2 \rightarrow m - l \; x$$
$$3 \rightarrow 0.$$

Using this function, we can define the weight function wf as follows:

$$wf \; x = -(white \; x).$$

This can be easily transformed into the following form:

$$wf = +/ \circ map \; f$$
$$\textbf{where } f \; x = \textbf{case } markKind \; x \textbf{ of}$$
$$1 \rightarrow l \; x$$
$$2 \rightarrow -m + l \; x$$
$$3 \rightarrow 0.$$

Now the paragraph formatting problem is written as follows:

$$mmm \; p \; wf \; 3.$$

By applying the Theorem 1 (by using the rule `mmmRule`), we can obtain an $O(mn)$ algorithm where n is the number of words. This complexity is achieved by the fact that the number of kinds of marks k is three, the size of the accumulating parameter $|Acc|$ is $3(m + 1)$, and the size of the function g (in this case id) $|Class|$ is 2.

5.2 Security Van Problem

The security van problem can be specified as follows [7]:

Suppose a bank has a known sequence of deposits and withdrawals. For security reasons the total amount of cash in the bank should never exceed some fixed amount N, assumed to be at least as large as any single *transaction. To cope with demand and supply, a security van can be called upon to deliver funds to the bank or to take away a surplus. The problem is to compute a schedule under which the van visits the bank a minimum number of times.*

In order to specify this problem as a maximum multi-marking problem, we consider the *security* of transactions. A sequence $[a_1, a_2, \ldots, a_n]$ of transactions is called *secure* if there is an amount r, indicating the total amount of cash in the bank at the beginning of the sequence of transactions, such that each of the sums

$$r, r + a_1, r + a_1 + a_2, \ldots, r + a_1 + \cdots + a_n$$

lies between zero and N. For example, taking $N = 10$, the sequence $[3, -5, 6]$ is secure because the van can take away or deliver enough cash to make an initial reserve of, for example, 5. Given the constraint that N is no smaller than any single transaction, every singleton sequence is secure, so a valid schedule certainly exists.

To formalize the constraint, define

$$ceiling = \uparrow_{+/} / \circ \; inits$$
$$floor \quad = \downarrow_{+/} / \circ \; inits$$

where *inits* is a function which takes as its argument a list and returns the list which has all the initial segments including empty list. A sequence x of transactions is secure if and only if

$$ceiling \; x - floor \; x \leq N.$$

Considering this condition, we can define property p in the following way. We express the time the van visits by marking 1 to a transaction after which the van visits. Transactions marked 2 represent the other transactions. The accumulating parameter holds a triple of sum, ceiling, and floor for each initial segment.

$$p \; xs = p' \; xs \; (0, 0, 0)$$
$$p' \; [] \; (s, c, f) = True$$
$$p' \; (x : xs) \; (s, c, f) =$$
$$\quad \textbf{let} \; (s', c', f') = (s + w \; x, \; c \uparrow_{id} s', \; f \downarrow_{id} s')$$
$$\quad \textbf{in case} \; markKind \; x \; \textbf{of}$$
$$\quad\quad 1 \rightarrow \textbf{if} \; c' - f' \leq N \; \textbf{then} \; p' \; xs \; (w \; x, 0 \uparrow_{id} w \; x, 0 \downarrow_{id} w \; x)$$
$$\quad\quad\quad \textbf{else} \; p' \; xs \; (w \; x, 0 \uparrow_{id} w \; x, 0 \downarrow_{id} w \; x)$$
$$\quad\quad 2 \rightarrow \textbf{if} \; c' - f' \leq N \; \textbf{then} \; p' \; xs \; (s', c', f'))$$
$$\quad\quad\quad \textbf{else} \; False$$

Here, the function w takes as its argument a marked transaction and returns the amount of it. We want to minimize the number of times the van visits, so we first define the function *times* which computes the times the van visits.

$$times = +/ \circ \; map \; f$$
$$\quad\quad \textbf{where} \; f \; x = \textbf{case} \; markKind \; x \; \textbf{of}$$
$$\quad\quad\quad\quad 1 \rightarrow 1$$
$$\quad\quad\quad\quad 2 \rightarrow 0$$

Using this function, we can define the weight function wf as follows:

$$wf\ x = -\ (times\ x).$$

This can be easily transformed into the following form:

$$wf = +/\ \circ\ map\ f$$
$$\mathbf{where}\ f\ x = \mathbf{case}\ markKind\ x\ \mathbf{of}$$
$$1 \to -1$$
$$2 \to 0.$$

Now the security van problem is written as follows:

$$mmm\ p\ wf\ 2.$$

The weight function wf is written in the required form, and the property p can be easily rewritten into the required form, though we omit the form. By applying Theorem 1, we obtain $O(N^3 n)$ algorithm because $|Acc| = (N+1)^2(2N+1)$, $k = 2$, and $|Class| = 2$.

5.3   Knapsack Problem

The knapsack problem [13] is a well known combinatorial optimization problem. There are several problems called knapsack problem such as 0-1 knapsack problem, 0-1 multiple knapsack problem, multidimensional knapsack problem, and so on. Here we consider the simplest one, the 0-1 knapsack problem.

Input of the 0-1 knapsack problem is a set of items each of which has weight and value. Output is a feasible selection of items whose value sum is maximum in all the feasible item selections. A selection is feasible when sum of weight of selected items does not exceed the given capacity C. We assume weight of items are integers. Without this assumption, this problem becomes NP-hard.

We express selection by marking 1 to selected items and 2 to the others. The property for 0-1 knapsack problem can be described as follows. The accumulating parameter holds a value from 0 to C, which indicates the remaining capacity of knapsack.

$$
\begin{aligned}
knap\ xs\quad &= knap'\ xs\ C \\
knap'\ []\ e\quad &= True \\
knap'\ (x : xs)\ e &= \mathbf{case}\ markKind\ x\ \mathbf{of} \\
&\quad 1 \to \mathbf{if}\ e \geq w\ x\ \mathbf{then}\ knap'\ xs\ (e - w\ x)\ \mathbf{else}\ False \\
&\quad 2 \to knap'\ xs\ e
\end{aligned}
$$

Here, the function w returns the weight of the item. We want to maximize the value of selected items, so we can define the weight function wf as follows:

$$wf = +/\ \circ\ map\ f$$
$$\mathbf{where}\ f\ x = \mathbf{case}\ markKind\ x\ \mathbf{of}$$
$$1 \to value\ x$$
$$2 \to 0.$$

Here, the function *value* returns the value of the item.

Now the 0-1 knapsack problem is written as follows:

$$mmm\ knap\ wf\ 2.$$

The weight function *wf* is written in the required form, and the property *knap* can be easily rewritten into the required form, though we omit the form. By applying Theorem 1, we obtain $O(Cn)$ algorithm because $|Acc| = C + 1$, $k = 2$, and $|Class| = 2$.

5.4   Weighted Interval Selection Problem

Given a set of weighted intervals, the weighted interval selection problem is to select a maximum-weight subset such that any two selected intervals are disjoint [14]. An application of this problem is a scheduling of jobs whose start and end times are fixed and only one job can be executed at a time. We assume that start and end times are represented by integers. This assumption is natural in real-world jobs, where we mean that the time unit is a day or an hour or a minute or a second, and so on.

Suppose the job set is given as a list of jobs in the order of start time, that is, if job A starts earlier than job B, then job A appears earlier than job B in the list. We express a job by a 3-tuple of the start time, the time which it takes, and the weight of the job. Here we express start time by the difference from the previous job in the job list except for the first job. We express the time of the first job as 0. This way of expressing start time is for applying Theorem 1. For example, the list

$$jobs = [(0, 3, 2), (2, 4, 3), (3, 2, 5)]$$

is a job list, and *jobs* represents three jobs where the second job starts at time 2, and the third job starts at time 5, provided that the first job starts at time 0. Feasible solutions are selecting the first and the third job or selecting only one job. So, the maximum solution is selecting the first and the third job. We express a selection by marking 1 to selected jobs and 2 to the others. For example, maximum solution for *jobs* is expressed as

$$[((0, 3, 2), 1), ((2, 4, 3), 2), ((3, 2, 5), 1)].$$

Property p checks that the selected jobs do not overlap each other. So, p can be defined as follows: The accumulating parameter represents the time the currently executed job takes until it ends.

$$
\begin{aligned}
&p\ xs &&= p'\ xs\ 0 \\
&p'\ [\ ]\ e &&= True \\
&p'\ (x : xs)\ e = \textbf{case}\ markKind\ x\ \textbf{of} \\
&\quad 1 \to \textbf{if}\ e - s\ x > 0\ \textbf{then}\ False\ \textbf{else}\ p'\ xs\ (t\ x) \\
&\quad 2 \to \textbf{if}\ e - s\ x > 0\ \textbf{then}\ p'\ xs\ (e - s\ x)\ \textbf{else}\ p'\ xs\ 0
\end{aligned}
$$

Here the function s takes as its argument a job x and returns the start time of it, that is, the first element of the 3-tuple. The function t takes as its argument a job x and returns the time it takes, that is, the second element of the 3-tuple.

We want to maximize the sum of weight of selected jobs, so we can define the weight function *wf* as follows:

$$wf = +/ \circ map\ f$$
$$\textbf{where } f\ x = \textbf{case } markKind\ x\ \textbf{of}$$
$$1 \rightarrow w\ x$$
$$2 \rightarrow 0.$$

Here the function *w* takes as its argument a job *x* and returns the weight of it, that is, the third element of the 3-tuple.

Now the weighted interval selection problem is written as follows:

$$mmm\ p\ wf\ 2.$$

The weight function *wf* is written in the required form, and the property *p* can be easily rewritten into the required form, though we omit the form. By applying Theorem 1, we obtain $O(Wn)$ algorithm, where W is the maximum length among all jobs, because $|Acc| = W + 1$, $|Class| = 2$, and $k = 2$.

6   Related Work

In addition to the related work given in the introduction, we show some others in this section.

Bird calculated a linear-time algorithm for solving the maximum segment sum problem on lists [6], which is a kind of maximum marking problem. Bird *et al.* studied optimization problems, which include maximum marking problems, in a more general way that uses relational calculus [7]. Using relational calculus, they developed a very general framework to treat optimization problems. Their approach is called *thinning theory*, and the *thinning theorem* plays the central role. But when applying the thinning theorem, one has to find two preorders which meet prerequisites of the thinning theorem, which makes it difficult for the theorem to be used for mechanical program generation. And they didn't show the relation between the complexity of derived algorithms and specifications, in return for discussing in a very general framework. We instead focus on a useful class of optimization problems, maximum multi-marking problems, propose a very simple way to derive efficient algorithms, and assure the complexity of the derived algorithms.

Johan Jeuring proposed several fusion theorems, each of which deals with a class of optimization problems such as subsequence problems on lists, partition problems on lists, and so on [15]. In order to derive an efficient program for a problem by his method, one has to select a suitable fusion theorem, which is not necessary in our method.

De Moor considered a generic program for sequential decision processes [16] which are specified as follows:

```
listmin r . filter p . fold (choice fs) [c].
```

The target problems are on lists and trees. They include maximum multi-marking problems by letting the list of functions fs, used in the above specification of sequential decision processes, be a list of marking functions. But property p is restricted to be suffix-closed. There are many examples whose property is not suffix-closed.

Recently, Bird showed that the maximum marking problems can be treated in the framework of thinning theory [2]. He assured the derived algorithm is a linear time algorithm, and showed the generic Haskell program for solving the maximum marking problems on polynomial data types. His method also requires that the property p should be suffix-closed.

In graph algorithms, Borie *et al.* proposed a method which enables the derivation of a linear time algorithm for solving the maximum marking problems on k-terminal graphs, a restricted class of graphs, from logical description of properties by a graph variant of monadic second order formula [5]. This graph variant of MSOL uses *Inc* (v, e), which means a vertex v is an incident of an edge e, instead of the use of a successor function in ordinary MSOL [17]. Although appealing in theory, these methods are hardly useful in practice due to a huge constant factor for space and time.

7   Conclusions

In this paper, we propose an important theorem (generation rule) for generating efficient algorithms for solving maximum multi-marking problems, which can efficiently handle multi-marking, general weight functions, and property description with an accumulating parameter. This theorem leads to a more *general* framework for automatically generating efficient programs for solving a wider class of combinatorial optimization problems, covering those in the previous work [3,2, 4,5].

Although this paper focuses on lists whereas the previous work [3] can treat any polynomial data structure, we believe that it is not difficult to extend this work to any polynomial data structure, and we leave it as our future work.

References

1. Andrew Gill, John Launchbury, and Simon L. Peyton Jones. A short cut to deforestation. In *Proceedings of the 6th International Conference on Functional Programming Languages and Computer Architecture (FPCA'93)*, pages 223–232, Copenhagen, Denmark, June 1993. ACM Press.
2. Richard Bird. Maximum marking problems, 2000. Available from http://www.comlab.ox.ac.uk/oucl/work/richard.bird/publications/mmp.ps.
3. Isao Sasano, Zhenjiang Hu, Masato Takeichi, and Mizuhito Ogawa. Make it practical: A generic linear-time algorithm for solving maximum-weightsum problems. In *Proceedings of the 5th ACM SIGPLAN International Conference on Functional Programming (ICFP'00)*, pages 137–149, Montreal, Canada, September 2000. ACM Press.

4. Marshall W. Bern, Eugene L. Lawler, and A. L. Wong. Linear-time computation of optimal subgraphs of decomposable graphs. *Journal of Algorithms*, 8:216–235, 1987.

5. Richard B. Borie, R. Gary Parker, and Craig A. Tovey. Automatic generation of linear-time algorithms from predicate calculus descriptions of problems on recursively constructed graph families. *Algorithmica*, 7:555–581, 1992.

6. Richard Bird. Algebraic identities for program calculation. *The Computer Journal*, 32(2):122–126, 1989.

7. Richard Bird and Oege de Moor. *Algebra of Programming.* Prentice Hall, 1996.

8. Oege de Moor and Ganesh Sittampalam. Generic program transformation. In *Proceedings of the 3rd International Summer School on Advanced Functional Programming (AFP'98)*, LNCS 1608, pages 116–149, Braga, Portugal, September 1998. Springer-Verlag.

9. Richard Bird. *Introduction to Functional Programming using Haskell (second edition)*. Prentice Hall, 1998.

10. Richard Bird. An introduction to the theory of lists. In Manfred Broy, editor, *Logic of Programming and Calculi of Discrete Design*, NATO ASI Series 36, pages 5–42. Springer-Verlag, 1987.

11. Maarten M. Fokkinga. *Law and Order in Algorithmics.* PhD thesis, University of Twente, Dept INF, Enschede, The Netherlands, 1992.

12. Zhenjiang Hu, Hideya Iwasaki, Masato Takeichi, and Akihiko Takano. Tupling calculation eliminates multiple data traversals. In *Proceedings of the 2nd ACM SIGPLAN International Conference on Functional Programming (ICFP'97)*, pages 164–175, Amsterdam, The Netherlands, June 1997. ACM Press.

13. Silvano Martello and Paolo Toth. *Knapsack Problems : Algorithms and Computer Implementations*. Wiley-Interscience series in discrete mathematics and optimization. John Wiley & Sons Ltd., 1990.

14. Thomas Erlebach and Frits Spieksma. Simple algorithms for a weighted interval selection problem. In *Proceedings of the 11th International Symposium on Algorithms and Computation (ISAAC'00)*, LNCS 1969, pages 228–240, Taipei, Taiwan, December 2000. Springer-Verlag.

15. Johan Jeuring. *Theories for Algorithm Calculation.* Ph.D thesis, Faculty of Science, Utrecht University, 1993.

16. Oege de Moor. A generic program for sequential decision processes. In *Proceedings of the 7th International Symposium on Programming Languages, Implementations, Logics, and Programs (PLILP'95)*, LNCS 982, pages 1–23, Utrecht, the Netherlands, September 1995.

17. Wolfgang Thomas. Automata on infinite objects. In Jan van Leeuwen, editor, *Handbook of Theoretical Computer Science*, volume B, chapter 4, pages 133–192. Elsevier Science Publishers, 1990.

Static Transition Compression

Daniel Damian and Olivier Danvy

BRICS[*]
Department of Computer Science, University of Aarhus
Ny Munkegade, Building 540, DK-8000 Aarhus C, Denmark
{damian,danvy}@brics.dk
http://www.brics.dk/~{damian,danvy}

Abstract. Starting from an operational specification of a translation from a structured to an unstructured imperative language, we point out how a compositional and context-insensitive translation gives rise to static chains of jumps. Taking an inspiration from the notion of continuation, we state a new compositional and context-sensitive specification that provably gives rise to no static chains of jumps, no redundant labels, and no unused labels. It is defined with one inference rule per syntactic construct and operates in linear time and space on the size of the source program (indeed it operates in one pass).

1   Introduction

The art of writing a compiler partly amounts to resolving the tensions between its various phases. For example, should each phase be simple, but generate redundancies that equally simple later phases would eliminate? Or should each phase avoid redundancies in order to avoid a later phase and save the resources spent processing the redundancies in between? Picturesquely, Richard Gabriel nicknamed this kind of choices "worse is better" and "the right thing" [8]. Worse is better yields results sooner, at the risk of never ending with the right thing. The right thing is the right thing, but takes longer to achieve, at the risk of funding running out. Resolving the tensions between these choices in a compiler is anything but easy due to its many circular dependencies.

In this article, we consider transition compression, i.e., collapsing chains of jumps into unique jumps. To this end, we formalize the translation of structured programs into unstructured programs with jumps (Section 2). We show how a compositional and context-insensitive translation naturally generates chains of jumps (Section 3). We then specify a compositional and context-sensitive translation that is parameterized by the labels of the current command and of the next command, and we prove that it generates no chains of jumps, no redundant labels and no unused labels (Section 4 and 5). It therefore compresses transitions at translation time—hence the title of this article.

The issue of transition compression is standard [1] [9, Section 4.4], but we are not aware of any other formalized characterization of generating chains of jumps

---

[*] Basic Research in Computer Science (www.brics.dk), funded by the Danish National Research Foundation.

W. Taha (Ed.): SAIG 2001, LNCS 2196, pp. 92–107, 2001.
© Springer-Verlag Berlin Heidelberg 2001

and avoiding them. Since we wrote this article, however, we became aware of Dybvig, Hieb, and Butler's work on destination-driven code generation [6], which shares the same goal as static transition compression and has been implemented as part of the back-end of an optimizing Scheme compiler.

2 Source and Target Languages

We consider the translation of structured programs that use conditional commands and while loops into unstructured programs that use labels and jumps.

2.1 An Unstructured Target Language

Our target language is defined in Figure 1. Unstructured commands can be (unspecified) atomic commands, skip commands, sequences of commands, conditional jumps, and unconditional jumps. Commands can be labeled, and labels are used as targets of jumps. Conditional jumps are triggered by either the truth (if) or the falsity (ifn) of a boolean expression. A program is an unstructured command ending with a stop instruction, optionally labeled.

$u \in$ UCom ::= a | skip | $u_1; u_2$ | $\ell:\ u$ | if b goto ℓ | ifn b goto ℓ | goto ℓ
$a \in$ ACom (atomic commands, omitted)
$b \in$ BExp (boolean expressions, omitted)
$\ell \in$ Lab   (code labels, unspecified)

Fig. 1. An unstructured target language

Valid programs are commands where labels are unique and targets of jumps always exist. Their semantics is state-based and straightforward. (We define it as a trace semantics since we omit the specification of atomic commands. A state is thus the series of atomic commands executed in the course of a program.)

2.2 A Structured Source Language

Our source language is defined in Figure 2. Structured commands can be atomic commands, sequences of commands, conditional commands, and while loops. Again, their (trace) semantics is state-based and straightforward [17].

$s \in$ SCom ::= a | $s_1; s_2$ | if b then s_1 else s_2 end | while b do s end
$a \in$ ACom (atomic commands, same as in Figure 1)
$b \in$ BExp (boolean expressions, same as in Figure 1)

Fig. 2. A structured source language

Implementing a compiler for such a language requires one to translate structured commands into unstructured commands in a language such as the one in Figure 1. This translation is the topic of the next section.

3   A Context-Insensitive Translation

We start with a compositional and context-insensitive translation. For each compound structured command, the translation generates code for all subcomponents, and combines them together with explicit conditional/unconditional jumps implementing the required flow of control. The translation is canonical [16, Section 2.8].

3.1   The Translation

The judgment

$$\vdash s \longrightarrow u$$

holds whenever the structured command s translates into the unstructured command u. Fresh labels may be generated during the translation. Label generation can be modeled, e.g., by threading a counter through the derivation tree.

At the top level, a structured program s is translated into an unstructured program u; stop if $\vdash s \longrightarrow u$ holds.

The inference rules are displayed in Figure 3. Let us describe each of them in words.

$$\vdash a \longrightarrow a$$

$$\frac{\vdash s_1 \longrightarrow u_1 \qquad \vdash s_2 \longrightarrow u_2}{\vdash s_1; s_2 \longrightarrow u_1; u_2}$$

$$\frac{\vdash s_1 \longrightarrow u_1 \qquad \vdash s_2 \longrightarrow u_2}{
\begin{array}{l} \vdash \text{if } b \\ \text{then } s_1 \\ \text{else } s_2 \\ \text{end} \end{array}
\longrightarrow
\begin{array}{l} \text{if } b \text{ goto } \ell_1; \\ u_2; \\ \text{goto } \ell_2; \\ \ell_1: u_1; \\ \ell_2: \text{skip} \end{array}
} \qquad \text{where } \ell_1 \text{ and } \ell_2 \text{ are fresh}$$

$$\frac{\vdash s \longrightarrow u}{
\begin{array}{l} \vdash \text{while } b \\ \text{do } s \\ \text{end} \end{array}
\longrightarrow
\begin{array}{l} \ell_1: \text{ifn } b \text{ goto } \ell_2; \\ u; \\ \text{goto } \ell_1; \\ \ell_2: \text{skip} \end{array}
} \qquad \text{where } \ell_1 \text{ and } \ell_2 \text{ are fresh}$$

Fig. 3. A compositional and context-insensitive translation

Atomic commands: An atomic command is translated into the same atomic command.

Sequences of commands: A sequence of commands is translated into the sequence of the translated commands.

Conditional commands: A conditional command is translated into a conditional jump determining whether to execute the translated then branch or the translated else branch. The translated branches merge into a labeled skip instruction. One branch jumps to it and the other one flows into it.

While loops: A while loop is translated into a labeled conditional jump determining whether to execute the translated body of the loop or to exit the loop. The translated body is followed by an unconditional jump to close the loop. A labeled skip instruction follows as the exit point of the loop.

In Figure 3, the translation judgments are deterministic and therefore the translation of a program always exists and is unique. Using rule induction [17] one can show that the translated program is valid and also that its semantics agrees with the semantics of the source program.

3.2 Variations

The translation defined in Figure 3 is only one among many in the range of choices for translating conditional commands and while loops. Let us take three examples.

- For conditional commands, the conditional branches could be swapped.
- For while loops, the translation starts with a conditional jump and finishes with an unconditional jump. More compact programs can be obtained by starting with an unconditional jump and finishing with a conditional jump:

$$\frac{\vdash s \longrightarrow u}{\vdash \text{while } b \longrightarrow \quad \begin{array}{l} \text{goto } \ell_2; \\ \ell_1 \colon u; \\ \ell_2 \colon \text{if } b \text{ goto } \ell_1 \end{array}} \quad \text{where } \ell_1 \text{ and } \ell_2 \text{ are fresh}$$

where on the left: $\vdash$ while b, do s, end

The two translations differ in the number of steps executed at run-time by the resulting programs.

- For while loops, one could also choose Baskett's technique [4], which duplicates b and mixes the two previous translations:

$$\frac{\vdash s \longrightarrow u}{\vdash \text{while } b \longrightarrow \quad \begin{array}{l} \text{ifn } b \text{ goto } \ell_2; \\ \ell_1 \colon u; \\ \text{if } b \text{ goto } \ell_1; \\ \ell_2 \colon \text{skip} \end{array}} \quad \text{where } \ell_1 \text{ and } \ell_2 \text{ are fresh}$$

where on the left: $\vdash$ while b, do s, end

These alternatives embody tradeoffs between the size and the speed of the resulting code. A compiler could decide among them based on compile-time information or on profiling information.

3.3 Analysis

A compositional and context-insensitive translation is simple to write and to reason about. By its very nature, however, it does not take into account the contexts of the translated terms and therefore, it gives rise to redundancies, e.g., when sequencing conditional commands and while loops, as illustrated next.

Example 1 (Sequencing).

$$
\begin{array}{ll}
\vdash \text{ if } b_1 \quad \longrightarrow \quad & \text{if } b_1 \text{ goto 1;} \\
\quad \text{then } a_1 & \quad a_2; \\
\quad \text{else } a_2 & \quad \text{goto 2;} \\
\quad \text{end;} & \text{1: } a_1; \\
\quad \text{while } b_2 & \text{2: skip;} \\
\quad \text{do } a_3 & \text{3: ifn } b_2 \text{ goto 4;} \\
\quad \text{end} & \quad a_3; \\
& \quad \text{goto 3;} \\
& \text{4: skip}
\end{array}
$$

Sequencing a conditional command and a while loop gives rise to a skip instruction (the one labeled by 2) that could be eliminated and to labels (2 and 3) that could be merged.   □

The translation also gives rise to further spurious skip instructions, e.g., for nested conditional commands, as illustrated next.

Example 2 (Then-nested conditional commands).

$$
\begin{array}{ll}
\vdash \text{ if } b_1 \quad \longrightarrow \quad & \text{if } b_1 \text{ goto 1;} \\
\quad \text{then if } b_2 & \quad a_3; \\
\qquad \text{then } a_1 & \quad \text{goto 2;} \\
\qquad \text{else } a_2 & \text{1: if } b_2 \text{ goto 3;} \\
\qquad \text{end} & \quad a_2; \\
\quad \text{else } a_3 & \quad \text{goto 4;} \\
\quad \text{end} & \text{3: } a_1; \\
& \text{4: skip;} \\
& \text{2: skip}
\end{array}
$$

Nesting a conditional command in the then branch of a conditional command gives rise to a spurious skip instruction (here, the one labeled with 4).   □

Given n then-nested conditional commands, the direct translation generates a chain of n consecutive skip instructions. It can also give rise to chains of jumps, as illustrated next.

Example 3 (Else-nested conditional commands).

$$
\begin{array}{ll}
\vdash \text{if } b_1 & \text{if } b_1 \text{ goto 1;} \\
\quad \text{then } a_1 & \text{if } b_2 \text{ goto 3;} \\
\quad \text{else if } b_2 & a_3; \\
\qquad \text{then } a_2 & \text{goto 4;} \\
\qquad \text{else } a_3 & 3: a_2; \\
\qquad \text{end} & 4: \text{skip;} \\
\quad \text{end} & \text{goto 2;} \\
& 1: a_1; \\
& 2: \text{skip}
\end{array}
$$

Nesting a conditional command in the else branch of a conditional command gives rise to a chain of skip instructions and unconditional jumps (label 4 is part of the chain here). □

Given n else-nested conditional commands, the direct translation generates a chain of n successive jumps.

Chains of jumps also arise when translating nested while loops, as illustrated next.

Example 4 (Nested while loops).

$$
\begin{array}{ll}
\vdash \text{while } b_1 & 1: \text{ifn } b_1 \text{ goto 2;} \\
\quad \text{do while } b_2 & 3: \text{ifn } b_2 \text{ goto 4;} \\
\qquad \text{do while } b_3 & 5: \text{ifn } b_3 \text{ goto 6;} \\
\qquad\quad \text{do } a & a; \\
\qquad\quad \text{end} & \text{goto 5;} \\
\qquad \text{end} & 6: \text{skip;} \\
\quad \text{end} & \text{goto 3;} \\
& 4: \text{skip;} \\
& \text{goto 1;} \\
& 2: \text{skip}
\end{array}
$$

Nesting a while loop in a while loop gives rise to a chain of skip instructions and unconditional jumps (labels 6 and 4 are part of the chain here). □

Given n nested while loops, the direct translation generates a chain of n successive jumps. The alternative translations for while loops mentioned in Section 3.1 share the same problem.

The redundancies add up when translating more complex code structures, as illustrated next.

Example 5 (Nested heterogeneous commands).

$$
\begin{array}{lll}
\vdash \text{while } b_1 & \longrightarrow & 1: \text{ifn } b_1 \text{ goto } 2; \\
\quad \text{do } a_1; & & \quad a_1; \\
\qquad \text{if } b_2 & & \quad \text{if } b_2 \text{ goto } 3; \\
\qquad \text{then while } b_3 & & \quad a_3; \\
\qquad\quad \text{do } a_2 & & \quad \text{goto } 4; \\
\qquad\quad \text{end} & & 3: \\
\qquad \text{else } a_3 & & 5: \text{ifn } b_3 \text{ goto } 6; \\
\qquad \text{end} & & \quad a_2; \\
\quad \text{end} & & \quad \text{goto } 5; \\
& & 6: \text{skip}; \\
& & 4: \text{skip}; \\
& & \quad \text{goto } 1; \\
& & 2: \text{skip}
\end{array}
$$

This example illustrates overlapping chains of jumps (the skip instruction labeled with 4 can both be flowed into and jumped to) and redundant aliased labels (3 and 5). □

Finding a proper strategy to eliminate overlapping chains of jumps increases the requirements on the post-processing phase. An extra phase is also necessary to eliminate redundant aliased labels.

3.4   Chains of Jumps

Chains of jumps are a classical issue. Compiler textbooks list two choices:

1. use backpatching [1, Chapter 8]; and
2. have a simple code-generation scheme and eliminate chains of jumps in a post-processing phase, e.g., peephole optimization [1, Chapter 9] or block reordering [12].

Post-unfolding chains of jumps is also known as *transition compression* in partial evaluation [9, Section 4.4].

On one hand, a simple code-generation scheme is easy to maintain and to extend. On the other hand, a post-processing phase is likely to be an expensive part of the compiler, since it requires one to identify the chains of jumps. As for backpatching, it requires one to maintain an additional list structure in the memory, potentially linear in the size of the source program. Ensuring correctness also becomes more difficult.

Other authors [2] propose using code blocks, exploring code traces and reshuffling blocks in order to minimize the amount of redundant jumps. On one hand, such an approach often leads to better code by optimizing the redundancies in the original code. On the other hand, it requires one to design and implement a code-reshuffling strategy.

In the following sections we present and prove a simple translation scheme that avoids generating redundant labels and chains of jumps, does not introduce additional computational steps, does not require allocation of additional space, and operates in one pass. Furthermore, the generated code is still amenable to code reshuffling and dynamic transition compression, as in Erosa and Hendren's work [7]. Our solution is not unique in the sense that it can be adapted to other translation rules.

4 Context Awareness

Examining Figure 3 makes it clear where chains of jumps can arise. For example, a conditional command is always punctuated with a labeled skip instruction, in order to establish a program point where the conditional branches can join. Therefore, as illustrated by Example 3, else-nested conditional commands give rise to chains of jumps—one for each joining program point.

4.1 Continuations and Duplication

To prevent these chains of jumps, and in the spirit of continuations [14], one can parameterize the translation with the label of the next instruction and generate explicit jumps to this label. The resulting translation, however, is not optimal because sequenced atomic commands yield redundant jumps to the next instruction. The problem is reminiscent of administrative redexes introduced by a Plotkin-style CPS transformation [5,11].

One could then duplicate the translation judgment. A first judgment would hold when the translated command ends with an explicit jump to the label of its next command, and a second would hold when the translated command flows into the next instruction. Duplication, however, is a slippery road because it leads one to uncomfortably large specifications. Alternatively, the translation judgment could be parameterized with an inherited attribute, and this is the topic of the next section.

4.2 Towards the Right Thing

We parameterize the translation judgment with attributes. The judgment relates a structured command s and an unstructured command u.

- Both conditional commands and while loops need a label for the next instruction. We therefore parameterize the judgment with an inherited label for the instruction following u (the 'next' label). On the other hand, atomic commands do not need a next label. We therefore parameterize the judgment with an inherited flag indicating whether u can flow into the next label or whether it must jump to it, and with a synthesized flag indicating whether or not the next label is used in u.
- While loops need a label for the current instruction, but other commands do not. We therefore parameterize the judgment with an inherited label for u (the 'current' label) and with a synthesized flag indicating whether or not the current label is used in u.

Thus equipped, we can specify a translation by combinatorially enumerating all the possible values of the flags. The next labels make it possible to short-cut static chains of jumps and the inherited flags to only declare the labels that are actually used. The translation avoids both chains of jumps and unused labels in translated programs, works in one pass, and is simple to prove correct.

On the other hand, the combinatorial enumeration gives rise to a large number of inference rules. We would rather have a solution with one inference rule per syntactic construct. Such a solution is the topic of the next section.

5   A Context-Sensitive Translation

We present a compositional and context-sensitive translation that has one inference rule per syntactic construct and that avoids generating chains of jumps as well as redundant or unused labels.

5.1   The Translation

Compared to Section 4.2, our insight is to combine inherited flags and inherited labels into *qualified labels*, and to reduce the two synthesized flags to one, for the next label.

The qualified current label, qcl, for a translated command u: qcl is inherited. It is either $MAY\ \ell$ or $MUST\ \ell$, for some label ℓ. The label ℓ is associated to the entry point of u. If ℓ is qualified as $MUST$, the translation must declare it at the entry point of u. Otherwise, ℓ is qualified as MAY and, unless necessary (e.g., for a while loop), the translation can ignore ℓ. Qualified current labels are attached (or not) to translated commands according to the judgment

$$\vdash_{\textbf{def}} \langle qcl, u \rangle \longrightarrow u'$$

where qcl is a qualified current label and u and u' are unstructured commands. If the qualifier is $MUST$, u is labeled in the result u'. Otherwise, the qualifier is MAY and u is not labeled in u'. This auxiliary judgment thus concerns the definition of labels for commands. It is defined in Figure 4.

The qualified next label, qnl, for a translated command u: qnl is inherited. It is either $FLOW\ \ell$ or $JUMP\ \ell$, for some label ℓ. The label ℓ is associated to the instruction following u. If ℓ is qualified as $JUMP$, the translation must generate an explicit jump to it. Otherwise, ℓ is qualified as $FLOW$ and, unless it needs it (e.g., for a conditional command or for a while loop), the translation can let u flow into the next instruction.

The result flag, r, for a translated command u: r is synthesized. It is either $USED$ or $UNUSED$. If it is $USED$, then the command following u must be labeled with the next label.

Qualified next labels are jumped to (or not) in translated commands according to the judgment

$$\vdash_{use} \langle qnl, u \rangle \longrightarrow \langle u', r \rangle$$

where qnl is a qualified next label, u and u' are unstructured commands, and r is a result flag. If the qualification is $FLOW$, then $u' = u$ and r is $UNUSED$. Otherwise, the qualification is $JUMP$, a jump to the next label is generated, and r is $USED$. This second auxiliary judgment thus concerns the use of a label after a command. It is defined in Figure 4.

Our translation is compositional, uses one inference rule per syntactic construct, and relates a structured command s into an unstructured command u. It is parameterized with two inherited attributes, qcl and qnl, and one synthesized attribute, r, and reads as follows:

$$\vdash \langle qcl, s, qnl \rangle \longrightarrow \langle u, r \rangle$$

The judgment is satisfied whenever s translates into u. It uses the two auxiliary judgments defined above.

At the top level, a structured program s is translated into an unstructured program u; u' as follows:

$$\frac{\vdash \langle MAY\ \ell_1, s, FLOW\ \ell_0 \rangle \longrightarrow \langle u, r \rangle \quad \vdash_{def} \langle qcl, \mathsf{stop} \rangle \longrightarrow u'}{\vdash s \longrightarrow u;\ u'}$$

where ℓ_0 and ℓ_1 are fresh and $qcl = transfer\ r\ \ell_0$

where $transfer$ is defined just below.

N.B.: u' is either stop or $\ell_0 :\ \mathsf{stop}$, depending on whether r is $UNUSED$ or $USED$.

We use the following auxiliary functions ($project$ is overloaded):

$$
\begin{aligned}
&transfer : result\text{-}flag \times \text{Lab} &&\rightarrow qualified\text{-}current\text{-}label \\
&transfer\ UNUSED\ \ell &&= MAY\ \ell \\
&transfer\ USED\ \ell &&= MUST\ \ell \\
\\
&project : qualified\text{-}current\text{-}label \rightarrow \text{Lab} \\
&project\ (MAY\ \ell) &&= \ell \\
&project\ (MUST\ \ell) &&= \ell \\
\\
&project : qualified\text{-}next\text{-}label &&\rightarrow \text{Lab} \\
&project\ (FLOW\ \ell) &&= \ell \\
&project\ (JUMP\ \ell) &&= \ell
\end{aligned}
$$

N.B.: In an implementation, since there is no ambiguity, one would probably represent qualified labels as pairs of tags and labels, and overload MAY, $FLOW$ and $UNUSED$ into one tag and $MUST$, $JUMP$ and $USED$ into another tag, at

$$\vdash_{\mathsf{def}} \langle MAY\ \ell, u \rangle \longrightarrow u \qquad \vdash_{\mathsf{def}} \langle MUST\ \ell, u \rangle \longrightarrow \ell :\ u$$

$$\vdash_{\mathsf{use}} \langle FLOW\ \ell, u \rangle \longrightarrow \langle u, UNUSED \rangle \qquad \vdash_{\mathsf{use}} \langle JUMP\ \ell, u \rangle \longrightarrow \langle (u;\ \mathsf{goto}\ \ell), USED \rangle$$

$$\frac{\vdash_{\mathsf{def}} \langle qcl, a \rangle \longrightarrow u \qquad \vdash_{\mathsf{use}} \langle qnl, u \rangle \longrightarrow \langle u', r \rangle}{\vdash \langle qcl, a, qnl \rangle \longrightarrow \langle u', r \rangle}$$

$$\frac{\vdash \langle qcl, s_1, FLOW\ \ell_1 \rangle \longrightarrow \langle u_1, r_1 \rangle \quad \vdash \langle qcl_2, s_2, qnl \rangle \longrightarrow \langle u_2, r_2 \rangle}{\vdash \langle qcl, (s_1;\ s_2), qnl \rangle \longrightarrow \langle (u_1;\ u_2), r_2 \rangle} \quad \begin{array}{l} \text{where } \ell_1 \text{ is fresh} \\ \text{and } qcl_2 = transfer\ r_1\ \ell_1 \end{array}$$

$$\frac{\vdash \langle MUST\ \ell_1, s_1, qnl \rangle \longrightarrow \langle u_1, r_1 \rangle \quad \vdash \langle MAY\ \ell_2, s_2, JUMP\ \ell \rangle \longrightarrow \langle u_2, r_2 \rangle \quad \vdash_{\mathsf{def}} \langle qcl, (\mathsf{if}\ b\ \mathsf{goto}\ \ell_1;\ u_2;\ u_1) \rangle \longrightarrow u}{\vdash \langle qcl, \mathsf{if}\ b\ \mathsf{then}\ s_1\ \mathsf{else}\ s_2\ \mathsf{end}, qnl \rangle \longrightarrow \langle u, USED \rangle} \quad \begin{array}{l} \text{where } \ell = project\ qnl \\ \text{and } \ell_1 \text{ and } \ell_2 \\ \text{are fresh} \end{array}$$

$$\frac{\vdash \langle MAY\ \ell_3, s, JUMP\ \ell_1 \rangle \longrightarrow \langle u, r \rangle \quad \vdash_{\mathsf{def}} \langle MUST\ \ell_1, (\mathsf{ifn}\ b\ \mathsf{goto}\ \ell_2;\ u) \rangle \longrightarrow u'}{\vdash \langle qcl, \mathsf{while}\ b\ \mathsf{do}\ s\ \mathsf{end}, qnl \rangle \longrightarrow \langle u', USED \rangle} \quad \begin{array}{l} \text{where } \ell_1 = project\ qcl \\ \ell_2 = project\ qnl \\ \text{and } \ell_3 \text{ is fresh} \end{array}$$

Fig. 4. A compositional and context-sensitive translation

the price of clarity. Then *transfer* would be the identity function and *project* would be the second projection function.

The inference rules are displayed in Figure 4. We describe each of them in words next.

Atomic commands: An atomic command is translated into the same atomic command. Depending on the qualified current label, the resulting atomic command might be labeled. Depending on the qualified next label, it might be followed by a jump to the next label and gives rise to the corresponding synthesized result flag.

Sequences of commands: A sequence of commands is translated into the sequence of the translated commands. The qualified current label is inherited by the translation of the first command, and the qualified next label by the translation of the second command. In the translation of the first command, to reflect sequencing, the qualification of the next label is *FLOW*. The result flag synthesized from the translation of the first command is transferred to the translation of the second command as an inherited attribute. The final result flag is inherited from the translation of the second command.

Conditional commands: A conditional command is translated into a conditional jump determining whether to execute the translated then branch or the translated else branch. The translated branches merge into the next label (the else branch must jump to it), and thus their result flags are not used.

While loops: A while loop is translated into a conditional jump labeled by the current label of the translation and determining whether to execute the translated body of the loop or to exit the loop. The current label serves as a next label to translate the body, to close the loop. The next label of the translation serves as the exit point of the loop.

In contrast to the context-insensitive translation of Figure 3, the context-sensitive translation of Figure 4 does not introduce any skip commands. Moreover, none of the generated unconditional jumps are labeled. The following theorem is straightforward to prove by rule induction [17].

Theorem 1 (No chains). *Let s be a program in* SCom *such that $\vdash s \longrightarrow u$ is satisfied. Then,*

1. *there exist no commands* goto ℓ *and* ℓ : goto ℓ' *in u;*
2. *there exist no commands* if b goto ℓ *and* ℓ : goto ℓ' *in u; and*
3. *there exist no commands* ifn b goto ℓ *and* ℓ : goto ℓ' *in u.*

Furthermore, the translation of Figure 4 generates no unused labels, as stated by the following theorem, which is also straightforward to prove.

Theorem 2 (All labels are used). *Let s be a program in* SCom *such that $\vdash s \longrightarrow u$ is satisfied. Then, for any label ℓ in u, at least one of the following conditions is true:*

1. *There exists a command* goto ℓ *in u.*
2. *There exists a command* if b goto ℓ *in u.*
3. *There exists a command* ifn b goto ℓ *in u.*

Finally, the translation of Figure 4 does not generate redundant aliased labels, as stated by the following theorem, which is also straightforward to prove.

Theorem 3 (No redundant labels). *Let s be a program in* SCom *such that $\vdash s \longrightarrow u$ is satisfied. Then there exist no labels ℓ_1 and ℓ_2 such that there exists a command ℓ_1 : ℓ_2 : u' in u.*

5.2   Variations

The translation defined in Figure 4 is only one among many in the range of choices for translating conditional commands and while loops. For instance, Baskett's translation of while loops [4] can be adapted as follows.

$$\frac{\vdash_{\text{def}} \langle qcl, \text{ifn } b \text{ goto } \ell_2 \rangle \longrightarrow u_0 \quad \vdash \langle MUST \; \ell_1, s, FLOW \; \ell_3 \rangle \longrightarrow \langle u_1, r_3 \rangle \quad \vdash_{\text{def}} \langle qcl_3, \text{if } b \text{ goto } \ell_1 \rangle \longrightarrow u_2}{\vdash \langle qcl, \text{while } b \text{ do } s \text{ end}, qnl \rangle \longrightarrow \langle (u_0; u_1; u_2), USED \rangle}$$

where $\ell_2 = project \; qnl$
ℓ_1, ℓ_3 are fresh
and $qcl_3 = transfer \; r_3 \; \ell_3$

The alternative translation of while loops from Section 3.2, however, does not blend as directly in the present context-sensitive translation. The guilty part is its opening unconditional jump.

5.3   Analysis

Let us revisit the examples of Section 3.3 and show that no redundancies occur.

Example 6 (Sequencing, revisited).

$$
\begin{array}{ll}
\vdash \text{ if } b_1 \longrightarrow & \text{if } b_1 \text{ goto 3;} \\
\quad \text{then } a_1 & \quad a_2; \\
\quad \text{else } a_2 & \quad \text{goto 2;} \\
\quad \text{end;} & 3: a_1; \\
\quad \text{while } b_2 & 2: \text{ifn } b_2 \text{ goto 0;} \\
\quad \text{do } a_3 & \quad a_3; \\
\quad \text{end} & \quad \text{goto 2;} \\
& 0: \text{stop}
\end{array}
$$

In contrast to Example 1, the translated code contains no additional labels or spurious skip instructions.   □

Example 7 (Then-nested conditional commands, revisited).

$$
\begin{array}{ll}
\vdash \text{ if } b_1 \longrightarrow & \text{if } b_1 \text{ goto 2;} \\
\quad \text{then if } b_2 & \quad a_3; \\
\qquad \text{then } a_1 & \quad \text{goto 0;} \\
\qquad \text{else } a_2 & 2: \text{if } b_2 \text{ goto 4;} \\
\qquad \text{end} & \quad a_2; \\
\quad \text{else } a_3 & \quad \text{goto 0;} \\
\quad \text{end} & 4: a_1; \\
& 0: \text{stop}
\end{array}
$$

In contrast to Example 2, no spurious skip instructions have been generated. □

Example 8 (Else-nested conditional commands, revisited).

$$
\begin{array}{ll}
\vdash \text{ if } b_1 \longrightarrow & \text{if } b_1 \text{ goto 2;} \\
\quad \text{then } a_1 & \text{if } b_2 \text{ goto 4;} \\
\quad \text{else if } b_2 & \quad a_3; \\
\qquad \text{then } a_2 & \quad \text{goto 0;} \\
\qquad \text{else } a_3 & 4: a_2; \\
\qquad \text{end} & \quad \text{goto 0;} \\
\quad \text{end} & 2: a_1; \\
& 0: \text{stop}
\end{array}
$$

In contrast to Example 3, all jumps to 0 are now direct, and the last statement flows directly to 0.   □

Example 9 (Nested while loops, revisited).

$$
\begin{array}{ll}
\vdash \text{while } b_1 & \quad\longrightarrow\quad 1: \text{ifn } b_1 \text{ goto } 0; \\
\quad \text{do while } b_2 & \quad 2: \text{ifn } b_2 \text{ goto } 1; \\
\qquad \text{do while } b_3 & \quad 3: \text{ifn } b_3 \text{ goto } 2; \\
\qquad\quad \text{do } a & \quad\quad a; \\
\qquad\quad \text{end} & \quad\quad \text{goto } 3; \\
\qquad \text{end} & \quad 0: \text{stop} \\
\quad \text{end} & \\
\text{end} &
\end{array}
$$

In contrast to Example 4, no additional labels or spurious skip instructions have been generated.   □

Example 10 (Nested heterogeneous commands, revisited).

$$
\begin{array}{ll}
\vdash \text{while } b_1 & \quad\longrightarrow\quad 1: \text{ifn } b_1 \text{ goto } 0; \\
\quad \text{do } a_1; & \quad\quad a_1; \\
\qquad \text{if } b_2 & \quad\quad \text{if } b_2 \text{ goto } 4; \\
\qquad \text{then while } b_3 & \quad\quad a_3; \\
\qquad\qquad \text{do } a_2 & \quad\quad \text{goto } 1; \\
\qquad\qquad \text{end} & \quad 4: \text{ifn } b_3 \text{ goto } 1; \\
\qquad \text{else } a_3 & \quad\quad a_2; \\
\qquad \text{end} & \quad\quad \text{goto } 4; \\
\quad \text{end} & \quad 0: \text{stop} \\
\text{end} &
\end{array}
$$

In contrast to Example 5, no chains of jumps, no useless labels, and no redundant aliased labels have been generated.   □

6   Conclusions

We have presented a context-sensitive translation from a language with structured control-flow constructs into a language with unstructured control-flow constructs. The translation is compositional and operates in linear time and space on the size of the input program. It is defined with one inference rule per syntactic construct and operates in one pass. The resulting program is semantically equivalent to the original program, contains the same atomic commands, and contains no chains of jumps, no unused labels, and no redundant labels. The translation should thus be useful in a JIT compiler for a structured language.

Compiling nested conditional commands naturally gives rise to chains of jumps to join their control flow if the translation is context-insensitive. We have pointed out how to avoid generating these chains of jumps. In SSA terms [3, 10,15], our translation naturally yields fewer merge points without duplicating contexts. It also generates fewer basic blocks and thus makes it faster to compute an SSA form.

Turning to the CPS transformation [5,13], we observe that the issue of chains of jumps arises there in the form of spurious η-redexes such as $\lambda v.k\ v$, where k

denotes a continuation. These η-redexes appear in the translation of tail calls and for nested conditional expressions, just like here for while loops and nested conditional commands. This coincidence should not come as a surprise since CPS and, more generally, functional programming are known to be connected to SSA [3,10].

Our closest related work is Dybvig, Hieb, and Butler's destination-driven code generation [6], where commands are also translated based on their context. While destination-driven code generation is not formalized and yields both redundant labels and unreferenced labels, it is defined for a richer source language and has been implemented in the back-end of a Scheme optimizing compiler, where it has been found very effective.

Acknowledgments. The idea of specifying operationally a translation from a structured language to an unstructured language (essentially Figure 3) originates in Andrzej Filinski's undergraduate semantics exam from January 2001 at the University of Aarhus. Thanks are also due to the anonymous referees for constructive comments and to Bernd Grobauer, Julia L. Lawall, Karoline Malmkjær, Lasse R. Nielsen, Norman Ramsey, Ulrik P. Schultz, and Zhe Yang for their feedback.

References

1. Alfred V. Aho, Ravi Sethi, and Jeffrey D. Ullman. *Compilers: Principles, Techniques and Tools.* Addison-Wesley, 1986.
2. Andrew W. Appel. *Modern Compiler Implementation in {C, Java, ML}.* Cambridge University Press, New York, 1998.
3. Andrew W. Appel. SSA is functional programming. *ACM SIGPLAN Notices,* 33(4):17–20, April 1998.
4. Forest Baskett. The best simple code generation technique for while, for, and do loops. *ACM SIGPLAN Notices,* 13(4):31–32, April 1978.
5. Olivier Danvy and Andrzej Filinski. Representing control, a study of the CPS transformation. *Mathematical Structures in Computer Science,* 2(4):361–391, 1992.
6. R. Kent Dybvig, Robert Hieb, and Tom Butler. Destination-driven code generation. Technical Report 302, Computer Science Department, Indiana University, Bloomington, Indiana, February 1990.
7. Ana M. Erosa and Laurie J. Hendren. Taming control flow: A structured approach to eliminating goto statements. In Henri Bal, editor, *Proceedings of the Fifth IEEE International Conference on Computer Languages,* pages 229–240, Toulouse, France, May 1994. IEEE Computer Society Press.
8. Richard P. Gabriel. LISP: Good news, bad news, how to win big. *AI Expert,* 6(6):30–39, June 1991.
9. Neil D. Jones, Carsten K. Gomard, and Peter Sestoft. *Partial Evaluation and Automatic Program Generation.* Prentice-Hall International, 1993. Available online at http://www.dina.kvl.dk/~sestoft/pebook/pebook.html.
10. Richard A. Kelsey. A correspondence between continuation passing style and static single assignment form. In Michael Ernst, editor, *ACM SIGPLAN Workshop on Intermediate Representations,* SIGPLAN Notices, Vol. 30, No 3, pages 13–22, San Francisco, California, January 1995. ACM Press.

11. Gordon D. Plotkin. Call-by-name, call-by-value and the λ-calculus. *Theoretical Computer Science*, 1:125–159, 1975.

12. M. V. S. Ramanath and Marvin H. Solomon. Jump minimization in linear time. *ACM Transactions on Programming Languages and Systems*, 6(4):527–545, 1984.

13. Guy L. Steele Jr. Rabbit: A compiler for Scheme. Technical Report AI-TR-474, Artificial Intelligence Laboratory, Massachusetts Institute of Technology, Cambridge, Massachusetts, May 1978.

14. Christopher Strachey and Christopher P. Wadsworth. Continuations: A mathematical semantics for handling full jumps. *Higher-Order and Symbolic Computation*, 13(1/2):135–152, 2000. Reprint of the technical monograph PRG-11, Oxford University Computing Laboratory (1974).

15. Mark N. Wegman and F. Ken Zadeck. Constant propagation with conditional branches. *ACM Transactions on Programming Languages and Systems*, 3(2):181–210, 1991.

16. Reinhard Wilhelm and Dieter Maurer. *Compiler Design*. Addison-Wesley, 1995.

17. Glynn Winskel. *The Formal Semantics of Programming Languages*. Foundation of Computing Series. The MIT Press, 1993.

A Unifying Approach to Goal-Directed Evaluation

Olivier Danvy, Bernd Grobauer, and Morten Rhiger

BRICS*
Department of Computer Science
University of Aarhus
Ny Munkegade, Building 540, DK-8000 Aarhus C, Denmark
{danvy,grobauer,mrhiger}@brics.dk
http://www.brics.dk/~{danvy,grobauer,mrhiger}

Abstract. Goal-directed evaluation, as embodied in Icon and Snobol, is built on the notions of backtracking and of generating successive results, and therefore it has always been something of a challenge to specify and implement. In this article, we address this challenge using computational monads and partial evaluation.

We consider a subset of Icon and we specify it with a monadic semantics and a list monad. We then consider a spectrum of monads that also fit the bill, and we relate them to each other. For example, we derive a continuation monad as a Church encoding of the list monad. The resulting semantics coincides with Gudeman's continuation semantics of Icon.

We then compile Icon programs by specializing their interpreter (i.e., by using the first Futamura projection), using type-directed partial evaluation. Through various back ends, including a run-time code generator, we generate ML code, C code, and OCaml byte code. Binding-time analysis and partial evaluation of the continuation-based interpreter automatically give rise to C programs that coincide with the result of Proebsting's optimized compiler.

1 Introduction

Goal-directed languages combine expressions that can yield multiple results through backtracking. Results are generated one at a time: an expression can either succeed and generate a result, or fail. If an expression fails, control is passed to a previous expression to generate the next result, if any. If so, control is passed back to the original expression in order to try whether it can succeed this time. Goal-directed programming specifies the order in which subexpressions are retried, thus providing the programmer with a succint and powerful control-flow mechanism. A well-known goal-directed language is Icon [11].

Backtracking as a language feature complicates both semantics and implementation. Gudeman [13] gives a continuation semantics of a goal-directed language; continuations have also been used in implementations of languages with

---

* Basic Research in Computer Science (www.brics.dk), funded by the Danish National Research Foundation.

W. Taha (Ed.): SAIG 2001, LNCS 2196, pp. 108–125, 2001.
© Springer-Verlag Berlin Heidelberg 2001

control structures similar to those of goal-directed evaluation, such as Prolog [3, 15,30]. Proebsting and Townsend, the implementors of an Icon compiler in Java, observe that continuations can be compiled into efficient code [1,14], but nevertheless dismiss them because "[they] are notoriously difficult to understand, and few target languages directly support them" [23, p.38]. Instead, their compiler is based on a translation scheme proposed by Proebsting [22], which is based on the four-port model used for describing control flow in Prolog [2]. Icon expressions are translated to a flow-chart language with conditional, direct and indirect jumps using templates; a subsequent optimization which, amongst other things, reorders code and performs branch chaining, is necessary to produce compact code. The reference implementation of Icon [12] compiles Icon into byte code; this byte code is then executed by an interpreter that controls the control flow by keeping a stack of expression frames.

In this article, we present a unified approach to goal-directed evaluation:

1. We consider a spectrum of semantics for a small goal-directed language. We relate them to each other by deriving semantics such as Gudeman's [13] as instantiations of one generic semantics based on computational monads [21]. This unified approach enables us to show the equivalence of different semantics simply and systematically. Furthermore, we are able to show strong conceptual links between different semantics: Continuation semantics can be derived from semantics based on lists or on streams of results by Church-encoding the lists or the streams, respectively.

2. We link semantics and implementation through semantics-directed compilation using partial evaluation [5,17]. In particular, binding-time analysis guides us to extract templates from the specialized interpreters. These templates are similar to Proebsting's, and through partial evaluation, they give rise to similar flow-chart programs, demonstrating that templates are not just a good idea—they are intrinsic to the semantics of Icon and can be provably derived.

The rest of the paper is structured as follows: In Section 2 we first describe syntax and monadic semantics of a small subset of Icon; we then instantiate the semantics with various monads, relate the resulting semantics to each other, and present an equivalence proof for two of them. In Section 3 we describe semantics-directed compilation for a goal-directed language. Section 4 concludes.

2   Semantics of a Subset of Icon

An intuitive explanation of goal-directed evaluation can be given in terms of lists and list-manipulating functions. Consequently, after introducing the subset of Icon treated in this paper, we define a monadic semantics in terms of the list monad. We then show that also a stream monad and two different continuation monads can be used, and we give an example of how to prove equivalence of the resulting monads using a monad morphism.

2.1 A Subset of the Icon Programming Language

We consider the following subset of Icon:

$$E ::= i \mid E_1 \text{ + } E_2 \mid E_1 \text{ to } E_2 \mid E_1 \text{ <= } E_2$$

Intuitively, an Icon term either fails or succeeds with a value. If it succeeds, then subsequently it can be resumed, in which case it will again either succeed or fail. This process ends when the expression fails. Informally, i succeeds with the value i; E_1 + E_2 succeeds with the sum of the sub-expressions; E_1 to E_2 (called a *generator*) succeeds with the value of E_1 and each subsequent resumption yields the rest of the integers up to the value of E_2, at which point it fails; E_1 <= E_2 succeeds with the value of E_2 if it is larger than the value E_1, otherwise it fails.

Generators can be nested. For example, the Icon term 4 to (5 to 7) generates the result of the expressions 4 to 5, 4 to 6, and 4 to 7 and concatenates the results.

In a functional language such as Scheme, ML or Haskell, we can achieve the effect of Icon terms using the functions map and concat. For example, if we define

```
fun to i j = if i<=j then i::(to (i+1) j) else nil
```

in ML, then evaluating concat (map (to 4) (to 5 7)) yields [4, 5, 4, 5, 6, 4, 5, 6, 7] which is the list of the integers produced by the Icon term 4 to (5 to 7).

2.2 Monads and Semantics

Computational monads were introduced to structure denotational semantics [21]. The basic idea is to parameterize a semantics over a monad; many language extensions, such as adding a store or exceptions, can then be carried out by simply instantiating the semantics with a suitable monad. Further, correspondence proofs between semantics arising from instantiation with different monads can be conducted in a modular way, using the concept of a monad morphism [28].

Monads can also be used to structure functional programs [29]. In terms of programming languages, a monad M is described by a unary type constructor M and three operations $unit_M$, map_M and $join_M$ with types as displayed in Figure 1. For these operations, the so-called monad laws have to hold.

In Section 2.4 we give a denotational semantics of the goal-directed language described in Section 2.1. Anticipating semantics-directed compilation by partial evaluation, we describe the semantics in terms of ML, in effect defining an interpreter. The semantics $[\![\cdot]\!]_M : Exp \to int\,M$ is parameterized over a monad M, where $\alpha\,M$ represents a sequence of values of type α.

$$unit_\mathsf{M} : \alpha \to \alpha\,\mathsf{M}$$
$$map_\mathsf{M} : (\alpha \to \beta) \to \alpha\,\mathsf{M} \to \beta\,\mathsf{M}$$
$$join_\mathsf{M} : (\alpha\,\mathsf{M})\,\mathsf{M} \to \alpha\,\mathsf{M}$$

Fig. 1. Monad operators and their types

Standard monad operations:

$$
\begin{aligned}
unit_\mathsf{L}\ x\quad\quad &= [x]\\[4pt]
map_\mathsf{L}\ f\ [\,]\quad &= [\,]\\
map_\mathsf{L}\ f\ (x :: xs) &= (f\ x) :: (map_\mathsf{L}\ f\ xs)\\[4pt]
join_\mathsf{L}\ [\,]\quad\ \ &= [\,]\\
join_\mathsf{L}\ (l :: ls)\ \ &= l\ @\ (join_\mathsf{L}\ ls)
\end{aligned}
$$

Special operations for sequences:

$$
\begin{aligned}
empty_\mathsf{L}\quad\quad\ \ &= [\,]\\
append_\mathsf{L}\ xs\ ys &= xs\ @\ ys
\end{aligned}
$$

Fig. 2. The list monad

2.3   A Monad of Sequences

In order to handle sequences, some structure is needed in addition to the three generic monad operations displayed in Figure 1. We add two operations:

$$empty_\mathsf{M} : \alpha\,\mathsf{M}$$
$$append_\mathsf{M} : \alpha\,\mathsf{M} \to \alpha\,\mathsf{M} \to \alpha\,\mathsf{M}$$

Here, $empty_\mathsf{M}$ stands for the empty sequence and $append_\mathsf{M}$ appends two sequences.

A straightforward instance of a monad of sequences is the list monad L, which is displayed in Figure 2; for lists, "join" is sometimes also called "flatten" or, in ML, "concat".

2.4   A Monadic Semantics

A monadic semantics of the goal-directed language described in Section 2.1. is given in Figure 3. We explain the semantics in terms of the list monad. A literal i is interpreted as an expression that yields exactly one result; consequently, i

$$[\![\cdot]\!]_\mathsf{M} \; : \; \mathit{Exp} \to \mathit{int}\,\mathsf{M}$$

$$[\![i]\!]_\mathsf{M} = \mathit{unit}_\mathsf{M}\; i$$
$$[\![E_1 \,\mathsf{to}\, E_2]\!]_\mathsf{M} = \mathit{bind2}_\mathsf{M}\;(\lambda xy.\mathit{to}_\mathsf{M}\; x\; y)\;[\![E_1]\!]_\mathsf{M}\;[\![E_2]\!]_\mathsf{M}$$
$$[\![E_1 \,\texttt{+}\, E_2]\!]_\mathsf{M} = \mathit{bind2}_\mathsf{M}\;(\lambda xy.\mathit{unit}_\mathsf{M}\;(x+y))\;[\![E_1]\!]_\mathsf{M}\;[\![E_2]\!]_\mathsf{M}$$
$$[\![E_1 \,\texttt{<=}\, E_2]\!]_\mathsf{M} = \mathit{bind2}_\mathsf{M}\;(\lambda xy.\mathit{leq}_\mathsf{M}\; x\; y)\;[\![E_1]\!]_\mathsf{M}\;[\![E_2]\!]_\mathsf{M}$$

where

$$\mathit{bind2}_\mathsf{M}\; f\; xs\; ys = \mathit{join}_\mathsf{M}\;(\mathit{map}_\mathsf{M}\;(\lambda x.\mathit{join}_\mathsf{M}\;(\mathit{map}_\mathsf{M}\;(f\; x)\; ys))\; xs)$$
$$\mathit{leq}_\mathsf{M}\; i\; j = \textbf{if}\; i \leq j \;\textbf{then}\; \mathit{unit}_\mathsf{M}\; j \;\textbf{else}\; \mathit{empty}_\mathsf{M}$$
$$\mathit{to}_\mathsf{M}\; i\; j = \textbf{if}\; i > j \;\textbf{then}\; \mathit{empty}_\mathsf{M}$$
$$\textbf{else}\; \mathit{append}_\mathsf{M}\;(\mathit{unit}_\mathsf{M}\; i)\;(\mathit{to}_\mathsf{M}\;(i+1)\; j)$$

Fig. 3. Monadic semantics for a subset of Icon

is mapped into the singleton list $[i]$ using *unit*. The semantics of to, + and <=
are given in terms of *bind2* and a function of type $\mathit{int} \to \mathit{int} \to \mathit{int}$ list. Function
$\mathit{bind2}_\mathsf{L}$ is of type $(\alpha \to \beta \to \gamma\,\mathsf{list}) \to \alpha\,\mathsf{list} \to \beta\,\mathsf{list} \to \gamma\,\mathsf{list}$, i.e., it takes two lists
containing values of type α and β, and a function mapping $\alpha \times \beta$ into a list of
values of type γ. The effect of the definition of $\mathit{bind2}_\mathsf{L}\; f\; xs\; ys$ is (1) to map
$f\,x$ over ys for each x in xs and (2) to flatten the resulting list of lists. Both
steps can be found in the example at the end of Section 2.1 of how the effect of
goal-directed evaluation can be achieved in ML using lists.

2.5   A Spectrum of Semantics

In the following, we describe four possible instantiations of the semantics given
in Figure 3. Because a semantics corresponds directly to an interpreter, we thus
create four different interpreters.

A list-based interpreter Instantiating the semantics with the list monad from
Figure 2 yields a list-based interpreter. In an eager language such as ML, a list-
based interpreter always computes all results. Such behavior may not be desirable
in a situation where only the first result is of interest (or, for that matter, whether
there exists a result): Consider for example a conditional that examines whether
a given expression yields at least one result or fails. An alternative is to use
laziness.

A stream-based interpreter Implementing the list monad from Figure 2
in a lazy language results in a monad of (finite) lazy lists; the corresponding
interpreter generates one result at a time. In an eager language, this effect can

Standard monad operations:

$$
\begin{aligned}
unit_{\mathsf{C}}\ x\ &= \lambda k.k\,x \\
map_{\mathsf{C}}\ f\ xs &= \lambda k.xs\,(\lambda x.k\,(f\,x)) \\
join_{\mathsf{C}}\ ls\ &= \lambda k.ls\,(\lambda x.x\,k)
\end{aligned}
$$

Special operations for sequences:

$$
\begin{aligned}
empty_{\mathsf{C}}\ &= \lambda k.\lambda l.l \\
append_{\mathsf{C}}\ xs\ ys &= \lambda k.(xs\,k) \circ (ys\,k)
\end{aligned}
$$

Fig. 4. The continuation monad

be achieved by explicitly implementing a data type of streams, i.e., finite lists built lazily: a thunk is used to delay computation.

$$\alpha\,\mathsf{stream}\ \equiv\ \mathsf{End}\mid\mathsf{More\ of}\ (\alpha\times(\mathbf{1}\rightarrow\alpha\,\mathsf{stream}))$$

The definition of the corresponding monad operations is straightforward.

A continuation-based interpreter Gudeman [13] gives a continuation-based semantics of a goal-directed language. We can derive this semantics by instantiating our monadic semantics with the continuation monad C as defined in Figure 4. The type-constructor $\alpha\,\mathsf{C}$ of the continuation monad is defined as $(\alpha\rightarrow R)\rightarrow R$, where R is called the *answer type* of the continuation.

A conceptual link between the list monad and the continuation monad with answer type $\beta\,\mathsf{list}\rightarrow\beta\,\mathsf{list}$ can be made through a Church encoding [4] of the higher-order representation of lists proposed by Hughes [16]. Hughes observed that when constructing the partially applied concatenation function $\lambda ys.xs\ @\ ys$ rather than the list xs, lists can be appended in constant time. In the resulting representation, the empty list corresponds to the function that appends no elements, i.e., the identity, whereas the function that appends a single element is represented by a partially applied cons function:

$$
\begin{aligned}
nil &= \lambda ys.ys \\
cons\ x &= \lambda ys.x :: ys
\end{aligned}
$$

Church-encoding a data types means abstracting over selector functions, in this case " :: ":

$$
\begin{aligned}
nil &= \lambda s_c.\lambda ys.ys \\
cons\ x &= \lambda s_c.\lambda ys.s_c\,x\,ys
\end{aligned}
$$

The resulting representation of lists can be typed as

$$(\alpha \to \beta \to \beta) \to \beta \to \beta,$$

which indeed corresponds to $\alpha\,C$ with answer type $\beta \to \beta$. Notice that *nil* and *cons* for this list representation yield $empty_C$ and $unit_C$, respectively. Similarly, the remaining monad operations correspond to the usual list operations.

Figure 5 displays the definition of $[\![\cdot]\!]_C$ where all monad operations have been inlined and the resulting expressions β-reduced.

$$[\![\cdot]\!]_C \ : \ Exp \to (int \to \beta \to \beta) \to \beta \to \beta$$

$$[\![i]\!]_C = \lambda k.k\,i$$
$$[\![E_1 \text{ to } E_2]\!]_C = \lambda k.[\![E_1]\!]_C\,(\lambda i.[\![E_2]\!]_C\,(\lambda j.to_C\ i\ j\ k))$$
$$[\![E_1 + E_2]\!]_C = \lambda k.[\![E_1]\!]_C\,(\lambda i.[\![E_2]\!]_C\,(\lambda j.k\,(i+j)))$$
$$[\![E_1 \text{ <= } E_2]\!]_C = \lambda k.[\![E_1]\!]_C\,(\lambda i.[\![E_2]\!]_C\,(\lambda j.leq_C\ i\ j\ k))$$

where

$$leq_C\ i\ j = \lambda k.\textbf{if}\ i \leq j\ \textbf{then}\ (k\ j)\ \textbf{else}\ (\lambda l.l)$$
$$to_C\ i\ j = \lambda k.\textbf{if}\ i > j\ \textbf{then}\ (\lambda l.l)$$
$$\textbf{else}\ (k\ i) \circ (to_C\ (i+1)\ j\ k)$$

Fig. 5. A continuation semantics

An interpreter with explicit success and failure continuations A tail-recursive implementation of a continuation-based interpreter for Icon uses explicit success and failure continuations. The result of interpreting an Icon expression then has type

$$(int \to (\mathbf{1} \to \alpha) \to \alpha) \to (\mathbf{1} \to \alpha) \to \alpha,$$

where the first argument is the success continuation and the second argument the failure continuation. Note that the success continuation takes a failure continuation as a second argument. This failure continuation determines the resumption behavior of the Icon term: the success continuation may later on apply its failure continuation to generate more results. The corresponding continuation monad C_2 has the same standard monad operations as the continuation monad displayed in Figure 4, and the sequence operations

$$empty_{C_2} = \lambda k.\lambda f.f\,()$$
$$append_{C_2}\ xs\ ys = \lambda k.\lambda f.(xs\ k)(\lambda().ys\ k\ f)$$

Just as the continuation monad from Figure 4 can be conceptually linked to the list monad, the present continuation monad can be linked to the stream monad by a Church encoding of the data type of streams:

$$end \quad\;\; = \lambda s_m.\lambda s_e.s_e()$$
$$more\; x\; xs = \lambda s_m.\lambda s_e.s_m\; x\; xs$$

The fact that the second component in a stream is a thunk suggests one to give the selector function s_m the type $int \to (\mathbf{1} \to \alpha) \to \beta$; the resulting type for end and $more\; x\; xs$ is then

$$(int \to (\mathbf{1} \to \alpha) \to \beta) \to (\mathbf{1} \to \beta) \to \beta.$$

Choosing α as the result type of the selector functions yields the type of a continuation monad with answer type $(\mathbf{1} \to \alpha) \to \alpha$.

The interpreter defined by the semantics $[\![\cdot]\!]_{C_2}$ is the starting point of the semantics-directed compilation described in Section 3. Figure 6 displays the definition of $[\![\cdot]\!]_{C_2}$ where all monad operations have been inlined and the resulting expressions β-reduced. Because the basic monad operations of C_2 are the same as those of C, the semantics based on C_2 and C only differ in the definitions of leq and to.

$$[\![\cdot]\!]_{C_2} \; : \; Exp \to (int \to (\mathbf{1} \to \alpha) \to \alpha) \to (\mathbf{1} \to \alpha) \to \alpha$$

$$[\![i]\!]_{C_2} = \lambda k.k\, i$$
$$[\![E_1\; \mathsf{to}\; E_2]\!]_{C_2} = \lambda k.[\![E_1]\!]_{C_2} (\lambda i.[\![E_2]\!]_{C_2} (\lambda j.to_{C_2}\; i\; j\; k))$$
$$[\![E_1 + E_2]\!]_{C_2} = \lambda k.[\![E_1]\!]_{C_2} (\lambda i.[\![E_2]\!]_{C_2} (\lambda j.k\, (i+j)))$$
$$[\![E_1\; \mathsf{<=}\; E_2]\!]_{C_2} = \lambda k.[\![E_1]\!]_{C_2} (\lambda i.[\![E_2]\!]_{C_2} (\lambda j.leq_{C_2}\; i\; j\; k))$$

where

$$leq_{C_2}\; i\; j = \lambda k.\lambda f.\mathbf{if}\; i \leq j\; \mathbf{then}\; k\; j\; f\; \mathbf{else}\; f\,()$$
$$to_{C_2}\; i\; j = \lambda k.\lambda f.\mathbf{if}\; i > j\; \mathbf{then}\; f\,()$$
$$\mathbf{else}\; (k\, i)\, (\lambda().to_{C_2}\; (i+1)\; j\; k\; f)$$

Fig. 6. A semantics with success and failure continuations

2.6   Correctness

So far, we have related the various semantics presented in Section 2.5 only conceptually. Because the four different interpreters presented in Section 2.5 were created by instantiating one parameterized semantics with different monads, a *formal* correspondence proof can be conducted in a modular way building on the concept of a monad morphism [28].

Definition 1 (Monad morphism). *If* M *and* N *are two monads, then* h : $\alpha\,M \to \alpha\,N$ *is a* monad morphism *if it preserves the monad operations[1], i.e.,*

$$h \circ unit_M = unit_N$$
$$h \circ map_M\, f = map_N\, f \circ h$$
$$h \circ join_M = join_N \circ h \circ map_M\, h$$
$$h\; empty_M = empty_N$$
$$h \circ append_M = \lambda xs.\lambda ys.append_N(h\, xs)(h\, ys)$$

The following lemma shows that the semantics resulting from two different monad instantiations can be related by defining a monad morphism between the two sequence monads in question.

Lemma 1. *Let* M *and* N *be monads of sequences as specified in Section 2.3. If* h *is a monad morphism from* M *to* N*, then* $(h\,\llbracket E\rrbracket_M) = \llbracket E\rrbracket_N$ *for every Icon expression* E.

Proof. By structural induction over E. A lemma to the effect that $h\,(to_M\; i\; j) = to_N\; i\; j$ is shown by induction over $i - j$ for $i \geq j$.

We use Lemma 1 to show that the list-based interpreter from Section 2.5 and the continuation-based interpreter from Section 2.5 always yield comparable results:

Proposition 1. *Let* $show : \alpha\,C \to \alpha\,L$ *be defined as*

$$show\; f = f\;(\lambda x.\lambda xs.append_L\;(unit_L\; x)\; xs)\; empty_L.$$

Then $(show\,\llbracket E\rrbracket_C) = \llbracket E\rrbracket_L$ *for all Icon expressions* E.

Proof. We show that (1) $h : \alpha\,L \to \alpha\,C$, which is defined as

$$h\;[\,] = empty_C$$
$$h\;(x :: xs) = append_C\;(unit_C\; x)\;(h\; xs)$$

is a monad morphism from L to C, and (2) the function $(show \circ h)$ is the identity function on lists. The proposition then follows immediately with Lemma 1.

2.7   Conclusion

Taking an intuitive list-based semantics for a subset of Icon as our starting point, we have defined a stream-based semantics and two continuation semantics. Because our inital semantics is defined as the instantiation of a monadic semantics with a list monad, the other semantics can be defined through a stream monad and two different continuation monads, respectively. The modularity of

---

[1] We strengthen the definition of a monad morphism somewhat by considering a *sequence-preserving* monomorphism that also preserves the monad operations specific to the monad of sequences.

the monadic semantics allows us to relate the semantics to each other by relating the corresponding monads, both conceptually and formally. To the best of our knowledge, the conceptual link between list-based monads and continuation monads via Church encoding has not been observed before.

It is known that continuations can be compiled into efficient code relatively easily [1,14]; in the following section we show that partial evaluation is sufficient to generate efficient code from the the continuation semantics derived in Section 2.5.

3 Semantics-Directed Compilation

The goal of partial evaluation is to specialize a source program $p : S \times D \to R$ of two arguments to a fixed "static" argument $s : S$. The result is a residual program $p_s : D \to R$ that must yield the same result when applied to a "dynamic" argument d as the original program applied to both the static and the dynamic arguments, i.e., $[\![p_s(d)]\!] = [\![p(s,d)]\!]$.

Our interest in partial evaluation is due to its use in semantics-directed compilation: when the source program p is an interpreter and the static argument s is a term in the domain of p then p_s is a compiled version of s represented in the implementation language of p. It is often possible to implement an interpreter in a functional language based on the denotational semantics.

Our starting point is a functional interpreter implementing the denotational semantics in Figure 6. The source language of the interpreter is shown in Figure 7. In Section 3.1 we present the Icon interpreter written in ML. In Section 3.1, 3.2, and 3.3 we use type-directed partial evaluation to specialize this interpreter to Icon terms yielding ML code, C code, and OCaml byte code as output. Other partial-evaluation techniques could be applied to yield essentially the same results.

```
structure Icon = struct
  datatype icon = LIT  of int
                | TO   of icon * icon
                | PLUS of icon * icon
                | LEQ  of icon * icon
end
```

Fig. 7. The abstract syntax of Icon terms

3.1 Type-Directed Partial Evaluation

We have used type-directed partial evaluation to compile Icon programs into ML. This is a standard exercise in semantics-directed compilation using type-directed partial evaluation [9].

Type-directed partial evaluation is an approach to off-line specialization of higher-order programs [8]. It uses a normalization function to map the (value of the) trivially specialized program $\lambda d.p(s, d)$ into the (text of the) target program p_s.

The input to type-directed partial evaluation is a binding-time separated program in which static and dynamic primitives are separated. When implemented in ML, the source program is conveniently wrapped in a functor parameterized over a structure of dynamic primitives. The functor can be instantiated with evaluating primitives (for running the source program) and with residualizing primitives (for specializing the source program).

In our case the dynamic primitives operations are addition (add), integer comparison (leq), a fixed-point operator (fix), a conditional functional (cond), and a quoting function (qint) lifting static integers into the dynamic domain. The signature of primitives is shown in Figure 8. For the residualizing primitives we let the partial evaluator produce functions that generate ML programs with meaningful variable names [8].

The parameterized interpreter is shown in Figure 9. The main function eval takes an Icon term and two continuations, k : tint $\rightarrow$ (tunit $\rightarrow$ res) $\rightarrow$ res and f : tunit $\rightarrow$ res, and yields a result of type res. We intend to specialize the interpreter to a static Icon term and keeping the continuation parameters k and f dynamic. Consequently, residual programs are parameterized over two continuations. (If the continuations were also considered static then the residual programs would simply be the list of the generated integers.)

```
signature PRIMITIVES = sig
  type tunit
  type tint
  type tbool
  type res

  val qint : int -> tint
  val add  : tint * tint -> tint
  val leq  : tint * tint -> tbool
  val cond : tbool * (tunit -> res) * (tunit -> res) -> res
  val fix  : ((tint -> res) -> tint -> res) -> tint -> res
end
```

Fig. 8. Signature of primitive operations

The output of type-directed partial evaluation is the text of the residual program. The residual program is in long beta-eta normal form, that is, it does

```
functor MakeInterp(P : PRIMITIVES) = struct
  fun loop (i, j) k f =
      P.fix
        (fn walk =>
            fn i =>
                P.cond (P.leq (i, j),
                        fn _ =>
                            k i (fn _ =>
                                    walk (P.add (i, P.qint 1))),
                        f))
        i

  fun select (i, j) k f =
      P.cond (P.leq (i, j), fn _ => k j f, f)

  fun sum (i, j) k = k (P.add (i, j))

  fun eval (LIT i)            k = k (P.qint i)
    | eval (TO(e1, e2))       k =
      eval e1 (fn i => eval e2 (fn j => loop (i, j) k))
    | eval (PLUS(e1, e2))     k =
      eval e1 (fn i => eval e2 (fn j => sum (i, j) k))
    | eval (LEQ(e1, e2))      k =
      eval e1 (fn i => eval e2 (fn j => select (i, j) k))
end
```

Fig. 9. Parameterized interpreter

not contain any beta redexes and it is fully eta-expanded with respect to its type.

Example 1. The following is the result of specializing the interpreter with respect to the Icon term 10 + (4 to 7).

```
fn k => fn f =>
   fix (fn loop0 =>
           fn i0 =>
               cond (leq (i0, qint 7),
                     fn () => k (add (qint 10, i0))
                               (fn () => loop0 (add (i0, qint 1))),
                     fn () => f ()))
       (qint 4)
```

3.2   Generating C Programs

Residual programs are not only in long beta-eta normal form. Their type

$$(\texttt{tint} \to (\texttt{tunit} \to \texttt{res}) \to \texttt{res}) \to (\texttt{tunit} \to \texttt{res}) \to \texttt{res}$$

imposes further restrictions: A residual program must take two arguments, a success continuation $\texttt{k} : \texttt{tint} \to (\texttt{tunit} \to \texttt{res}) \to \texttt{res}$ and a failure continuation $\texttt{f} : \texttt{tunit} \to \texttt{res}$, and it must produce a value of type $\texttt{res}$. When we also consider the types of the primitives that may occur in residual programs we see that values of type $\texttt{res}$ can only be a result of

- applying the success continuation $\texttt{k}$ to an integer n and function of type $\texttt{tunit} \to \texttt{res}$;
- applying the failure continuation $\texttt{f}$;
- applying the primitive $\texttt{cond}$ to a boolean and two functions of type $\texttt{tunit} \to \texttt{res}$;
- applying the primitive $\texttt{fix}$ to a function of two arguments, $\texttt{loop}_n : \texttt{tint} \to \texttt{res}$ and $\texttt{i}_n : \texttt{tint}$, and an integer; or
- (inside a function passed to $\texttt{fix}$) applying the function $\texttt{loop}_n$ to an integer.

A similar analysis applies to values of type $\texttt{tint}$: they can only arise from evaluating an integer n or a variable $\texttt{i}_n$ or from applying $\texttt{add}$ to two argument of type $\texttt{tint}$. As a result, we observe that the residual programs of specializing the Icon interpreter using type-directed partial evaluation are restricted to the grammar in Figure 10. (The restriction that the variables $\texttt{loop}_n$ and $\texttt{i}_n$ each must occur inside a function that binds them cannot be expressed using a context-free grammar. This is not a problem for our development.) We have expressed the grammar as an ML datatype and used this datatype to represent the output from type-directed partial evaluation. Thus, we have essentially used the type system of ML as a theorem prover to show the following lemma.

Lemma 2. *The residual program generated from applying type-directed partial evaluation to the interpreter in Figure 9 can be generated by the grammar in Figure 10.*

The idea of generating grammars for residual programs has been studied by, e.g., Malmkjær [20] and is used in the run-time specializer Tempo to generate code templates [6].

The simple structure of output programs allows them to be viewed as programs of a flow-chart language. We choose C as a concrete example of such a language. Figure 11 show the translation from residual programs to C programs.

The translation replaces function calls with jumps. The name of a function uniquely determines the corresponding label to jump to. Calls to $\texttt{loop}_n$ pass an argument. The name of the formal parameter is known ($\texttt{i}_n$) and therefore arguments are passed by assigning the variable before the jump. In each translation of a conditional a new label l must be generated. The entire translated term must be wrapped in a context that defines the labels $\texttt{succ}$ and $\texttt{fail}$ (corresponding to

$$I ::= \texttt{fn k => fn f =>} \; S$$
$$S ::= \texttt{k} \; E \; \texttt{(fn () =>} \; S\texttt{)}$$
$$\mid \; \texttt{f ()}$$
$$\mid \; \texttt{cond} \; (E, \; \texttt{fn () =>} \; S, \; \texttt{fn () =>} \; S)$$
$$\mid \; \texttt{fix (fn loop}_n \; \texttt{=> fn i}_n \; \texttt{=>} \; S) \; E$$
$$\mid \; \texttt{loop}_n \; E$$
$$E ::= \texttt{qint} \; n \mid \texttt{i}_n \mid \texttt{add} \; (E, \; E) \mid \texttt{leq} \; (E, \; E)$$

Fig. 10. Grammar of residual programs

the initial continuations). The statements following the label succ are allowed to jump to resume. The translation in Figure 11 generates a C program that successively prints the produced integers one by one. A lemma to the effect that the translation from residual ML programs into C is semantics preserving would require giving semantics to C and to the subset of ML presented in Figure 10 and then showing equivalence.

Example 2. Consider again the Icon term 10 + (4 to 7) from Example 1. It is translated into the following C program.

```
          i0 = 4;
loop0:    if (i0 <= 7) goto L0;
          goto fail;

L0:       value = 10 + i0;
          goto succ;

resume:   i0 = i0 + 1;
          goto loop0;

succ:     printf("%d ", value);
          goto resume;

fail:     printf("\n");
          exit(0);
```

The C target programs corresponds to the target programs of Proebsting's optimized template-based compiler [22]. In effect, we are automatically generating flow-chart programs from the denotation of an Icon term.

3.3 Generating Byte Code

In the previous two sections we have developed two compilers for Icon terms, one that generates ML programs and one that generates flow-chart programs. In this

$$|\text{fn k => fn f => } S|_\text{I} = \begin{cases} & |S|_\text{S} \\ \text{succ:} & \text{printf("\%d ", value);} \\ & \text{goto resume;} \\ \text{fail:} & \text{printf("\textbackslash n");} \\ & \text{exit(0);} \end{cases}$$

$$|\text{k } E \text{ (fn () => } S)|_\text{S} = \begin{cases} & \text{value = } |E|_\text{E}; \\ & \text{goto succ;} \\ \text{resume:} & |S|_\text{S} \end{cases}$$

$$|\text{f ()}|_\text{S} = \{\text{goto fail;}$$

$$|\text{cond } (E, \text{ fn () => } S, \text{ fn () => } S')|_\text{S} = \begin{cases} & \text{if } (|E|_\text{E}) \text{ goto } l; \\ & |S'|_\text{S} \\ l: & |S|_\text{S} \end{cases}$$

$$|\text{fix (fn loop}_n \text{ => fn i}_n \text{ => } S) \text{ } E|_\text{S} = \begin{cases} & \text{i}_n \text{ = } |E|_\text{E}; \\ \text{loop}_n: & |S|_\text{S} \end{cases}$$

$$|\text{loop}_n \text{ } E|_\text{S} = \begin{cases} \text{i}_n \text{ = } |E|_\text{E}; \\ \text{goto loop}_n; \end{cases}$$

$$|\text{qint } n|_\text{E} = n$$
$$|\text{i}_n|_\text{E} = \text{i}_n$$
$$|\text{add } (E, \text{ } E')|_\text{E} = |E|_\text{E} \text{ + } |E'|_\text{E}$$
$$|\text{leq } (E, \text{ } E')|_\text{E} = |E|_\text{E} \text{ <= } |E'|_\text{E}$$

Fig. 11. Translating residual programs into C

section we unify the two by composing the first compiler with the third author's automatic run-time code generation system for OCaml [25] and by composing the second compiler with a hand-written compiler from flow charts into OCaml byte code.

Run-time code generation in OCaml Run-time code generation for OCaml works by a deforested composition of traditional type-directed partial evaluation with a compiler into OCaml byte code. Deforestation is a standard improvement in run-time code generation [6,19,26]. As such, it removes the need to manipulate the text of residual programs at specialization time. As a result, instead of generating ML terms, run-time code generation allows type-directed partial evaluation to directly generate executable OCaml byte code.

Specializing the Icon interpreter from Figure 9 to the Icon term 10 + (4 to 7) using run-time code generation yields a residual program of about 110 byte-code instructions in which functions are implemented as closures and calls are implemented as tail-calls. (Compiling the residual ML program using the OCaml compiler yields about 90 byte-code instructions.)

Compiling flow charts into OCaml byte code We have modified the translation in Figure 11 to produce OCaml byte-code instructions instead of C programs. The result is an embedding of Icon into OCaml.

Using this compiler, 10 + (4 to 7) yields 36 byte-code instructions in which functions are implemented as labelled blocks and calls are implemented as an assignment (if an argument is passed) followed by a jump. This style of target code was promoted by Steele in the first compiler for Scheme [27].

3.4   Conclusion

Translating the continuation-based denotational semantics into an interpreter written in ML and using type-directed partial evaluation enables a standard semantics-directed compilation from Icon terms into ML. A further compilation of residual programs into C yields flow-chart programs corresponding to those produced by Proebsting's Icon compiler [22].

4   Conclusions and Issues

Observing that the list monad provides the kind of backtracking embodied in Icon, we have specified a semantics of Icon that is parameterized by this monad. We have then considered alternative monads and proven that they also provide a fitting semantics for Icon. Inlining the continuation monad, in particular, yields Gudeman's continuation semantics [13].

Using partial evaluation, we have then specialized these interpreters with respect to Icon programs, thereby compiling these programs using the first Futamura projection. We used a combination of type-directed partial evaluation and code generation, either to ML, to C, or to OCaml byte code. Generating code for C, in particular, yields results similar to Proebsting's compiler [22].

Gudeman [13] shows that a continuation semantics can also deal with additional control structures and state; we do not expect any difficulties with scaling up the code-generation accordingly. The monad of lists, on the other hand, does not offer enough structure to deal, e.g., with state. It should be possible, however, to create a rich enough monad by combining the list monad with other monads such as the state monad [10,18].

In the full version of this article, we also consider conditional expressions. It is our observation that the traditional (in partial evaluation) generalization of the success continuation avoids the code duplication that Proebsting presents as problematic in his own compiler. We are also studying the results of defunctionalizing the continuations, à la Reynolds [24], to obtain stack-based specifications and the corresponding run-time architectures.

Acknowledgments. Thanks are due to the anonymous referees for comments and to Andrzej Filinski for discussions.

References

1. Andrew W. Appel. *Compiling with Continuations*. Cambridge University Press, New York, 1992.
2. Lawrence Byrd. Understanding the control of Prolog programs. Technical Report 151, University of Edinburgh, 1980.
3. Mats Carlsson. On implementing Prolog in functional programming. *New Generation Computing*, 2(4):347–359, 1984.
4. Alonzo Church. *The Calculi of Lambda-Conversion*. Princeton University Press, 1941.
5. Charles Consel and Olivier Danvy. Tutorial notes on partial evaluation. In Susan L. Graham, editor, *Proceedings of the Twentieth Annual ACM Symposium on Principles of Programming Languages*, pages 493–501, Charleston, South Carolina, January 1993. ACM Press.
6. Charles Consel and François Noël. A general approach for run-time specialization and its application to C. In Guy L. Steele, editor, *Proceedings of the Twenty-Third Annual ACM Symposium on Principles of Programming Languages*, pages 145–156, St. Petersburg Beach, Florida, January 1996. ACM Press.
7. Ron K. Cytron, editor. *Proceedings of the ACM SIGPLAN'97 Conference on Programming Languages Design and Implementation*, SIGPLAN Notices, Vol. 32, No 5, Las Vegas, Nevada, June 1997. ACM Press.
8. Olivier Danvy. Type-directed partial evaluation. In John Hatcliff, Torben Æ. Mogensen, and Peter Thiemann, editors, *Partial Evaluation – Practice and Theory; Proceedings of the 1998 DIKU Summer School*, number 1706 in Lecture Notes in Computer Science, pages 367–411, Copenhagen, Denmark, July 1998. Springer-Verlag.
9. Olivier Danvy and René Vestergaard. Semantics-based compiling: A case study in type-directed partial evaluation. In Herbert Kuchen and Doaitse Swierstra, editors, *Eighth International Symposium on Programming Language Implementation and Logic Programming*, number 1140 in Lecture Notes in Computer Science, pages 182–197, Aachen, Germany, September 1996. Springer-Verlag. Extended version available as the technical report BRICS-RS-96-13.
10. Andrzej Filinski. Representing layered monads. In Alex Aiken, editor, *Proceedings of the Twenty-Sixth Annual ACM Symposium on Principles of Programming Languages*, pages 175–188, San Antonio, Texas, January 1999. ACM Press.
11. Ralph E. Griswold and Madge T. Griswold. *The Icon Programming Language*. Prentice Hall, Inc., 1983.
12. Ralph E. Griswold and Madge T. Griswold. *The Implementation of the Icon Programming Language*. Princeton University Press, 1986.
13. David A. Gudeman. Denotational semantics of a goal-directed language. *ACM Transactions on Programming Languages and Systems*, 1992.
14. Robert Hieb, R. Kent Dybvig, and Carl Bruggeman. Representing control in the presence of first-class continuations. In Bernard Lang, editor, *Proceedings of the ACM SIGPLAN'90 Conference on Programming Languages Design and Implementation*, SIGPLAN Notices, Vol. 25, No 6, pages 66–77, White Plains, New York, June 1990. ACM Press.

15. Ralf Hinze. Prological features in a functional setting—axioms and implementations. In Masahiko Sato and Yoshihito Toyama, editors, *Third Fuji International Symposium on Functional and Logic Programming (FLOPS'98)*, pages 98–122, Kyoto, Japan, April 1998. World Scientific.

16. John Hughes. A novel representation of lists and its application to the function "reverse". *Information Processing Letters*, 22(3):141–144, 1986.

17. Neil D. Jones, Carsten K. Gomard, and Peter Sestoft. *Partial Evaluation and Automatic Program Generation.* Prentice-Hall International, 1993. Available online at http://www.dina.kvl.dk/~sestoft/pebook/pebook.html.

18. David J. King and Philip Wadler. Combining Monads. In John Launchbury and Patrick M. Sansom, editors, *Glasgow Workshop on Functional Programming*, Workshops in Computing, Ayr, Scotland, 1992. Springer, Berlin.

19. Mark Leone and Peter Lee. Optimizing ML with run-time code generation. In *Proceedings of the ACM SIGPLAN'96 Conference on Programming Languages Design and Implementation*, SIGPLAN Notices, Vol. 31, No 5, pages 137–148. ACM Press, May 1996.

20. Karoline Malmkjær. *Abstract Interpretation of Partial-Evaluation Algorithms.* PhD thesis, Department of Computing and Information Sciences, Kansas State University, Manhattan, Kansas, March 1993.

21. Eugenio Moggi. Computational lambda-calculus and monads. In *Proceedings of the Fourth Annual IEEE Symposium on Logic in Computer Science*, pages 14–23, Pacific Grove, California, June 1989. IEEE Computer Society Press.

22. Todd A. Proebsting. Simple translation of goal-directed evaluation. In Cytron [7], pages 1–6.

23. Todd A. Proebsting and Gregg M. Townsend. A new implementation of the Icon language. Technical Report 99-13, University of Arizona, Department of Computer Science, 1999.

24. John C. Reynolds. Definitional interpreters for higher-order programming languages. *Higher-Order and Symbolic Computation*, 11(4):363–397, 1998. Reprinted from the proceedings of the 25th ACM National Conference (1972).

25. Morten Rhiger. PhD thesis, BRICS PhD School, University of Aarhus, Aarhus, Denmark, 2001. Forthcoming.

26. Michael Sperber and Peter Thiemann. Two for the price of one: composing partial evaluation and compilation. In Cytron [7], pages 215–225.

27. Guy L. Steele Jr. Compiler optimization based on viewing LAMBDA as RENAME + GOTO. In Patrick Henry Winston and Richard Henry Brown, editors, *Artificial Intelligence: An MIT Perspective*, volume 2. The MIT Press, 1979.

28. Philip Wadler. Comprehending monads. *Mathematical Structures in Computer Science*, 2(4):461–493, December 1992.

29. Philip Wadler. Monads for functional programming. In Johan Jeuring and Erik Meijer, editors, *Advanced Functional Programming*, number 925 in Lecture Notes in Computer Science, pages 24–52. Springer-Verlag, 1995.

30. Richard S. Wallace. An easy implementation of pil (PROLOG in LISP). *Association for Computing Machinery Special Interest Group on Artificial Intelligence. SIGART NEWSL.*, (85):29–32, July 1983.

Integrating Partial Evaluators into Interpreters

Kenichi Asai

Department of Information Science, Faculty of Science, University of Tokyo
7-3-1 Hongo Bunkyo-ku 113-0033 Japan
`asai@is.s.u-tokyo.ac.jp`
"Information and Human Activity," PRESTO, JST

Abstract. This paper describes our first step towards the integration of partial evaluation into standard interpretation. The two main issues in this integration are the treatment of heap objects and side-effects. To enable specialization with respect to the heap objects that are allocated beforehand in standard evaluation, specialization is performed with respect to *the heap state at specialization time* rather than based on a program text input so far. To avoid duplication of heap objects, *direct references to heap objects* are allowed in the specialized programs, in addition to the use of the conventional let-insertion technique. Despite our modest approach on side-effects that we allow partial evaluation of only side-effect free portions of a program, the resulting system covers some typical cases, such as the use of partial evaluation during an interactive debugging session. It also enables us to specialize a (side-effect free) program with respect to cyclic data structures, which was not easy before. We formalize this integration using store semantics and state its correctness. The system is implemented in Scheme and various examples are tested. Among them, we show specialization of a ray tracing program.

1 Introduction

Given a function $f(x, y)$ and a part of its input $x = a$, partial evaluation [19] (or program specialization) produces a specialized (and usually more efficient) program $f_a(y)$ by precomputing the parts of f that depend only on the known input x. The central strategy used in partial evaluation is strong normalization: given $f(x, y)$ and $x = a$, partial evaluation builds the specialization by strongly normalizing $\lambda y.f(a, y)$. In contrast to the standard interpretation (of call-by-value functional languages such as Scheme) which evaluates higher-order programs only up to the weak head normal form, the eager behavior of partial evaluation is suited for program optimization performed before actual execution. It is also well-known that this optimization amounts to compilation when applied to interpreters [13].

The conventional partial evaluation assumes that the program text to be transformed is given as a whole. Users are asked to prepare in a file the entire program, and then partial evaluation is applied to the designated function in it. In the language like Scheme, however, users input and execute programs one

W. Taha (Ed.): SAIG 2001, LNCS 2196, pp. 126–145, 2001.
© Springer-Verlag Berlin Heidelberg 2001

by one. In such an interactive interpreter environment, it is more desirable that users can apply partial evaluation *on the fly* during the interactive session.

As the first step towards this integration of partial evaluation and standard interpretation, this paper tries to identify the problems that arise during the integration and show possible solutions to them. The target language is a subset of Scheme. The two main issues are the treatment of heap objects and side-effects.[1] In the interpreter environment, because objects are already allocated in heap and the pointer equality (eq-ness) is important in Scheme, partial evaluation must be performed in such a way that the identity of objects are preserved. For this purpose, we propose two techniques: partial evaluation with respect to *the heap state at specialization time* and *direct reference to heap objects* in the specialized program.

The other issue is the treatment of side-effects. Side-effects are inevitable in an interactive interpreter environment. Users will redefine functions and variables, construct data structures in heap, and modify them. As for the treatment of side-effects, however, we take rather a modest approach. Rather than solving various problems caused by side-effects, we simply identify them and show how to circumvent them. This causes several (rather severe) restriction on the use of partial evaluation: the current system allows partial evaluation of only side-effect free portions of a program.

We took this approach because we have no feasible solution for dealing with side-effects in an interactive environment. The previous work [3,26] requires a program analysis on the whole program text. Even with this restriction, however, it covers some interesting cases, such as specialization with respect to circular data structures. It would also serve as a basis for more sophisticated techniques to weaken the restriction.

As a specializer, we employ *online* partial evaluation [16,23] that inspects the availability of values *during* specialization process. The *offline* approach where availability of values are analyzed beforehand in a separate phase (called a binding-time analysis) was not employed because it usually requires a whole program text for the global program analysis. If we made use of a separate binding-time analysis [8], we might be able to employ the offline approach as well.

We formalize the specializer in store-passing style to make special emphasis on the behavior of heap. We then state its correctness: the execution of programs with and without specialization produce a congruent result and store.

Three versions of the specializer together with the interpreter are implemented in Scheme. Various extensions are implemented, including controlling termination and residualization via user annotation (filters [7]), the multilevel specialization [14], and other language extensions. Various examples are tested on the implementation. Among them, we show a ray tracing example in this paper.

---

[1] By side-effects, we mean assignments (set!) and destructive updates (set-car! and set-cdr!). When we refer to I/O-type side-effects (such as read and write), we will explicitly say so.

The paper is organized as follows. In the next section, we describe in detail various issues that arise during the integration of partial evaluation and standard interpretation. The formal description then starts by showing the language in Sect. 3 and describing the standard interpreter in Sect. 4. The specializer is presented in detail in Sect. 5, whose correctness is mentioned in Sect. 6. The extensions employed in the implementation are discussed in Sect. 7. Specialization of ray tracing is detailed in Sect. 8. Related work is in Sect. 9 and the paper concludes in Sect. 10.

2   Issues

In this section, we describe what issues arise during the integration of partial evaluation and interpretation. We will use the following interactive session as an example:

```
> (define (nth n lst)
    (if (= n 0) (car lst) (nth (- n 1) (cdr lst))))
> (define circular-list
    (let ((aux (cons 1 (cons 2 '()))))
      (set-cdr! (cdr aux) aux)
      aux))
> (define nth2
    (pe (lambda (n) (nth n circular-list))))
```

After `nth` is defined which takes the n'th element of `lst`, a circular list (1 2 1 2 ...) is constructed. Then, we specialize `nth` with respect to the circular list. Here, `pe` initiates a partial evaluation of its argument closure.

2.1   Side-Effects before Specialization

In the above session, we used two kinds of side-effects before specialization: definition of variables (`nth` and `circular-list`) and a destructive update. Although the presence of side-effects is not preferable from the partial evaluation point of view, we allow arbitrary side-effects *before* specialization. This is because we want the integrated interpreter to be a standard interpreter if the specialization construct `pe` was not used at all. In the above example, we actually define `nth`, destructively update the cdr of `aux`, and define `circular-list`. Note that the definition of variables can be modification of variables if they were already defined beforehand.

2.2   Specialization with Respect to the Current Heap State

The decision that arbitrary side-effects are allowed before specialization does not make the later specialization process complicated. We simply perform specialization *with respect to the current heap state*.

In the conventional partial evaluators, specialization of programs containing side-effects requires a side-effect analysis [3,26]. In particular, if we want to statically evaluate side-effects at specialization time, a partial evaluator has to be able to decide that it can be safely done at partial evaluation time (using a complex region-based binding-time analysis [26]). This complication can be avoided if we perform specialization with respect to the specialization-time heap state rather than the program text input so far in the interactive session. Whatever side-effects occur before specialization, they simply change the heap state, and when the specialization begins, the heap state is fixed (if no side-effects are used during specialization).

By taking the current heap state static, we can perform interesting partial evaluation which was not easy before: specialization with respect to a circular-list. In the above example, the value of `nth2` becomes:[2]

```
> nth2
(letrec ((f1 (lambda (n) (if (= n 0) 1 (f2 (- n 1)))))
         (f2 (lambda (n) (if (= n 0) 2 (f1 (- n 1))))))
  f1)
```

Not only the elements of `circular-list` are inlined but also its circular structure is reflected to the recursive structure of the specialized program.

2.3   Side-Effects during Specialization

Although side-effects before specialization can be handled nicely, side-effects *during* specialization is difficult. The situation is essentially the same as the conventional partial evaluation: a side-effect analysis is inevitable [3,26]. Furthermore, because we are interested in the interactive environment, such an analysis would have to be able to cope with pre-allocated objects and interactive redefinition of programs. In this paper, we propose no solution to it but simply restrict that specialization can be applied only to pure side-effect free programs. One possible future direction would be to investigate a modular side-effect analysis, so that it can be applied to interactively input programs on the fly.

Even with this restriction, it covers some typical cases. For example, suppose a user is writing and debugging a program in a pure functional manner. He first inputs functions some of which are erroneous, executes them, finds that something was wrong, and then redefines the erroneous functions and executes them again. At every stage, the whole program does not contain any side-effects, yet the definition of functions changes as the user redefines them. In such a case, he is allowed to perform specialization at any time he wants.

2.4   Side-Effects after Specialization

In the previous subsections, we have allowed side-effects before specialization and prohibited side-effects during specialization. There is one other possibility of

---

[2] The definition of `f2` will be inlined into the definition of `f1` in the actual output.

side-effects: side-effects *after* specialization. Because specialization with respect
to the current heap state means that the information on the current heap state
is used for specialization, the modification of heap can invalidate specialization.
For example, if we destructively modify `circular-list` after we obtained the
above `nth2`:

```
> (set-car! circular-list 3)
```

the original program (`nth 0 circular-list`) now returns 3 but the specialized
program (`nth2 0`) returns 1 because the element of the old `circular-list` is
already inlined into `nth2`.

Rather than providing a sophisticated mechanism to detect which specialization is invalidated and should be respecialized, we again take rather a modest
approach. We decide on two principles: (1) specialization is performed assuming that the heap state will never be modified, and (2) the future modification
on heap does not have any effects on specialized programs. The first principle
is reasonable. In the interactive environment, users can modify any (accessible)
data structures after specialization. If we take the side-effects after specialization
into account during specialization, we can perform very little specialization. We
cannot even take car or cdr of a cons cell since it might be modified later.

The second principle is not very satisfactory. We could design more sophisticated techniques, such as automatic detection of invalidation and respecialization [17,27]. In this paper, however, we do not pursue this approach further but
accept the second principle as the first step towards the integration of partial
evaluation and standard interpretation. One of the reasons for this decision is
its simplicity and expectation that the other techniques could be built on top of
it. Another reason is that invalidation is not so straightforward. Since Scheme
does not provide any ways to indicate mutable data structures (in contrast to
ML where only references are mutable), we have to maintain a set of *all* the
data structures referenced during specialization to judge invalidation, which can
be very large. This situation is in contrast to the run-time specialization [9,21]
where whole the program is given beforehand and an analysis can estimate which
data structures are mutable. To keep the set small, we feel that some kind of
user assistance is required — our future work.

2.5   Direct Reference to Heap Objects

The presence of pre-allocated heap objects has impact on the output of partial
evaluation: care must be taken not to duplicate them. In the conventional partial
evaluators, let-insertion [6] has been used to avoid code duplication. In addition
to that, we need direct reference to heap objects.

Consider the following specialization where `circular-list` is already allocated in heap:

```
> (define p (pe (lambda () (cdr circular-list))))
```

The result should not produce code that reconstructs a different circular list than
`circular-list`, but should refer to the second cell of `circular-list` directly.

$$AExp := (Preaction; \ldots; Preaction, Var)$$
$$Preaction := Var = Exp \mid Var \stackrel{r}{=} (\mathsf{lambda}\ (Var^*)\ AExp)$$
$$Exp := Const \mid Var \mid (\mathsf{if}\ Var\ AExp\ AExp) \mid (\mathsf{set!}\ Var\ Var) \mid$$
$$(\mathsf{lambda}\ (Var^*)\ AExp) \mid (Var\ Var^*) \mid (\mathsf{pe}\ AExp)$$

Fig. 1. Language

Otherwise, in the later interaction, the result of applying the specialized program may be compared its identity with the cdr of `circular-list`:

```
> (eq? (p) (cdr circular-list))
```

which should return #t (true). The problem here is that the cdr of `circular-list` does not have a name. To refer directly to anonymous heap objects, we assume that every heap object has a unique global name. In our example, we assume that `circular-list` was constructed something like:

```
> (define a (cons 2 '()))
> (define circular-list (cons 1 a))
> (set-cdr! a circular-list)
```

giving a global name a to `(cons 2 '())`. Then, we can write the result of specializing p as follows:

```
> p
(lambda () a)
```

In the implementation, we do not have to give a unique global name to every anonymous object explicitly. It can be thought of as the address of the object in memory (or location in the store semantics). Rather than creating a new name to each anonymous object, we will allow to write explicitly its memory address in the result of partial evaluation. In other words, we will use the memory address as a global name to the object.

3   The Language

The language we consider is a higher-order subset of Scheme expressed in A-normal form [12]. Its syntax is displayed in Fig. 1. We call an expression in A-normal form an *A-expression*. An A-expression (*AExp*) consists of a sequence of *preactions* [3] (separated by ";") and a variable. A preaction builds a let-binding (the first form) or a letrec-binding (the second form). In the latter case, the bound expression is required to be a lambda expression. For example,

$$(a = 3; f \stackrel{r}{=} (\mathsf{lambda}\ (x)\ \ldots); b = (f\ a), b)$$

is equivalent to the following Scheme expression:

```
(let ((a 3)) (letrec ((f (lambda (x) ...))) (let ((b (f a))) b))).
```

$$\mathcal{E} \; : \; AExp \to Env \to Store \to (\, Value \times Store)$$
$$\mathcal{E}_p \; : \; Exp \to Env \to Store \to (\, Value \times Store)$$
$$\rho \in \; Env \; = \; Var \to Name$$
$$\sigma \in \; Store \; = \; Name \to Value$$
$$Value = Const + Closure$$

$$\mathcal{E}[\![(\cdot, y)]\!]\rho\,\sigma = (\sigma(\rho(y)), \sigma)$$
$$\mathcal{E}[\![(x = e; P, y)]\!]\rho\,\sigma = \textbf{let } (v_1, \sigma_1) = \mathcal{E}_p[\![e]\!]\rho\,\sigma$$
$$n = new(\sigma_1)$$
$$\textbf{in } \mathcal{E}[\![(P, y)]\!]\rho[n/x]\,\sigma_1[v_1/n]$$
$$\mathcal{E}[\![(x \stackrel{r}{=} (\mathsf{lambda}\ (x^*)\ (P_0, x_0)); P, y)]\!]\rho\,\sigma = \textbf{let } l = new(\sigma)$$
$$n = new(\sigma[\star/l])$$
$$clo = cl(l, x^*, (P_0, x_0), \rho[n/x])$$
$$\textbf{in } \mathcal{E}[\![(P, y)]\!]\rho[n/x]\,\sigma[\star/l, clo/n]$$

$$\mathcal{E}_p[\![const]\!]\rho\,\sigma = (const, \sigma)$$
$$\mathcal{E}_p[\![x]\!]\rho\,\sigma = (\sigma(\rho(x)), \sigma)$$
$$\mathcal{E}_p[\![(\mathsf{if}\ x_0\ (P_1, x_1)\ (P_2, x_2))]\!]\rho\,\sigma = \textbf{if } \sigma(\rho(x_0)) \textbf{ then } \mathcal{E}[\![(P_1, x_1)]\!]\rho\,\sigma$$
$$\textbf{else } \mathcal{E}[\![(P_2, x_2)]\!]\rho\,\sigma$$
$$\mathcal{E}_p[\![(\mathsf{set!}\ x\ y)]\!]\rho\,\sigma = (\star, \sigma[\sigma(\rho(y))/\rho(x)])$$
$$\mathcal{E}_p[\![(\mathsf{lambda}\ (x^*)\ (P_0, x_0))]\!]\rho\,\sigma = \textbf{let } l = new(\sigma)$$
$$\textbf{in } (cl(l, x^*, (P_0, x_0), \rho), \sigma[\star/l])$$
$$\mathcal{E}_p[\![(x_0\ y_0^*)]\!]\rho\,\sigma = \textbf{let } v_y^* = \sigma(\rho(y_0^*))$$
$$\textbf{in case } \sigma(\rho(x_0)) \textbf{ of}$$
$$prim : (prim(v_y^*), \sigma)$$
$$cl(l, x^*, (P', x'), \rho') :$$
$$\textbf{let } l^* = new^*(\sigma)$$
$$\textbf{in } \mathcal{E}[\![(P', x')]\!]\rho'[l^*/x^*]\,\sigma[v_y^*/l^*]$$
$$\mathcal{E}_p[\![(\mathsf{pe}\ (P_0, x_0))]\!]\rho\,\sigma = \textbf{let } (P_1, n_1, v_1, \gamma_1) = \mathcal{P}[\![(P_0, x_0)]\!]\rho\,\sigma$$
$$\textbf{in } \mathcal{E}[\![(P_1, n_1)]\!]\rho_{id}\,\sigma$$

Fig. 2. Standard interpreter

The last expression (pe $AExp$) initiates partial evaluation.

Because standard Scheme programs can be converted into A-normal form in linear time [12], we will use expressions not necessarily in A-normal form for the presentation of examples.

4   Standard Interpreter

The interpreter, giving the standard operational semantics of the language, is shown in Fig. 2. It is written in store-passing style. Given an A-expression (P, y), an environment ρ, and a store σ, the interpreter $\mathcal{E}$ evaluates (P, y) under ρ and σ, and returns the final value (which is either a constant or a closure) together with the store after the evaluation.

In the figure, we use the following notations. An empty sequence of preactions is denoted by a dot $\cdot$. $new(\sigma)$ generates a name (location) which is not bound in σ. We use the word 'name' rather than 'location' because the generated names are used as the unique names of the objects allocated there. $\rho[n/x]$ is an environment identical to ρ except that $\rho(x) = n$. $\sigma[l/n]$ is similar. The constant $\star$ denotes an unspecified value. cl is a closure constructor.[3] x^* represents a sequence of variables. If $x^* = x_1 \ldots x_k$ and $l^* = l_1 \ldots l_k$, then $l^* = new^*(\sigma)$ creates k new names and assign them to l^*, $\rho(x^*)$ represents a sequence $\rho(x_1) \ldots \rho(x_k)$, $\rho[l^*/x^*]$ is equivalent to ρ except that $\rho(x_i) = l_i$ for $1 \leq i \leq k$.

The evaluation of an A-expression proceeds by evaluating each preaction in the A-expression in order. The evaluation of each expression in preactions is done by the auxiliary function $\mathcal{E}_p$. The interpreter is completely standard.[4] The only non-standard rule is the last one for the evaluation of the pe construct, which will be described after the specializer $\mathcal{P}$ is shown in the next section.

5   Specializer

The specializer is shown in Figs. 3 and 4. It is also written in store-passing style. Given an A-expression (P, y), an environment ρ, and a partial evaluation time store γ (pe-store, for short), $\mathcal{P}$ partially evaluates (P, y) under ρ and γ. The returned value is a tuple of four elements (P', n', v', γ'). P' and n' are a sequence of preactions and a variable, respectively, which constitute the specialized program. (We treat a name n' as a variable; see below.) v' is a partial evaluation time value (pe-value, for short) of (P, y). If (P, y) can be reduced completely, the resulting value is stored in v' and is used for further specialization. If not, v' is bound to a name. Finally, γ' is a modified pe-store.

Here, we assume that $Name$ is a subset of Var and hence of Exp. Whenever we create a new name n, we also use n as a variable that refers to the object allocated at the location n. This is the same as the name creation of the conventional partial evaluation. Remember that names are created during the standard evaluation, too, when objects are allocated in heap. If such names are referred to in a specialized program, it indicates direct references to heap objects that are created before specialization. This use of names avoids duplication of pre-allocated heap objects. If we had used code that reconstruct heap objects instead, it would have duplicated them and destroyed their identity.

Like the standard evaluation, partial evaluation of an A-expression proceeds by partially evaluating each preaction in the A-expression in order. Specialization of an A-expression with an empty preaction $(\cdot, y)$ returns $(\cdot, \rho(y), \gamma(\rho(y)), \gamma)$. Here, the name $\rho(y)$ is used as a specialized program to refer directly to the object $\gamma(\rho(y))$ allocated in heap (store). This means that all the variable lookups are

---

[3] The first element l of a closure indicates where in memory the closure is allocated. It works as an identity when the language is extended with pointer equality.

[4] The recursion is realized in the rule for $x \stackrel{r}{=} \cdots$ by using $\rho[n/x]$ in clo where x is bound to n which will later be bound to the recursive closure itself.

$$\mathcal{P} : AExp \to Env \to PEStore \to (Preaction^* \times Name \times PEValue \times PEStore)$$
$$\mathcal{P}_p : Exp \to Env \to PEStore \to (Preaction^* \times Exp \times PEValue \times PEStore)$$
$$\rho \in \quad Env \quad = Var \to Name$$
$$\gamma \in PEStore = Name \to PEValue$$
$$PEValue = Const + Closure + Name$$

$$\mathcal{P}[\![(\cdot, y)]\!]\rho\,\gamma = (\cdot, \rho(y), \gamma(\rho(y)), \gamma)$$
$$\mathcal{P}[\![(x = e; P, y)]\!]\rho\,\gamma = \textbf{let}\ (P_1, e_1, v_1, \gamma_1) = \mathcal{P}_p[\![e]\!]\rho\,\gamma$$
$$n = new(\gamma_1)$$
$$\gamma_1' = \textbf{if}\ v_1 = \textsf{dyn}\ \textbf{then}\ \gamma_1[n/n]\ \textbf{else}\ \gamma_1[v_1/n]$$
$$(P_2, n_2, v_2, \gamma_2) = \mathcal{P}[\![(P, y)]\!]\rho[n/x]\,\gamma_1'$$
$$\textbf{in}\ (P_1; n = e_1; P_2, n_2, v_2, \gamma_2)$$
$$\mathcal{P}[\![(x \stackrel{r}{=} (\textsf{lambda}\ (x^*)\ (P_0, x_0)); P, y)]\!]\rho\,\gamma$$
$$= \textbf{let}\ l = new(\gamma)$$
$$n = new(\gamma[\star/l])$$
$$clo = cl(l, x^*, (P_0, x_0), \rho[n/x])$$
$$(P_1, n_1, v_1, \gamma_1) = \mathcal{P}[\![(P, y)]\!]\rho[n/x]\,\gamma[\star/l, clo/n]$$
$$p^* = new^*(\gamma_1)$$
$$(P_2, n_2, v_2, \gamma_2) = \mathcal{P}[\![(P_0, x_0)]\!]\rho[n/x, p^*/x^*]\,\gamma_1[p^*/p^*]$$
$$\textbf{in}\ (n \stackrel{r}{=} (\textsf{lambda}\ (p^*)\ (P_2, n_2)); P_1, n_1, v_1, \gamma_2)$$

Fig. 3. Partial evaluator (part 1)

done at this specialization time, and the resulting specialized program contains only the memory address.

Specialization of an A-expression (P, y) proceeds by partially evaluating all the preactions in P in order using the auxiliary function $\mathcal{P}_p$ shown in Fig. 4. $\mathcal{P}_p$ partially evaluates a given expression in a preaction and returns a tuple $(P_1, e_1, v_1, \gamma_1)$ consisting of a preaction P_1, a specialized expression e_1, a specialized value v_1, and a modified pe-store γ_1. v_1 may be a special name dyn which indicates that the result cannot be computed at partial evaluation time.

The specialization of a recursive binding includes not only creation of a recursive closure but also creation of a recursive specialized closure. It is done by specializing the body of the lambda expression with respect to the unknown parameter p^*. This can be regarded as the online realization of both static and dynamic values [2]. The creation of specialization can be postponed until it turns out that it is actually required (residualized), in a way similar to performing the backward analysis [18].

$\mathcal{P}_p$ is shown in Fig. 4. Specialization of a constant is itself. Here, the first *const* is a program text to appear in the specialized program while the second one is the value to be used in the later specialization. Specialization of a variable x returns a program text[5] $\rho(x)$ and a pe-value $\gamma(\rho(x))$. Specialization of a conditional is delegated to specialization of the then- or else-branch when the condition $\gamma(\rho(x))$ reduces to true (#t) or false (#f), respectively. If the value

---

[5] Or a name, a location, or a memory address.

$$\mathcal{P} \; : \; AExp \to Env \to PEStore \to (Preaction^* \times Name \times PEValue \times PEStore)$$
$$\mathcal{P}_p \; : \; Exp \to Env \to PEStore \to (Preaction^* \times Exp \times PEValue \times PEStore)$$
$$\rho \; \in \; Env \;\; = Var \to Name$$
$$\gamma \; \in PEStore = Name \to PEValue$$
$$PEValue = Const + Closure + Name$$

$$\mathcal{P}_p[\![const]\!]\rho\,\gamma = (\cdot, const, const, \gamma)$$
$$\mathcal{P}_p[\![x]\!]\rho\,\gamma = (\cdot, \rho(x), \gamma(\rho(x)), \gamma)$$
$$\mathcal{P}_p[\![(\text{if } x_0 \; (P_1, x_1) \; (P_2, x_2))]\!]\rho\,\gamma = \textbf{case } \gamma(\rho(x_0)) \textbf{ of}$$
$$\quad \#\text{t} : \mathcal{P}[\![(P_1, x_1)]\!]\rho\,\gamma$$
$$\quad \#\text{f} : \mathcal{P}[\![(P_2, x_2)]\!]\rho\,\gamma$$
$$\quad \textbf{otherwise} :$$
$$\quad\quad \textbf{let } (P_1', n_1, v_1, \gamma_1) = \mathcal{P}[\![(P_1, x_1)]\!]\rho\,\gamma$$
$$\quad\quad\quad\quad (P_2', n_2, v_2, \gamma_2) = \mathcal{P}[\![(P_2, x_2)]\!]\rho\,\gamma_1$$
$$\quad\quad \textbf{in } (\cdot, (\text{if } \rho(x_0) \; (P_1', n_1) \; (P_2', n_2)), \text{dyn}, \gamma_2)$$
$$\mathcal{P}_p[\![(\text{lambda } (x^*) \; (P_0, x_0))]\!]\rho\,\gamma = \textbf{let } l = new(\gamma)$$
$$\quad\quad clo = cl(l, x^*, (P_0, x_0), \rho)$$
$$\quad\quad p^* = new^*(\gamma[\star/l])$$
$$\quad\quad (P_1, n_1, v_1, \gamma_1) =$$
$$\quad\quad\quad\quad \mathcal{P}[\![(P_0, x_0)]\!]\rho[p^*/x^*]\,\gamma[\star/l, p^*/p^*]$$
$$\quad\quad \textbf{in } (\cdot, (\text{lambda } (p^*) \; (P_1, n_1)), clo, \gamma_1)$$
$$\mathcal{P}_p[\![(x_0 \; y_0^*)]\!]\rho\,\gamma = \textbf{let } n_x = \rho(x_0), \; v_x = \gamma(n_x)$$
$$\quad\quad n_y^* = \rho(y_0^*), \; v_y^* = \gamma(n_y^*)$$
$$\quad\quad \textbf{in case } v_x \textbf{ of}$$
$$\quad\quad prim : \textbf{if } v_y^* \textit{ are all known}$$
$$\quad\quad\quad\quad \textbf{then let } v = prim(v_y^*) \textbf{ in } (\cdot, v, v, \gamma)$$
$$\quad\quad\quad\quad \textbf{else } (\cdot, (n_x \; n_y^*), \text{dyn}, \gamma)$$
$$\quad\quad cl(l, x^*, (P', x'), \rho') :$$
$$\quad\quad\quad \textbf{if } \textit{unfold?}$$
$$\quad\quad\quad \textbf{then let } l^* = new^*(\gamma)$$
$$\quad\quad\quad\quad (P_1, n_1, v_1, \gamma_1) =$$
$$\quad\quad\quad\quad\quad \mathcal{P}[\![(P', x')]\!]\rho'[l^*/x^*]\,\gamma[v_y^*/l^*]$$
$$\quad\quad\quad \textbf{in } (l^* = n_y^*; P_1, n_1, v_1, \gamma_1)$$
$$\quad\quad\quad \textbf{else } (\cdot, (n_x \; n_y^*), \text{dyn}, \gamma)$$
$$\quad\quad\quad \textbf{otherwise} : (\cdot, (n_x \; n_y^*), \text{dyn}, \gamma)$$
$$\mathcal{P}_p[\![(\text{pe } (P_0, x_0))]\!]\rho\,\gamma = \mathcal{P}[\![(P_0, x_0)]\!]\rho\,\gamma$$

Fig. 4. Partial evaluator (part 2)

of the condition is not obtained during specialization, both the then- and else-branches are specialized and a conditional expression is returned. This is one of the places where a binding-time of a value is examined online.

Specialization of a lambda expression creates a closure and its specialized version. The former is used when the lambda expression is applied to arguments while the latter is used when it appears in the specialized program.

Specialization of application proceeds by first examining online the value of its function part. If it is *not* available at specialization time, an application expression is returned. If the function is a primitive, it computes the result if its arguments are all available, otherwise returns an application expression. If the function is a closure, one of two actions is taken: unfold the application or returns an application expression without unfolding. We can obtain more specialized results if application is unfolded. However, if we blindly unfold all the application, it is more likely that the specialization does not terminate. Here, we do not specify how to control this termination behavior of specialization. It is discussed in Sect. 7.1.

Finally, pe during specialization is simply ignored, and specialization is continued to its argument. In Sect. 7.2, we slightly change this rule to accommodate the multilevel specialization [14].

The specialization process itself is launched by executing pe during standard evaluation. Let us go back to the last rule in Fig. 2. The execution of (pe (P_0, x_0)) results in the partial evaluation of (P_0, x_0), whose result (an A-expression) is then executed by the standard interpreter (under the identity environment $\rho_{id} = \lambda n.n$; see below). Although the argument (P_0, x_0) can be any A-expression, only the lambda expression $(y = (\mathsf{lambda}\ (x^*)\ (P_0, x_0)), y)$ is sensible, because otherwise the specialized program is executed only once and in this case, standard evaluation is faster than partial evaluation.

Three points are noticed here for the rule of pe. First, the same standard store σ is used for the pe-store of specialization. Namely, we specialize a program with respect to the current heap state. (We regard a standard store as a special kind of pe-store where the stored values are only constants or closures and not names.) Secondly, the final pe-store resulting from the specialization is discarded and the specialized program is executed under the original store σ. In the implementation, this means that all the objects allocated during specialization can be garbage collected. Finally, the obtained specialized program is executed under the identity environment ρ_{id}. Remember that all the environment lookups are performed during specialization and the specialized program contains only names (locations) which directly refer to heap objects. Thus, ρ_{id} is used to map these names (regarded as variables in the specialized program) to names (locations) themselves.

6   Correctness

We have defined a congruence relation between values and proved that the result of partial evaluation of any side-effect free program is congruent to the original program in the store semantics, if the partial evaluation terminates. Details are omitted, however, for the lack of space.

7   Implementation and Extensions

We have implemented three versions[6] of the specializer together with the interpreter in Scheme. Below, we describe the extensions that we implemented.

7.1   Controlling Termination and Residualization

The specializer shown in Fig. 3 does not specify when to unfold a closure. In the implementation, we employ the user-annotation approach (filters [7]). Whenever a closure is *not* to be unfolded, a filter is attached to indicate it. Currently, filters are attached manually. This makes the implementation simpler releasing from sophisticated termination detection mechanisms. There seems to be a version of Schism that supports automatic insertion of filters.

A filter has two parts. The first part indicates when the closure is unfolded whereas the second part indicates which parameter values are used to make specialization when the closure is not unfolded. For example, consider the following power program using an accumulator parameter:

```
(define power-acc (lambda (m n acc)
  '(filter (static? n) '(- D D))
  (if (= n 0) acc (power-acc m (- n 1) (* m acc)))))
```

The first part of the filter indicates that the function is unfolded when the value of n is known. This reflects the fact that it is safe to unfold it when the recursion variable is known. A special construct static? is supported to check the availability of values at partial evaluation time. When n is unknown, the second part of the filter is examined and a specialized closure is created. The list (- D D) corresponds to the list of parameters (m n acc) and indicates if the value of each parameter should be propagated or not when constructing specializations. The directive - means "propagate" and D "not propagate". Even though the directive is -, the value is not propagated if it is unknown. Propagated parameters are inlined and disappear from the parameters of specializations. One specialization is created for each variation of the value of propagated parameters.

In the above example, the value of m is propagated and inlined into specialization (if its value is known) but acc is not. Acc is not propagated because otherwise infinite specializations (corresponding to infinite variations of acc) are created leading to non-termination of partial evaluation if both m and acc are known.

---

[6] One is the faithful implementation of $\mathcal{P}$ and $\mathcal{E}$, and the other two implement a store using the real memory. In the latter, let-insertion is realized via explicit continuation passing [20] or delimited continuation operators [2,25].

7.2 Multilevel Partial Evaluation

The occurrence of pe during specialization is simply ignored in Fig. 3. If the last rule in Fig. 3 is changed to the following rule:

$$\mathcal{P}_p[\![(\text{pe } (P_0, x_0))]\!]\rho\,\gamma = \textbf{let } (P_1, n_1, v_1, \gamma_1) = \mathcal{P}[\![(P_0, x_0)]\!]\rho\,\gamma$$
$$\textbf{in } (\cdot, (\text{pe } (P_1, n_1)), \text{dyn}, \gamma_1)$$

we can perform the multilevel specialization [14]. We left the pe construct in the specialized program. For example,

```
(pe (lambda (x) .....(pe (lambda (y) .....)).....))
```

will first produce a closure where computation not dependent on x (nor y) is performed. Since the resulting program now keeps the pe construct:

```
(lambda (x) ...(pe (lambda (y) ...))...)
```

the inner closure is further specialized using the value of x when the outer closure is applied. If the inner closure contains computation that can be specialized significantly only after the value of x is known (and the closure is used sufficiently many times), specializing it at this time would improve the overall execution time.

The practical evaluation of this multilevel partial evaluation has not yet been done.

7.3 Language Extension

Most standard primitives and special forms are supported for standard evaluation. For partial evaluation, primitives that have no side-effects are supported by simply putting them in the initial environment. Even the primitives that test the pointer equality, such as eq?, are supported because the specialized program is congruent to the original one with respect to the store semantics. Since our partial evaluator is online, cons naturally realizes partially known data structures. Among side-effecting primitives, I/O-type primitives are supported by blindly residualizing them in the specialized program. This is justified because the order of preactions is preserved during specialization.

The use of assignments (set!) and destructive updates (set-car! and set-cdr!) during partial evaluation are currently prohibited completely. However, the restricted form of assignments and destructive updates could be supported for the case where the names (locations) of the updated variables/objects are identified (known) and their values are unknown at partial evaluation time.

In all cases, side-effects would be blindly residualized in the specialized program. Execution of side-effects during specialization requires a sophisticated program analysis [26].

8   Experiments

We have tested various examples on our implementation. We obtained expected results for the standard examples, such as specialization of a power function, Ackermann's function, and compilation of various kinds of interpreters by specialization. For the compilation of interpreters, the specializer passes Neil Jones' optimality test [19]. In this section, we show our experience on the specialization of ray tracing as a bigger example.

Ray tracing produces a realistic image of 3D objects by calculating the color of each pixel on the screen. Fig. 5 shows a sample output of ray tracing. Given a configuration of 3D objects, we trace light in the reverse direction from the viewpoint (V-point) to each pixel on the screen. When it intersects with an object, we collect various light that reaches that intersecting point, such as ambient light (uniform light whose intensity is the same at all places), diffuse reflection (light coming directly from the light-point (L-point); effective only when the point is visible from the light-point), and specular reflection (reflected light coming from the direction of mirror-reflection; computed using recursion). Here goes the psuedo code for it:

```
(define (main V-point screen L-point object)
  (foreach pixel on the screen
    ; let V-vector be the vector from V-point to the pixel
    (ray-trace V-point V-vector L-point object)))
(define (ray-trace V-point V-vector L-point object)
  ; calculate if V-vector intersects with object
  ; if it does not, return background color
  ; otherwise, return the sum of
  ; - ambient light
  ; - diffuse reflection if the intersecting point
  ;                            is visible from L-point
  ; - specular reflection (via recursion)
  ; of the intersecting point
  )
```

For each pixel on the screen, ray-trace is called with L-point and object being constants. Since the number of times ray-trace is called is proportional to the number of pixels on the screen which can be quite large, specializing ray-trace with respect to fixed L-point and object will have benefits.

For specialization, we made the following changes. First, we insert a filter '(filter #f '(D D - -)) to ray-trace. #f says that ray-trace is never unfolded. Since the recursion structure of ray-trace is dependent on how objects are arranged and reflected-light runs, it is difficult to predict it. Here, we decide not to unfold at all. '(D D - -) means that the values of L-point and object are propagated to make specialization. Filters are inserted for other recursive functions, too. Then, we replace ray-trace in main with ray-trace2 and include the following:

Fig. 5. A sample image (128×128 pixels)

```
(define compiled? #f)
(define compiled-ray-trace 0)
(define (ray-trace2 V-point V-vector L-point object)
  (if (not compiled?)
    (begin (set! compiled-ray-trace
             (pe (lambda (V-point V-vector)
                   (ray-trace V-point V-vector L-point object)))))
           (set! compiled? #t)))
  (compiled-ray-trace V-point V-vector))
```

When `ray-trace2` is called for the first time, it calls a partial evaluator to specialize `ray-trace` and memoise it in the global variable `compiled-ray-trace`. During the specialization, `V-point` and `V-vector` are unknown since they are abstracted by `lambda` while `L-point` and `object` are bound to their values when the specializer is called. The specialization is done only once. The next time `ray-trace2` is called, it simply uses the specialization stored in `compiled-ray-trace`. The use of side-effects to store the specialized program is permitted since it is outside the `ray-trace` function and the updated variables are never referenced there.

We executed the original and specialized programs for the image in Fig. 5 with the screen size 32×32 pixels and compared their execution times. The experiment was done using MacGambit 2.2.2 on Macintosh PowerBook (PowerPC G3, 500MHz, 64MB memory for Scheme among 128MB). The specializer (together with the interpreter) is compiled by the MacGambit Compiler. The result is summarized in Table 1. The row (A) shows the execution time (in seconds) of the original program without performing specialization. (B) shows the execution time and the specialization time for the program with the changes for specialization described above. We can observe speedup of more than 16 for the main execution time excluding the specialization time. Even with the specialization time, speedup is almost the same, indicating that the specialization time is ignorable.

Table 1. Effect of specialization for `ray-trace`. The image size is 32×32 pixels. All produce the same image.

	specialization	execution	total
(A) orig (sec.)	-	6377.3	6377.3
(B) spec1 (sec.)	9.7	388.3	398.0
ratio (A/B)	-	16.4	16.0
(C) Trick (sec.)	21.9	347.0	368.9
ratio (A/C)	-	18.4	17.3
(D) spec2 (sec.)	4.5	547.5	552.0
ratio (A/D)	-	11.6	11.6

Notice that the experiment was done *interactively*: we first input the whole program and execute it; we then redefine parts of it to include the changes for specialization; finally the modified program is executed again with specialization. We will further modify the program below. This is achieved through the integration of partial evaluation into standard interpretation.

The row (C) shows the time for the program after we applied so-called "The Trick" [19]. In the calculation of diffuse reflection and specular reflection, we need a normal vector at the intersecting point. It is calculated from an object on which the intersecting point resides. Since the object is unknown until the intersecting point is known, and the intersecting point is unknown until the view-vector is known, the calculation of a normal vector cannot be done during specialization at all under the unknown view-vector. However, knowing that the object is one of the objects in the original configuration, we can make a case branch for each object in the configuration and perform some computation that depends on each object only. This replacement of unknown value with a case branch on all the possible variations is called "The Trick."

We implemented "The Trick" as follows. Suppose that we want to calculate a normal vector of `an-object` at `intersecting-point`:

```
(get-normal-vector an-object intersecting-point)
```

We first replace the above program with the following:

```
(let ((obj (bounded-variation an-object object)))
  (get-normal-vector obj intersecting-point))
```

where `object` is a (known) list of all the objects in the original configuration. Then, we add the following definition:

```
(define (bounded-variation obj lst)
  (if2 (null? (cdr lst))
       (car lst) ; the last element
       (if2 (eq? obj (car lst))
            (car lst)
            (bounded-variation obj (cdr lst)))))
```

where if2 is a special kind of conditional described soon. The function **bounded-variation** extracts obj from a known lst and returns the object found in lst. From the standard evaluation point of view, the returned object is the same as the original one (assuming that obj is always found in lst). From the partial evaluation point of view, however, there is a significant difference between the input and the output: the input is unknown, but the output is known. This enables further specialization in the calculation of normal vectors.

A special form if2 is supported in our specializer. In the standard evaluation, it is the same as if. During partial evaluation, it behaves like if except that it duplicates and propagates its continuation into the then- and else-branches. For example, (+ (if d 1 2) 3) where d is unknown is specialized into itself because the value of (if d 1 2) is unknown at specialization time, while specialization of (+ (if2 d 1 2) 3) becomes (if d 4 5) where the continuation "add 3" is duplicated and propagated into then- and else-branches. Duplication and propagation of continuation is easily implemented if a specializer is written in continuation-passing style or if we use delimited continuation operators [11, 20].

The use of if2 has positive and negative effects. The positive side is more specialization. Since the result of each branch is propagated to the continuation, we can expect more specialized output if the value of each branch is useful for the continuation. The negative side is the code explosion and hence the longer specialization time. Since whole the continuation is duplicated, the code size may be doubled if no specialization could be done at all. Nested if2 would make the code size further bigger. In fact, we tried to execute the ray tracing program where all the if special forms are treated as if2, but could not obtain the result. Since the use of if2 is not always effective, both if and if2 are supported in the implementation.

We use if2 to make a case branch for the possible objects in the configuration. In each branch of if2, one of the known objects is returned and used in the continuation (where the calculation of a normal vector is specialized). The resulting program is a big case statement, each branch of which contains a specialized normal vector calculation program.

The effect of "The Trick" is shown in Table 1 (C). Because the continuation of **bounded-variation** is duplicated and executed as many times as the number of objects, the specialization time becomes larger. Once the specialization is done, however, the execution time is further reduced from the case (B).

Finally, the row (D) in Table 1 shows the specialization and execution time where only the function that calculates intersection is specialized. We changed the intersection function in the same way as we did for **ray-trace**. Since we specialize only the intersection function, the specialization time is very small, yet we achieve rather significant speedup compared to the original case. This shows that the specialization of intersection is the major factor of the speedup.

9   Related Work

Applying specialization during standard evaluation (in-place partial evaluation) is studied by Balat and Danvy [5]. They use type-directed partial evaluation [10] to achieve strong normalization. We use the standard partial evaluation without any type information to achieve the similar goal.

Currently, we do not detect when a specialized program is invalidated by side-effects after the specialization. More sophisticated mechanisms would be possible, e.g., the one proposed by Volanschi et al. [27], where respecialization occurs when the heap objects that the specialized program depends on are modified. Hölzle et al. [17] describes the deoptimization technique that transforms compiled code into new versions when it is invalidated. We hope to introduce such mechanisms on top of the current framework in the future.

Although the original motivation of this work was to use partial evaluation in the interactive environment, it seems that the technique proposed here can be regarded as a foundation of run-time specialization [9,21]. What we did in the ray tracing experiment was the specialization of a part of the program at run-time. Although our specializer is very heavy compared to the existing run-time specialization systems, it addresses one of the important characteristics of run-time specialization, namely, sharing of heap objects between standard and partial evaluation.

MetaML [24] allows one to manually separate a program into multiple stages. So to speak, it allows one to manually perform binding-time analysis. Although MetaML is not suited for partially evaluating programs interactively (since one has to annotate programs every time he wants to perform specialization), MetaML and our work have one important technique in common: the sharing of objects between standard and partial evaluation corresponds to *cross-stage persistence* in MetaML.

Specialization of ray tracing was first done by Mogensen [22]. Andersen [1] specialized an already efficient ray tracer written in C. The realistic application of specialization in graphics is also found in [15].

10   Conclusion

This paper described our first step towards the integration of partial evaluation into standard interpretation. The two main issues in this integration are the treatment of heap objects and side-effects. To enable specialization with respect to the heap objects that are allocated beforehand in standard evaluation, specialization is performed with respect to *the heap state at specialization time* rather than based on a program text input so far. To avoid duplication of heap objects, *direct references to heap objects* are allowed in the specialized programs, in addition to the use of the conventional let-insertion technique. Despite our modest approach on side-effects that we allow partial evaluation of only side-effect free portions of a program, the resulting system covers some typical cases, such as the use of partial evaluation during an interactive debugging session. It also enables us to specialize a (side-effect free) program with respect to cyclic data structures, which was not easy before. We formalized this integration using store semantics and stated its correctness. The system is implemented in Scheme and various examples are tested. Among them, we have shown the specialization of a ray tracing program, and reported significant speedup.

In the future, we are planning to (1) develop the relationship between the preaction-based specialization and the conventional continuation-based let-insertion, (2) use the integrated specializer as a compiler for reflective languages [4], and (3) investigate the run-time specialization aspects of our system.

Acknowledgements. I would like to thank Olivier Danvy and Robert Glück for many comments and suggestions to the earlier versions of this paper.

References

1. Andersen, P. H. "Partial Evaluation Applied to Ray Tracing," *Software Engineering in Scientific Computing*, pp. 78–85, DIKU report D-289 (1996).
2. Asai, K. "Binding-Time Analysis for Both Static and Dynamic Expressions," In A. Cortesi and G. Filé, editors, *Static Analysis (LNCS 1694)*, pp. 117–133 (September 1999).
3. Asai, K., H. Masuhara, and A. Yonezawa "Partial Evaluation of Call-by-value λ-calculus with Side-effects," *ACM SIGPLAN Symposium on Partial Evaluation and Semantics-Based Program Manipulation (PEPM '97)*, pp. 12–21 (June 1997).
4. Asai, K., S. Matsuoka, and A. Yonezawa "Duplication and Partial Evaluation — For a Better Understanding of Reflective Languages —," *Lisp and Symbolic Computation*, Vol. 9, Nos. 2/3, pp. 203–241, Kluwer Academic Publishers (May/June 1996).
5. Balat, V., and O. Danvy "Strong Normalization by Type-Directed Partial Evaluation and Run-Time Code Generation," In X. Leroy and A. Ohori editors, *Types in Compilation (LNCS 1473)* pp. 240–252 (March 1998).
6. Bondorf, A., and O. Danvy "Automatic autoprojection of recursive equations with global variables and abstract data types," *Science of Computer Programming*, Vol. 16, pp. 151–195, Elsevier (1991).
7. Consel, C. "A Tour of Schism: A Partial Evaluation System for Higher-Order Applicative Languages," *Proceedings of the Symposium on Partial Evaluation and Semantics-Based Program Manipulation (PEPM'93)*, pp. 145–154 (June 1993).
8. Consel, C., P. Jouvelot, and P. Ørbæk "Separate Polyvariant Binding Time Reconstruction," Ecole des Mines, CRI Report A/261 (October 1994).
9. Consel, C., and F. Noël "A General Approach for Run-Time Specialization and its Application to C," *Conference Record of the 23rd Annual ACM Symposium on Principles of Programming Languages*, pp. 145–156 (January 1996).
10. Danvy, O. "Type-Directed Partial Evaluation," *Conference Record of the 23rd Annual ACM Symposium on Principles of Programming Languages*, pp. 242–257 (January 1996).
11. Danvy, O., and A. Filinski "Abstracting Control," *Proceedings of the 1990 ACM Conference on Lisp and Functional Programming*, pp. 151–160 (June 1990).

12. Flanagan, C., A. Sabry, B. F. Duba, and M. Felleisen "The Essence of Compiling with Continuations," *Proceedings of the ACM SIGPLAN '93 Conference on Programming Language Design and Implementation (PLDI)*, pp. 237–247 (June 1993).

13. Futamura, Y. "Partial evaluation of computation process – an approach to a compiler-compiler," *Systems, Computers, Controls*, Vol. 2, No. 5, pp. 45–50, (1971), reprinted as *Higher-Order and Symbolic Computation*, Vol. 12, No. 4, pp. 381–391, Kluwer Academic Publishers (December 1999).

14. Glück, R., and J. Jørgensen "An Automatic Program Generator for Multi-Level Specialization," *Lisp and Symbolic Computation*, Vol. 10, No. 2, pp. 113–158, Kluwer Academic Publishers (July 1997).

15. Guenter, B., T. B. Knoblock, E. Ruf "Specializing Shaders," *Proceedings of SIGGRAPH 95 (Computer Graphics Proceedings)* pp. 343–350 (1995).

16. Hatcliff, J. "An Introduction to Online and Offline Partial Evaluation Using a Simple Flowchart Language," In J. Hatcliff, T. Æ. Mogensen, and P. Thiemann editors, *Partial Evaluation, Practice and Theory (LNCS 1706)*, pp. 20–82 (1999).

17. Hölzle, U., C. Chambers, and D. Ungar "Debugging Optimized Code with Dynamic Deoptimization," *Proceedings of the ACM SIGPLAN '92 Conference on Programming Language Design and Implementation (PLDI)*, pp. 32–43 (June 1992).

18. Hornof, L., C. Consel, and J. Noyé "Effective Specialization of Realistic Programs via Use Sensitivity," In Van Hentenryck P., editor, *Static Analysis (LNCS 1302)*, pp. 63–73 (1997).

19. Jones, N. D., C. K. Gomard, and P. Sestoft *Partial Evaluation and Automatic Program Generation*, New York: Prentice-Hall (1993).

20. Lawall, J. L., and O. Danvy "Continuation-Based Partial Evaluation," *Proceedings of the 1994 ACM Conference on Lisp and Functional Programming*, pp. 227–238 (June 1994).

21. Lee, P., and M. Leone "Optimizing ML with run-time code generation," *Proceedings of the ACM SIGPLAN '96 Conference on Programming Language Design and Implementation (PLDI)*, pp. 137–148 (May 1996).

22. Mogensen, T. Æ. "The Application of Partial Evaluation to Ray-Tracing," Master's thesis, DIKU, University of Copenhagen (1986).

23. Ruf, E. *Topics in Online Partial Evaluation*, Ph.D. thesis, Stanford University (March 1993). Also published as Stanford Computer Systems Laboratory technical report CSL-TR-93-563.

24. Taha, W. *Multi-Stage Programming: Its Theory and Applications*, Ph.D. thesis, Oregon Graduate Institute of Science and Technology (November 1999).

25. Thiemann, P. J. "Cogen in Six Lines," *Proceedings of the ACM SIGPLAN International Conference on Functional Programming (ICFP'96)*, pp. 180–189 (May 1996).

26. Thiemann, P. J., and D. Dussart "Partial Evaluation for Higher-Order Languages with State," Available at http://www.informatik.uni-freiburg.de/~thiemann /papers/mlpe.ps.gz.

27. Volanschi, E. N., C. Consel, G. Muller, and C. Cowan "Declarative Specialization of Object-Oriented Program," *Proceedings of the 1997 ACM SIGPLAN Conference on Object-Oriented Programming Systems, Languages, and Applications (OOPSLA '97)*, pp. 286–300, (October 1997).

A Design Methodology for Functional Programs

David Wakeling

School of Engineering and Computer Science
University of Exeter
Exeter, EX4 4PT
United Kingdom
D.Wakeling@exeter.ac.uk

Abstract. An increasingly significant weakness of declarative programming is that it lacks a design methodology. In this paper, we attempt to provide one by showing how methodologies commonly used to develop object-oriented programs might also be used to develop functional ones. This involves mapping from a restricted subset of the diagrammatic notation used with these methodologies, the Unified Modeling Language (UML), to the standard lazy functional programming language, Haskell. As an example, we develop a small electronic mail system.

1 Introduction

In his position paper to the First Symposium on the Practical Aspects of Declarative Languages, Schmidt pointed out that an increasingly significant weakness of declarative programming is that it lacks a *design methodology* [19]. In this paper, we attempt to provide one by showing how methodologies, such as Catalysis [7], OPEN [11], and the Rational Unified Process [13], commonly used to develop object-oriented programs might also be used to develop functional ones. This involves mapping from a restricted subset of the diagrammatic notation used with these methodologies, the Unified Modeling Language (UML) [2], to the standard lazy functional programming language, Haskell [17].

The remainder of this paper is organised as follows. Section 2 introduces a restricted subset of the UML. Section 3 shows how designs in this restricted subset can be mapped to incomplete Haskell programs. Section 4 presents a small example. Section 5 mentions some related work. Section 6 considers some possible future work. Section 7 concludes.

2 The Unified Modeling Language

The UML is a diagrammatic notation with nine kinds of diagram. This section introduces the three that we will deal with, and then comments briefly on the six that we will not. Those familiar with the UML should find it easy going; others may need to consult [2].

W. Taha (Ed.): SAIG 2001, LNCS 2196, pp. 146–161, 2001.
© Springer-Verlag Berlin Heidelberg 2001

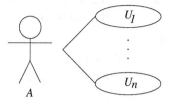

Fig. 1. The form of a use case diagram.

2.1 Use Case Diagrams

Figure 1 shows the form of a use case diagram. Use case diagrams capture the functional requirements of the system being developed. The stick person represents an *actor* — a user of the system in a particular role, and each oval represents a *use case* — a task to be performed with the aid of the system that yields an observable result of value to the actor. A use case diagram is accompanied by a textual description of the different courses of action possible in the use case. Both the diagram and the textual description are intended to be simple enough that all stakeholders in the project can readily agree on what they mean.

2.2 Class Diagrams

Once the use cases have been determined, a collection of *classes* can be designed to provide the required functionality. A class describes *objects* with common features. Figure 2 shows the form of a class in a *class diagram*. To start with, a

Fig. 2. The form of a class in a class diagram.

rectangle containing the name is all that is needed to represent a class. Later, *features* are added, and the rectangle is divided into three smaller ones. The top one contains the name, C, the middle one any *attributes* $A_1, \ldots A_i$, and the bottom one any *operations* $O_1, \ldots O_j$. Simplifying somewhat, the syntax of an attribute may be described by the BNF grammar

   visibility name [*multiplicity*] : *type*

and that of an operation by the grammar

   visibility name ({ *name* : *type* }) : *return-type*

Access to features is controlled by prefixing them with a *visibility* — either '+' or '–', standing for public or private. A public feature can be accessed from any class, and a private feature from only its own class. An attribute may also have a *multiplicity* saying how many there will be. A multiplicity can be written as two numbers separated by two dots that are the lower and upper limits of a range, with a * standing for zero or more.

There is an *association* between two classes if objects of the first "know about" objects of the second. Figure 3 shows the form of an association in a class diagram. An arrowhead on the association line specifies its *navigability* in

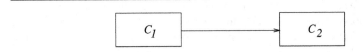

Fig. 3. The form of an association in a class diagram.

a particular direction; that is, that objects of the source class "know about" objects of the destination class, but not the other way round. An absence of arrowheads means navigability in both directions. Like attributes, associations can have both a visibility and a multiplicity.

2.3 Sequence Diagrams

After the classes have been designed, *sequence diagrams* can be drawn to show how they realise the use cases. Figure 4 shows the form of a sequence diagram. In a sequence diagram, labelled objects are placed at the top of vertical dashed *lifelines*. A stick person now represents an actor object — an instance of the actor from the use case diagram, and a rectangle represents an ordinary object — an instance of a class from the class diagram. An object may interact with another (or itself) by sending a *message*. A message is represented by an arrow from the lifeline of the sender to that of the receiver, labelled with the name and argument values for one of the receiver's operations. Later messages appear further down the page, and the lifeline of an object is thickened while it is engaged in interaction. A special message, **new**, indicates the creation of an object with certain attribute values. The symbol := can be used to give a name to a value returned in response to a message, and this name may then be used in subsequent messages.

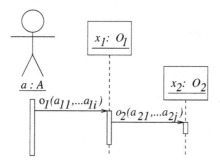

Fig. 4. The form of a sequence diagram.

2.4   Other Diagrams

There are six other diagrams that we do not deal with. An *object diagram* is an instance of a class diagram that contains no more information, and a *collaboration diagram* can be automatically converted to a sequence diagram that contains the same information. A *state chart* diagram describes a state machine and the events that cause transitions between states, of which an *activity diagram* is a special case. In our view, these state-based diagrams do not provide a natural way to describe the design of functional programs. A *component diagram* describes the relationships between program components, and a *deployment diagram* describes the relationships between these components and processors or devices. Although a component diagram could map to a script for a configuration management system, it is hard to see what more could be done with either diagram.

3   A Mapping to Haskell

In this section we present a series of rules for mapping from the restricted subset of the UML that we have described to Haskell. Applying these rules to a design will give an incomplete program because some operations are not fully described. A programmer must then complete the program by adding code for these operations.

3.1   Use Case Diagrams

In the Rational Unified Process, use case diagrams are used to generate test cases [13]. Taking this idea on board, we map use case diagrams to functions that can be used for testing. Currently, "black box" testing is performed interactively. Eventually, though, we plan to supplement this with "white box" testing performed automatically using QuickCheck [5]. Figure 5 shows the $\mathcal{U}$ rule. This

```
𝒰⟦ A ⇒ U₁,...Uₙ ⟧ =
  module Main_𝒩⟦ A ⟧ where
  import 𝒩⟦ U₁ ⟧
    ⋮
  import 𝒩⟦ Uₙ ⟧
  main_𝒩⟦ A ⟧ :: IO ()
  main_𝒩⟦ A ⟧ =
    menu [ ("U₁", do_𝒩⟦ U₁ ⟧ )
             ⋮
         , ("Uₙ", do_𝒩⟦ Uₙ ⟧ )
         ]
```

Fig. 5. The $\mathcal{U}$ rule.

rule produces the function main_$\mathcal{N}$⟦ A ⟧ that allows an actor, A, to choose which of its associated use cases, $U_1,\ldots U_n$, is done next. Here and elsewhere, the $\mathcal{N}$ rule maps the name of a UML entity, which may include punctuation, spaces, and line breaks, to a Haskell name, which may not. Each use case will have its own module, which must be imported. The menu function for menu selection is defined in Appendix A.

Every use case has some observable result of value in the real world. Figure 6 shows the $\mathcal{D}$ rule. This rule produces the function do_$\mathcal{N}$⟦ U ⟧ that does a use

```
𝒟⟦ U ⟧ =
  do_𝒩⟦ U ⟧ :: IO ()
  do_𝒩⟦ U ⟧ =
    do { args    <- prompt [ "a₁" ⋯ "aₘ" ]
       ; output <- run_𝒩⟦ U ⟧ 𝒩⟦ U ⟧ (pick "a₁" args) ⋯ (pick "aₘ" args)
       ; putStrLn output
       }
  in which
    run_𝒩⟦ U ⟧(a₁,...aₘ)
  ─────────────────────→ x : 𝒩⟦ U ⟧ ▷ IS ∈ interactions
```

Fig. 6. The $\mathcal{D}$ rule.

case, U, by prompting for any arguments, producing the observable result of value, and then printing the output string that is returned.

In this rule, and others which follow, we write $M \triangleright I_1,\ldots I_n$ to describe an interaction that has a *cause* — a message, M, is received — and an *effect* —

further interactions $I_1, \ldots I_n$ (in that order) then take place. The message M can be shown in more detail by writing it as an operation name and arguments above an arrow, $\xrightarrow{o(a_1, \ldots a_i)}$, followed by the label of the receiver, $x : C$. All interactions are assumed to be available in the set *interactions*.

Here, an object of the "use case controller" (or "boundary") class $\mathcal{N}[\![\, U \,]\!]$ is created with the constructor $\mathcal{N}[\![\, U \,]\!]$. This class has an operation $\mathtt{run}\_\mathcal{N}[\![\, U \,]\!]$ that gets the use case U done. More will be said about the mapping for classes below. Again, the `prompt` and `pick` auxiliaries for collecting and selecting use case arguments are defined in Appendix A.

3.2   Class Diagrams

A class maps to a module containing a datatype and some functions. The datatype has a single constructor with a field for each attribute and navigable association. There is a function on values of this datatype for each operation. Figure 7 shows the $\mathcal{C}$ rule. This rule produces the module $\mathcal{N}[\![\, C \,]\!]$ for the class

---

$\mathcal{C}[\![\, C \,]\!] =$
  $\mathtt{module}\ \mathcal{N}[\![\, C \,]\!]\ (\ \mathcal{N}[\![\, C \,]\!](..),\ \mathcal{N}[\![\, O_1 \,]\!],\ \cdots \mathcal{N}[\![\, O_p \,]\!]\ )\ \mathtt{where}$
  $\mathcal{A}[\![\, C \,]\!]$
  $\mathcal{O}[\![\, O_1 \,]\!]\ C \cdots \mathcal{O}[\![\, O_p \,]\!]\ C \quad \mathcal{O}[\![\, O_{p+1} \,]\!]\ C \cdots \mathcal{O}[\![\, O_j \,]\!]\ C$
  in which
  $\{O_1, \quad \ldots O_p\} = public\ operations(C)$
  $\{O_{p+1}, \ldots O_j\} = private\ operations(C)$

Fig. 7. The $\mathcal{C}$ rule.

C, using the $\mathcal{A}$ rule to produce the datatype, and the $\mathcal{O}$ rule to produce the functions. The visibility of operations is dealt with directly by including public ones in the export list of the module. The visibility of attributes and navigable associations is dealt with indirectly by preventing private ones from being named in patterns outside of the module, although our rules cannot show this.

Figure 8 shows the $\mathcal{A}$, $\mathcal{T}$, $\mathcal{M}$ and $\mathcal{B}$ rules. Together, these rules produce a datatype, $\mathcal{N}[\![\, C \,]\!]$, for a class, C. This datatype that has single constructor, $\mathcal{N}[\![\, C \,]\!]$, with a field for each attribute and navigable association. The $\mathcal{T}$ rule translates an attribute or navigable association to a field type. It uses the $\mathcal{M}$ rule to translate three of the most common multiplicities, and the $\mathcal{B}$ rule to translate basic types.

Figure 9 shows the $\mathcal{O}$ and $\mathcal{V}$ rules. Together, these rules produce the function for an operation, O, of class C. The type of the function is derived from that of the operation, with the "receiver" class, C, added as a first argument, and the result type wrapped in an `IO` type. Adding the receiver class is common in the

$\mathcal{A}[\![\ C\ ]\!] =$
   data $\mathcal{N}[\![\ C\ ]\!] = \mathcal{N}[\![\ C\ ]\!]\ \mathcal{T}[\![\ A_1\ ]\!]\cdots\mathcal{T}[\![\ A_i\ ]\!]$
   in which
   $\{A_1,\ldots A_i\} = attributes\ and\ navigable\ associations(C)$

$\mathcal{T}[\![\ v\ n\ m:t\ ]\!] = \mathcal{M}[\![\ m:t\ ]\!]$

$\mathcal{M}[\![\ 1..1:t\ ]\!] = \mathcal{B}[\![\ t\ ]\!]$
$\mathcal{M}[\![\ 0..1:t\ ]\!] = (\ \texttt{Maybe}\ \mathcal{B}[\![\ t\ ]\!]\ )$
$\mathcal{M}[\![\ 0..*:t\ ]\!] = [\ \mathcal{B}[\![\ t\ ]\!]\ ]$

$\mathcal{B}[\![\ \texttt{Void}\quad\ ]\!] = ()$
$\mathcal{B}[\![\ \texttt{Integer}\ ]\!] = \texttt{Int}$
$\mathcal{B}[\![\ \texttt{Boolean}\ ]\!] = \texttt{Bool}$
$\vdots$
$\mathcal{B}[\![\ other\quad\ ]\!] = \mathcal{N}[\![\ other\ ]\!]$

Fig. 8. The $\mathcal{A}$, $\mathcal{T}$, $\mathcal{M}$ and $\mathcal{B}$ rules.

$\mathcal{O}[\![\ o(a_1:t_1,\ldots a_m:t_m):r\ ]\!]\ C =$
   $\mathcal{N}[\![\ o\ ]\!]\ ::\ \mathcal{N}[\![\ C\ ]\!]\ \text{->}\ \mathcal{B}[\![\ t_1\ ]\!]\ \cdots\ \text{->}\ \mathcal{B}[\![\ t_m\ ]\!]\ \text{->}\ \texttt{IO}\ \mathcal{B}[\![\ r\ ]\!]$
   $\mathcal{N}[\![\ o\ ]\!]\ \texttt{this@}(\mathcal{N}[\![\ C\ ]\!]\ \mathcal{V}[\![\ A_1\ ]\!]\cdots\mathcal{V}[\![\ A_i\ ]\!]\ )\ a_1\ \ldots\ a_m = \mathcal{E}[\![\ IS\ ]\!]$
   in which
   $\{A_1,\ldots A_i\} = attributes\ and\ navigable\ associations(C)$
   $\xrightarrow{\ o(a_1,\ldots a_m)\ }\ \underline{x:C}\ \triangleright\ IS\ \in\ interactions$

$\mathcal{V}[\![\ v\ n\ m:t\ ]\!] = \mathcal{N}[\![\ n\ ]\!]$

Fig. 9. The $\mathcal{O}$ and $\mathcal{V}$ rules.

---

implementation of object-oriented programming languages. Wrapping the result type allows the function to have a side-effect that contributes to the observable result of value. These rules produce the left-hand side of a function. The right-hand side is produced from the interaction diagram — see below.

For each use case, U, there must be at least a "use case controller" (or "boundary" class), $\mathcal{N}[\![\ U\ ]\!]$. This class has no attributes or navigable associations, and a single operation, $\texttt{run\_}\mathcal{N}[\![\ U\ ]\!]$, that gets the use case U done, and then returns an output string.

3.3   Interaction Diagrams

An interaction diagram maps to the right-hand side of the function for an operation. Figure 10 shows the $\mathcal{E}$ and $\mathcal{S}$ rules. If an operation has an interaction

---

$\mathcal{E}[\![I_1, \ldots I_n]\!] =$
  do { $\mathcal{S}[\![I_1]\!]$; $\cdots \mathcal{S}[\![I_n]\!]$; return -?- }

$\mathcal{S}[\![\xrightarrow{o(a_1, \ldots a_m)} x : C \triangleright IS]\!] =$
  $\mathcal{N}[\![o]\!] \; \mathcal{N}[\![x]\!] \; \mathcal{N}[\![a_1]\!] \cdots \mathcal{N}[\![a_m]\!]$

$\mathcal{S}[\![\xrightarrow{v := o(a_1, \ldots a_m)} x : C \triangleright IS]\!] =$
  $\mathcal{N}[\![v]\!]$ <- $\mathcal{N}[\![o]\!] \; \mathcal{N}[\![x]\!] \; \mathcal{N}[\![a_1]\!] \cdots \mathcal{N}[\![a_m]\!]$

$\mathcal{S}[\![\xrightarrow{\texttt{new}(a_1, \ldots a_m)} x : C \triangleright IS]\!] =$
  let $\mathcal{N}[\![x]\!]$ = new_$\mathcal{N}[\![C]\!] \; \mathcal{N}[\![a_1]\!] \cdots \mathcal{N}[\![a_m]\!]$

Fig. 10. The $\mathcal{E}$ and $\mathcal{S}$ rules.

---

diagram, then the $\mathcal{E}$ rule produces a do block, using the $\mathcal{S}$ rule to fill it with a sequence of function applications and variable bindings. In this case, the programmer need only complete the return type. If an operation has no interaction diagram, it is considered to have an empty interaction diagram, and the $\mathcal{E}$ rule produces an empty do block. In this case, the programmer must complete the entire block on their own.

3.4   Restrictions

A number of restrictions are required to make these rules work. These require the designer to adopt a functional style.

The first restriction is on class diagrams, where generalisation relationships between classes are not allowed. Originally, we took the view that they would not be useful in the design of Haskell programs because the language does not support inheritance. However, many have since disagreed with this view, and so now we plan to allow them after all using the scheme described in [21].

The second restriction is also on class diagrams, where only the multiplicities 1..1, 0..1, and 0..* are allowed — the latter two mapping to the predefined Maybe and list types. This restriction could be lifted by introducing new types. However, as Fowler notes, the multiplicities allowed are the most common in practice [9].

The third restriction is on sequence diagrams, where operations must obey the *Law of Demeter*, which aims to describe good object-oriented design [14]. This law says that in any interaction diagram, on receiving a message, M, an object, O, may only send messages to:

1. object O;
2. objects directly accessible from O via its attributes;
3. objects created by O as a result of receiving M;
4. objects passed as arguments of M.

As well as describing good object-oriented design, this restriction is one way to ensure that an operation maps to a Haskell function with no free variables.

The final restriction is also on sequence diagrams, where an operation can have a "global" side-effect on the state of the world, but not a "local" side-effect on the state of an object. Global side-effects are allowed because the functions for operations have IO types, but local side-effects are disallowed because the fields of a Haskell datatype may not be updated. A change in state can only be brought about by creating a new object.

4   An Example

In this section we develop a small example system to give something of the flavour of our work. This system, called notmail, allows electronic mail to be sent and received. Figure 11 shows the design diagram. Quite deliberately, we say nothing more about this design. Recall, that it is supposed to be simple enough that all stakeholders in the notmail project can readily agree on what it means.

Our mapping can now be applied to the design to produce an incomplete program. Figure 12 shows the code for the use case diagram. This testing code does not need to be completed by the programmer. Figure 13 shows the code for the Send and Receive classes. The run_ operations of these two use case controller classes both have interaction diagrams, and the programmer need only complete the imports (which could, in fact, have been done by a more sophisticated mapping) and the return type. Some code that they might write to do so is shown underlined. Figure 14 shows the code for the Box and Message classes. None of the operations of these classes has an interaction diagram, and so the programmer must complete them on their own. Again, some code that they might write to do so is shown underlined. This code assumes a directory boxes that contains a mail box file for each user. The add and remove operations append and delete messages from this file, where a message begins with a line that begins with the word "From:". A trick is used in code for the remove operation: comparing the length of the mail box file with 0 ensures that the entire file is read into memory, so that the same file can then be written without corruption.

As even this small example shows, the incomplete code produced by our mapping looks much more imperative that functional. The advantage of this is that it is easy to relate diagrams and code, and so to complete the program. The disadvantage of this is that the elegance and power of functional programming seem to go unused. However, it is worth noting that all of this elegance and power can still be used to complete the program. In this example, unfortunately, this is not obvious because the code to complete the program simply deals with

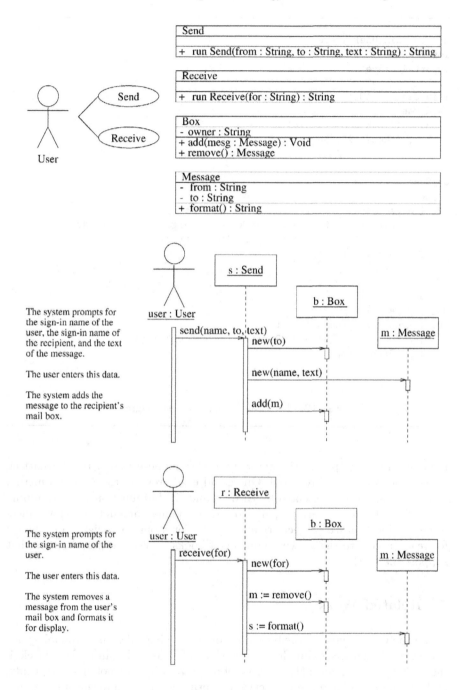

Fig. 11. The `notmail` design diagram.

```
module Main_User where
import Send
import Receive

main_User :: IO ()
main_User =
 menu [ ("Send",    do_Send)
      , ("Receive", do_Receive)
      ]

do_Send :: IO ()
do_Send =
 do { args    <- prompt [ "from", "to", "text" ]
    ; output <- run_Send Send (pick "from" args) (pick "to" args)
                              (pick "text" args)
    ; putStrLn output
    }

do_Receive :: IO ()
do_Receive =
 do { args    <- prompt [ "for" ]
    ; output <- run_Receive Receive (pick "for" args)
    ; putStrLn output
    }
```

Fig. 12. The code for the use case diagram.

input from and output to the file system. But suppose that better formatting of messages were to be required. One could easily rewrite the **format** function to use the algorithm presented by Bird [1] and the full functional programming repertoire. Overall, we are prepared to accept a small amount of awkwardness in converting from the object-oriented to the functional paradigm in exchange for ready access to the growing number of books, tools, and practitioners that support the UML.

5   Related Work

As yet, no work seems to have been done on developing a design methodology for declarative languages. Schmidt suggests that this may be because when developing declarative programs: (1) the crisis of program scale does not arise so quickly; and (2) the same language can serve for both design and implementation, and so the two activities merge almost invisibly [19]. The idea that a specification can be written as an inefficient functional program and then transformed to an efficient one goes back at least as far as Burstall and Darlington [4]. Turner

```
module Send (Send(..), run_Send) where
import Box
import Message
data Send = Send

send :: Send -> String -> String -> String -> IO String
send this@(Send) from to text =
  do { let b = Box to
     ; let m = Message from text
     ; add b m
     ; return "OK"
     }

module Receive (Receive(..), run_Receive) where
import Box
import Message
data Receive = Receive

receive :: Receive -> String -> IO String
receive this@(Receive) for =
  do { let b = Box for
     ; m <- remove b
     ; s <- format m
     ; return s
     }
```

Fig. 13. The completed code for the Send and Receive classes.

takes functional programs as executable specifications as the theme of his paper to the Royal Society [22]. Non-executable specifications have also been *animated* to check their correctness by translating them to functional programs. Borba and Meira [3] and O'Neill [16] have considered the animation of VDM specifications, and Johnson and Sanders [12], Diller [6], and Sherrell and Carver [20] the animation of Z specifications.

A problem that we have encountered throughout this work is that although the *syntax* of UML diagrams can be easily understood from [2], their *semantics* cannot. Both the Object Management Group and the Precise UML group are working to provide a formal semantics for the UML by developing a meta-model description of the language [15,8]. So whereas we describe the semantics by a mapping from the UML to Haskell, they describe them by a model of the UML in UML.

Many Computer Aided Software Engineering (CASE) tools already exist to support the drawing, cross-checking, and sharing of UML diagrams. We mention Rational Rose [18] as just one example. Tools like Rose are far more advanced

```
module Box (Box(..), add, remove) where
import List
import Message
data Box = Box String

add :: Box -> Message -> IO ()
add this@(Box owner) mesg =
 do { s <- format mesg
      appendFile ("boxes/" ++ owner) s
    ; return ()
    }

remove :: Box -> IO Message
remove this@(Box owner) =
 do { cs <- readFile ("boxes/" ++ owner)
    ; if length cs == 0 then
        return (Message "system" "no messages")
      else
        do { let ws        = words cs
           ; let ls        = lines cs
           ; let from      = head (tail ws)
           ; let (tls,rls) = break (isPrefixOf "From:") (tail ls)
           ; let text      = unlines tls
           ; let rest      = unlines rls
           ; writeFile ("boxes/" ++ owner) rest
           ; return (Message from text)
           }
    }

module Message (Message(..), format) where
data Message = Message String String

format :: Message -> IO String
format this@(Message from text) =
 do { return ("From: " ++ from ++ "\n" ++ text ++ "\n")
    }
```

Fig. 14. The completed code for the Box and Message classes.

that what we have described here. Typically, they support not only *forward engineering* (the production of incomplete code from diagrams), but also *reverse engineering* (the production of diagrams from code) and *round-trip engineering* (the reproduction of diagrams from completed code). These tools, of course, work with object-oriented programming languages like C++ and Java, rather than with functional programming languages like Haskell.

6   Future Work

There are a number of ways in which this work could be continued.

As we have shown, even with a restricted subset of the UML it is possible to develop interesting programs in Haskell. Clearly, though, we need to try more designs that use more of the UML, and in doing so to further develop our mapping to Haskell. Our hope is that certain *design patterns* for functional programs will then emerge in the same way that they have done for object-oriented ones [10].

Currently, we map designs to incomplete programs by hand. Eventually, of course, we want a CASE tool to do this automatically. Our current plan is to develop one from scratch, rather than to try and interface with an existing one. Clearly, this will be more work, but a "Haskell aware" tool will also be able to provide much better support for forward, reverse, and round-trip engineering.

7   Conclusions

In this paper, we have shown how methodologies commonly used to develop object-oriented programs might also be used to develop functional ones. This involved mapping from a restricted subset of the diagrammatic notation used with these methodologies, the Unified Modeling Language (UML), to the standard lazy functional programming language, Haskell. As our example electronic mail system showed, there is some awkwardness in converting from the object-oriented to the functional paradigm. However, we a prepared to accept this in exchange for ready access to the growing number of books, tools, and practitioners that support the UML.

Acknowledgements. An early draft of this paper was written while the author was on study leave at the University of York, working in the Department of Computer Science. The author would like to thank the Department for its hospitality, and Professor Colin Runciman and the Programming Languages and Systems Group for some lively discussions. The author would also like to thank the anonymous referees for some useful comments and suggestions.

This research was funded by the EPSRC under grant number GR/N20041 *Formal Description of the Software Life Cycle for Functional Programming Languages (Feasibility Study)*.

References

1. R. S. Bird. Transformational programming and the paragraph problem. *Science of Computer Programming*, 6(2):159–89, March 1986.

2. G. Booch, J. Rumbaugh, and I. Jacobson. *The Unified Modeling Language User Guide*. Addison Wesley, July 1998. ISBN 0201571684.

3. P. Borba and S. Meira. From VDM specifications to functional prototypes. *Journal of Systems and Software*, 21(3):267–78, June 1993.

4. R. M. Burstall and J. Darlington. A transformation system for developing recursive programs. *Journal of the Association of Computing Machinery*, 24(1):44–67, 1977.

5. K. Claessen and J. Hughes. QuickCheck: A lightweight tool for random testing of Haskell programs. In *Proceedings of the International Conference on Functional Programming*, pages 268–279. ACM Press, September 2000. ISBN 1581132026.

6. A. Diller. *Z: An Introduction to Formal Methods (Second Edition)*. John Wiley, 1994. ISBN 0471939730.

7. D. F. D'Souza and A. C. Wills. *Objects, Components and Frameworks with UML: The Catalysis Approach*. Addison Wesley, October 1998. ISBN 0201310120.

8. A. Evans and S. Kent. Core meta-modelling semantics of UML: The pUML approach. In *Proceedings of the Second International Conference on The Unified Modeling Language*, pages 140–155. Springer Verlag, October 1999. LNCS 1723.

9. M. Fowler and K. Scott. *UML Distilled (Second Edition)*. Addison Wesley, October 1999. ISBN 020165783X.

10. E. Gamma, R. Helm, R. Johnson, and J. Vlissides. *Design Patterns*. Addison Wesley, December 1994. ISBN 0201633612.

11. B. Henderson-Sellers and B. Unhelkar. *OPEN Modeling with UML*. Addison Wesley, June 2000. ISBN 0201675129.

12. M. Johnson and P. Sanders. From Z specifications to functional implementations. In J. E. Nicholls, editor, *Proceedings of the 4th Annual Z User Meeting*, pages 86–112. Springer Verlag, 1990.

13. P. Krutchen. *The Rational Unified Process: An Introduction (Second Edition)*. Addison Wesley, April 2000. ISBN 201707101.

14. Karl J. Lieberherr and Ian Holland. Assuring good style for object-oriented programs. *IEEE Software*, pages 38–48, September 1989.

15. Object Management Group. *OMG Unified Modeling Language Specification (Version 1.3)*, October 2000. See http://www.omg.org.

16. G. O'Neill. VDM - automatic translation of VDM specifications into Standard ML programs (short note). *Computer Journal*, 35(6):623–624, 1992.

17. S. Peyton Jones and J. Hughes. The Haskell 98 Language Report, February 1999.

18. Rational. Rational Rose, April 2001. See http://www.rational.com.

19. D. A. Schmidt. A return to elegance: The reapplication of declarative notation to software design. In *Proceedings of the Conference on the Practical Application of Declarative Languages*, pages 360–364. Springer Verlag, January 1999. LNCS 1551, ISBN 3540655271.

20. L. B. Sherrell and D. L. Carver. FunZ: An intermediate specification language. *Computer Journal*, 38(3):193–206, 1995.

21. M. Shields and S. L .Peyton Jones. Object-oriented sytle overloading for Haskell, July 2001. Submitted to the Workshop on Multi-Language Infrastructure and Interoperability.

22. D. A. Turner. Functional programs as executable specifications. In C. A. R. Hoare and J. Shepherdson, editors, *Mathematical Logic and Programming Languages*, pages 29–54. Prentice-Hall, 1985. ISBN 0135614651.

A   Auxiliary Function Definitions

This appendix defines some auxiliary functions used in the main text.

```
menu :: [ (String, IO ()) ] -> IO ()
menu options =
 do { mapM option (zip [1..] ss)
    ; n <- readLn
    ; head (drop (n - 1) xs)
    ; menu options
    }
    where (ss, xs) = unzip options

option :: (Int, String) -> IO ()
option (n,s) =
 putStrLn (show n ++ ") " ++ s)

prompt :: [ String ] -> IO [ (String, String) ]
prompt =
 mapM ask
 ask :: String -> IO (String, String)
 ask question =
   do { putStr question
      ; putStr "? "
      ; answer <- getLine
      ; return (question, answer)
      }

pick :: String -> [ (String, String) ] -> String
pick x ((n,v):nvs)
   | x == n    = v
   | otherwise = pick x nvs
```

A   Auxiliary Function Definitions

This appendix defines some auxiliary functions used in the main text.

```
menu :: [ (String, IO ()) ] -> IO ()
menu options =
 do { mapM option (zip [1..] ss)
    ; n <- readLn
    ; head (drop (n - 1) xs)
    ; menu options
    }
    where (ss, xs) = unzip options

option :: (Int, String) -> IO ()
option (n,s) =
 putStrLn (show n ++ ") " ++ s)

prompt :: [ String ] -> IO [ (String, String) ]
prompt =
 mapM ask
 ask :: String -> IO (String, String)
 ask question =
  do { putStr question
     ; putStr "? "
     ; answer <- getLine
     ; return (question, answer)
     }

pick :: String -> [ (String, String) ] -> String
pick x ((n,v):nvs)
  | x == n    = v
  | otherwise = pick x nvs
```

Dynamically Adaptable Software with Metacomputations in a Staged Language

Bill Harrison and Tim Sheard

Pacific Software Research Center
OGI School of Science and Engineering
Oregon Health & Science University
{wlh,sheard}@cse.ogi.edu
http://www.cse.ogi.edu/ wlh,sheard

Abstract. *Profile-driven* compiler optimizations take advantage of information gathered at runtime to re-compile programs into more efficient code. Such optimizations appear to be more easily incorporated within a semantics-directed compiler structure than within traditional compiler structure. We present a case study in which a metacomputation-based reference compiler for a small imperative language converts easily into a compiler which performs a particular profile-driven optimization: *local register allocation*. Our reference compiler is implemented in the staged, functional language MetaML and takes full advantage of the synergy between metacomputation-style language definitions and the staging constructs of MetaML. We believe that the approach to implementing profile-driven optimizations presented here suggests a useful, formal model for dynamically adaptable software.

1   Introduction

Dynamically adaptable software—software which can reconfigure itself at runtime in response to changes in the environment—is the focus of much current interest [2,13,18]. A classic example is the Synthesis Kernel [19] which dynamically specializes operating system kernel code to take advantage of runtime information. Staged programming [24] provides high-level abstractions for modeling such behavior. In this paper, we consider a particular kind of dynamically adaptable software, namely programming language compilers with profile-driven dynamic recompilation. The idea is to use staged programming to build a compiler for a language where the compiled code may periodically re-compile itself to take advantage of runtime information. A compiler constructed using staged programming does not have to rely on *ad hoc* techniques for specifying such optimizations.

Profile-driven compiler optimizations use information about a program's runtime behavior gathered during test executions to re-compile the program into more efficient code. An example of a profile-driven optimization is *local register allocation* [15,1]. The idea behind this optimization is that, if the memory location bound to a program variable x is accessed sufficiently often during testing

W. Taha (Ed.): SAIG 2001, LNCS 2196, pp. 163–182, 2001.
© Springer-Verlag Berlin Heidelberg 2001

runs of the program, then it may improve the runtime performance of the program to recompile it with x stored in a register because access time for x would be reduced. This "usage count" heuristic may also be used to guide the inlining of procedures.

This paper makes two contributions. (1) We present a case study which suggests that profile-driven optimizations can be remarkably straightforward to implement in a semantics-directed compilation scheme based on metacomputations [7,6]. We will demonstrate that the metacomputation structure makes it possible to achieve interoperability between static computation (e.g., program compilation) and dynamic computation (e.g., program execution), and we exploit this ability to implement a compiler which performs local register allocation. (2) We believe that the use of a staged language to construct code that reconfigures itself in response to dynamic stimuli illustrates an instance of a general model for constructing dynamically adaptable software in a concise and high level manner.

1.1   Compilation as Staged Computation

The usual semantics-directed paradigm is to write an interpreter and stage it, thereby producing a compiler. Typically, one may use a partial evaluator [11,3] or a staged language [23,21] to accomplish this. A compiler based on *metacomputations* and staging [7,6] factors the language specification into separate static and dynamic parts, where each of these parts is represented as a distinct monad. For a language L, the compiler typically has type (L->(Value D)S) where monads S and D represent the static and dynamic parts of L. We use ML-style postfix type constructor application (e.g., "Value D" instead of "D Value"). The metacomputation (S ∘ D) is a S-computation which produces a D-computation, and although it is defined in terms of monads, it is generally not a monad itself.

A logical next step is to express metacomputation-style compilers within a staged functional language like MetaML. The effect of staging is visible in the type of the compiler, which is now (L->(<Value D> S)). Here the brackets (< ... >) indicate the MetaML *code* type constructor. Code values are first-class in MetaML and may be inspected as any other program data. An immediate advantage of using MetaML in this endeavor is that object code produced by the metacomputation-based compiler (i.e., code values of type <Value D>) are both observable as data and executable as MetaML programs.

When one applies a staged interpreter to a source program, a code valued object program is obtained which is a compiled version of the source program. That object program expresses instructions of an abstract machine, that is closer to the hardware than the source language. The dynamic monad plays an important role by encapsulating the abstract machine of the object code [21,6,14], and cleanly separating dynamic computation from static computation.

Although the guiding principle of previous work [7,6] was to separate static from dynamic explicitly, we intentionally mix static with dynamic in one monad M = S+D[1] and use the MetaML code annotation <...> to distinguish static from

---

[1] Please pardon our abuse of language. The monads discussed here are constructed from monad transformers [14] and thus the additive notation is appropriate.

dynamic. Doing so allows us to compile using S features, execute using D features, and then re-compile, etc., all within the single monad M, and this interoperability between compilation and execution is *essential* to the current undertaking.

Because the static monad and the dynamic monad are the same, a very flexible approach to compilation is made possible. Dynamic computations can be performed at compile time (when information is available), and the dynamic computation can re-compile sub-components when needed. The use of a staged language makes the expression of such programs concise, high-level and natural.

When the abstract machine is able to perform staging, an object program can take advantage of this ability to adapt to runtime information. The following illustrates this matter concretely:

```
interpret      : Program -> input -> Value M
compile        : Program -> <input -> Value M> M
adaptcompile   : Program -> training -> <input -> Value M'> M'
```

where M' contains profiling information along with features from M. The function interpret is a monadic interpreter for the Program language, which when staged using metacomputation-style staging, produces compile. Enriching the monad M to M' yields a setting in which adaptable compilation becomes possible. Here, training is a set of training data to be used as an input. The compiled program is run on the training data collecting profile information, and is then recompiled to take advantage of the information learned in the training run. Using metacomputation and staging, this is easy to express, and can be added as a small delta to the program compile. It is the thesis of this paper that this technique can describe a wide variety of dynamically adaptable software.

2   Related Work

Traditionally constructed compilers [1,15] have one key virtue: they can produce very high-quality target code through sophisticated program analysis techniques and aggressive code optimization. But their complicated structure makes them infamously difficult to prove correct. In contrast, semantics-based approaches to compilation [4,7,12,28] are more amenable to formal proofs of correctness, but they fall short by comparison in the area of code optimization. The compiler writer appears to be in a dilemma, having to choose between performance (traditional compilers) and formal correctness (semantics-directed approaches). One purpose of this paper is to show that certain compiler optimizations may be easier to incorporate within a semantics-directed compilation scheme than within a traditional approach.

There is a synergy between the metacomputation-based approach to compilation and the staged language MetaML making it straightforward to implement profile-driven compiler optimizations. We found MetaML to be ideal because:

- Metacomputation-based language specifications, being explicitly staged, can be easily translated into the staged, functional language MetaML.

The first author developed metacomputation-based compilation as part of his thesis [6]. Previously, implementing the approach involved first translating the metacomputation-based specification into standard ML to ensure type correctness, and then translating it to Scheme by hand to apply partial evaluation. This involved annotating the resulting Scheme code (again by hand) with type information (and some black magic as well) to enable type-directed partial evaluation [3]. The result of partial evaluation is an observable Scheme program representing target code.

Given the same metacomputation-based specification written in standard ML, in contrast, achieving compilation is merely a matter of supplying the explicit staging annotations. This is orders of magnitude easier than the above process.

- MetaML's meta and object languages are the same making it easy to test metacomputation-based compilers written in MetaML and to test the object programs that they produce as well because both compiler and object code are MetaML programs.
- Metacomputation-based compiler specifications in MetaML are typechecked, thereby avoiding all sorts of latent errors.
- Profiling information may be added easily to metacomputation-based compiler specifications because metacomputations are structured by monad transformers [14].

Our framework for dynamically adaptable software may be viewed as an alternative to the "architectural composition" problem, where rich "architectures" are composed from modules or components. Such components need general interfaces which may be redundant or unnecessary in a larger composite architecture, and removing unnecessary component code is critical to making the approach practical for large systems. Architectural optimization usually consists of performing cross-component inlining to remove these unused interface components. The optimizer must treat the component code as data, observing their structure to determine which pieces to fuse. Treating "code as data" is integral to staged programming, and so in a dynamically adaptable software system as we have described, this "code as data" problem is handled at a much higher level of abstraction.

The remainder of this paper describes our case study in dynamically adaptable software and discusses its relevance as a model for such software. Section 3 defines a metacomputation-based compiler for a small imperative language with loops. Section 4 defines **adaptcompile** and discusses the minimal changes necessary to add dynamic reconfigurability to our reference compiler. Section 5 presents an example compilation. Section 6 outlines the general approach to adding a profile-driven optimization to a metacomputation-based compiler. Finally, Section 7 concludes with a discussion of how the techniques developed in this paper apply to adaptable software in general. In Appendix A, we have placed a short tutorial on the staging annotations and use of monads in MetaML. Appendix B gives an overview of the abstract machine and the monads used in the paper.

```
*********** Source Language ************
datatype Src = IntLit of int | Negate of Src | Add of Src*Src
             | Leq of Src*Src | ProgVar of Name | Assign of Name*Src
             | Seq of Src*Src | WhileDo of Src*Src;
datatype Program = Program of (Name list)*Src;


*********** Static Operations **********
datatype Location = Loc of int | Reg;     rdEnv  : Env M
datatype Env = env of Name -> Location;   rdAddr : Addr M
type Addr = int;                          inEnv  : Env -> a M -> a M
type Label = int;                         inAddr : Addr -> a M -> a M
                                          newlabel : Label M


***** Abstract Machine Operations *****
datatype Value = code of <Value M> | Z of int | Void;
push : int -> Value M      branch : Label -> Label -> Value M
pop  : Value M             read,store        : Addr -> Value M
ADD,LEQ,NEG : Value M      pushReg,loadReg : Value M
jump : Label -> Value M    newSeg,endlabel : Label->Value M->Value M
```

Fig. 1. Source, Static & Abstract Machine Operations for the Reference Compiler

3   The Metacomputation-Based Reference Compiler

Figure 1 presents the source language for our compiler. We have deliberately kept this language quite simple, because we wish to keep our metacomputation-based compiler as simple as possible. Src is a simple imperative language with while loops. A program is represented as (Program (globals,body)), where globals are the globally-defined integer program variables with command body of type Src. body is either an assignment (Assign(x,e)), a loop (WhileDo(b,c)), or a sequence of such statements (Seq(c1,c2)). Variables are defined only in the declarations in the top-level Program phrase. Src has integer expressions (IntLit i), (Negate e), and (Add(e1,e2)) representing integer constants, negation, and addition, respectively. (ProgVar x) is the program variable x when used as an expression. Src has only one boolean expression (Leq(e1,e2)) standing for ($\leq$).

In this Section we present a staged metacomputation-based compiler for Program. We use the combined monad approach discussed earlier. The monad M has two sets of operations, a set for static operations and another for dynamic operations. The static operations encapsulate the information needed at compile-time (e.g., mapping variable names to runtime locations), and the dynamic operations are the operations of the abstract machine.

The static operations of the monad M include mechanisms for manipulating environments, keeping track of free addresses, and generating fresh labels. They are given in the second part of Figure 1. The combinator rdEnv returns the current environment and rdAddr returns the current free address. For environment r, (inEnv r x) evaluates computation x in r. For address a, (inAddr a x) evaluates computation x with the "next free" address set to a. The combinator newlabel returns a fresh label.

The abstract machine targeted by our compiler is a simple stack machine with one general purpose register Reg. This is typical of target machines found in standard compiler textbooks [1,15]. The key differences are that we give executable definitions for the abstract machine operations as monadic functions in MetaML, and we rely on MetaML's staging annotations to produce inspectable code. Our approach is similar to the way that type-directed partial evaluation was used in previous work [4,8,7,6]. The operations of the targeted abstract machine are shown in the third part of Figure 1.

The MetaML definitions of these operations and of the monad M are given in Appendix B. The instruction (push i) pushes i onto the runtime stack and pop pops the runtime stack. The arithmetic instruction, ADD, pops the top two elements off of the stack, adds them, and pushes the result back on. The boolean test, LEQ, is defined similarly, although booleans are encoded as integer values (see the definitions of encode/decode in Appendix B.2 for further details). The jump (jump L) sends control to the code at label L, while (branch L1 L2) pops the stack and sends control to label L1 (L2) if that value is true (false). Memory operation (read a) pushes the contents of address a onto the stack, while (store a) pops the top value from the stack and stores it in address a. Instructions pushReg and loadReg are similar to read and store, except that the source and target of the respective operation is the register Reg. Code store operation (newSeg L pi) defines a new code segment at L. Note that (newSeg L pi) does not execute pi, because pi is only executed if control is sent to label L with a jump or a branch. A *forward jump* is an instruction (jump L), where the label L occurs after the jump instruction. Following Reynolds [20], we define a binding mechanism (endlabel L pi) defines a label L "at the end" of the code pi. One would pretty-print (endlabel L pi) as "pi ; L:". Forward jumps (jump L) within (endlabel L pi) simply branch to the "end" of pi.

Figure 2 presents the first compiler for the source language corresponding to the function compile from Section 1. compile is a MetaML function with type (Program -> <int list -> Value M> M). Given a Program, it performs a computation which produces a piece of code with type (int list -> Value M). The (int list) corresponds to the input to the program, which are the initial values for the global variables of the program.

Our reference compiler is similar to previous metacomputation-based compilers [7,6] with two differences. Firstly, MetaML staging annotations appear explicitly in the definition of compile thereby eliminating the need for a partial evaluator to generate code (because compile produces "residual" code values <...> itself). The use of staging annotations in compile is evident in its type— note that the range of compile is a MetaML code value. A second difference between compile and previous metacomputation-based compilers [8,7,6] is that compile is not explicitly derived from a denotational semantics for Program. We believe that this will make compile easier to understand.

```
(* ccsrc : Src -> <Value M> M *)
fun ccsrc e =
case e of
  (IntLit i) => Return M <push (~(lift i))>
| (Negate e) => Do M { pi <- (ccsrc e)   ; Return M <Do M { ~pi ; NEG }>}
| (Add (e1,e2)) => Do M { phi1 <- (ccsrc e1)
                        ; phi2 <- (ccsrc e2)
                        ; Return M <Do M { ~phi1 ; ~phi2 ; ADD }>}
| (Leq (e1,e2)) => Do M { phi1 <- (ccsrc e1)
                        ; phi2 <- (ccsrc e2)
                        ; Return M <Do M { ~phi1 ; ~phi2 ; LEQ }>}
| (Seq (c1,c2)) =>  Do M { phi1 <- ccsrc c1
                         ; phi2 <- ccsrc c2
                         ; Return M <Do M { ~phi1 ; ~phi2 }> }
| (WhileDo (b,c)) =>
   Do M { Lk <- newlabel ; Lc <- newlabel ; Lb <- newlabel
        ; phi_b <- ccsrc b
        ; phi_c <- ccsrc c
        ; Return M
                <endlabel ~(lift Lk)
                     (Do M { (newSeg ~(lift Lc)
                                 (Do M { ~phi_c
                                       ; jump ~(lift Lb) }))
                           ; (newSeg ~(lift Lb)
                                 (Do M { ~phi_b
                                       ; branch  ~(lift Lc) ~(lift Lk) }))
                           ; jump ~(lift Lb)    })>  }
| (ProgVar n) =>   Do M { (env rho) <- rdEnv
                        ; let val bnd_x = rho n
                          in case bnd_x of
                                Loc a => Return M <read ~(lift a)>
                              | Reg   => Return M <pushReg> end}
| (Assign (x,e)) =>
   Do M { phi_e <- (ccsrc e)
        ; env rho <- rdEnv
        ; let val bnd_x = (rho x)
          in case bnd_x of
                Loc a => Return M <Do M { ~phi_e ; store ~(lift a) }>
              | Reg   => Return M <Do M { ~phi_e ; loadReg}> end}

(* compile : Program -> <int list -> Value M> M *)
fun compile (Program (globals,main)) =
   Do M { fcode <- AllocVars (zip globals (upto (length globals - 1)))
                            (ccsrc main)
        ; Return M <fn input => ~(fcode <input>)>  };
```

Fig. 2. Compiler for Src and Program

The MetaML function `ccsrc` is a monadic version of what are sometimes called *semantic translation schemas* [1]. To see what is meant by this, consider first how the integer literals and negation in `Src` would be typically compiled into a stack language. Source expression (`IntLit i`) would be translated into the operation (`push i`). Compiling (`Negate e`) would produce the stack code "pi ; NEG", where pi is the stack code translation of e and NEG is a command which pops the top value off of the stack and pushes its negation back on. It is assumed that executing pi results in the value for e being pushed on the stack.

Both of these translation schemas are easily made formal in MetaML. The code for (`IntLit i`) is just <push (~(lift i))>[2], and so (`ccsrc (IntLit i)`) is just: (`Return M <push (~(lift i))>`). If (pi : <Value M>) is the code for the expression e, then <~pi ; NEG> is the code for (`Negate e`). Note that we had to splice pi into this code (i.e., use ~pi instead of pi) because it is a MetaML code value. Now (`ccsrc (Negate e)`) can be simply defined as:

```
Do M { pi <- (ccsrc e) ; Return M <Do M { ~pi ; NEG }>}
```

The other arithmetic and boolean expressions are compiled in a similar fashion.

| Before Profiling Transformation: x and y are stored on stack |

```
<(fn a =>
  Do M { push (nth (a,0))
       ; push (nth (a,1))
       ; endlabel 100
               (Do M { newSeg 101
                          (Do M { read 0 ; push 1 ; ADD ; store 0
                                ; read 0 ; store 1 ; jump 102 })
                     ; newSeg 102 (Do M { read 0 ; push 3 ; LEQ ; branch 101 100 })
                     ; jump 102
                     })
       ; pop
       ; pop })>
```

| After Profiling Transformation: x is now stored in Reg |

```
<(fn a =>
  Do M' { push (nth (a,0))
        ; loadReg
        ; push (nth (a,1))
        ; endlabel 103
                (Do M' { newSeg 104
                           (Do M' { pushReg ; push 1 ; ADD ; loadReg
                                  ; pushReg ; store 0 ; jump 105 })
                      ; newSeg 105 (Do M' { pushReg ; push 3 ; LEQ ; branch 104 103 })
                      ; jump 105
                      })
        ; pop })>
```

Fig. 3. Compiling (`Program([x,y], while x<=3 { x:=x+1 ; y:=x })`)

---

[2] Here, the ~(lift i) merely inlines the stage-0 value i into the stage-1 value <push...>.

Command sequencing (Seq (c1,c2)) is a straightforward formalization of the translation:

$$(\text{Seq}(c1, c2)) \mapsto \text{"code for c1"};\text{"code for c2"}$$

(WhileDo (b,c)) is a formalization of the following translation schema:

$(\text{WhileDo}(b, c)) \mapsto$ For three new labels Lk, Lc, and Lb, emit:

> Lc: "code for c" ; jump Lb
> Lb: "code for b" ; branch Lc Lk
> jump Lb
> Lk:

The interesting cases for this compiler are the constructs involving use of program variables, because these may be stored in either stack locations or the register Reg. Specifically, these are (ProgVar x), (Assign(x,e)), and (Program (globals,main)). (ccsrc (ProgVar x)) must emit code either reading the current value of x. It checks whether x has been assigned a stack location a or the register Reg, and emits appropriate instruction (read a) or loadReg, respectively). Similarly, (ccsrc (Assign(x,e))) must determine where to store the top of stack (i.e., where x is kept). Initially, we assume that all program variables are stored on the stack, and ((compile (Program (globals,main))) input) uses the function AllocVars to allocate stack locations for the global variables globals. The helper function (var2loc x g) allocates a new address a, and then runs the computation g in an extended environment in which x is bound to a:

```
(* var2loc : ['a]. string -> 'a M -> 'a M *)
fun var2loc x g = Do M { a <- rdAddr
                       ; r <- rdEnv
                       ; initProfile x a
                       ; inAddr (a+1) (inEnv ((xEnv x (Loc a)) r) g) };

(* AllocVars : ['a]. (string * int) list -> (string * 'a ) Maybe ->
                          <Value M> M -> <int list> -> <Value M> M *)
fun AllocVars vars phi =
  case vars of
    [] => Do M { body <- phi ; Return M (fn input => body) }
  | (x,n)::xs =>
            var2loc x
              (Do M { fcode <- (AllocVars xs phi)
                    ; (Return M (fn input =>
                                  <Do M { push (nth(~input,~(lift n)))
                                        ; ~(fcode input)
                                        ; pop
                                        }>))});
```

In a call (AllocVars vars phi), (vars : (Name*int)list) is a list of global variables paired with an index into the input list of initial values, while (phi : <Value M>M) is a code generator (i.e., an M-computation which produces code of type <Value M>). For each (x,n) in vars, the code produced by phi (i.e., ~(fcode input) above) is enclosed within instructions which allocate and deallocate storage for x. Respectively, these instructions are a push of the n-th element of the input list to allocate and a pop to deallocate. Within the code produced by phi, x will be bound to the appropriate stack location.

A sample compilation is presented in the top half of Figure 3 (marked "Before"). In that figure, the accesses to x (which is bound to stack location 0) are underlined.

3.1   Why Use MetaML <...> Instead of Concrete Syntax?

We could have defined an abstract syntax for the target stack language (e.g., `datatype Target = Push of int...`) and made `compile` a `Target`-valued computation. That is, `compile` could have been given type `Src -> Target M` and been defined as `compile (IntLit i) = Return M (Push i)`, etc. However, `Target` programs would not be immediately executable.

Because the target is an abstract machine parameterized by the monad M, simple changes to this machine can be used to collect profile information. We can extend the monad M to contain the material for both compiling `Src` programs, executing target machine programs, and profiling. This lays the foundation for dynamic adaptability.

4   Introducing Dynamic Profiling

What extensions are necessary to add dynamic profiling to the compiler in Figure 2? Having written `compile` in metacomputation-style, it is a simple matter to construct `adaptcompile`. We would like to write the following function and be done:

```
fun adaptcompile e training =
        Do M { pi <- compile e ; (run pi) training ; compile e };
```

As this point, however, the second call to `compile` would return the same code (modulo different `Labels`) as the first call (assuming `((run pi) training)` terminates). But remember, `(compile e)` is a monadic computation and can be affected by any states encapsulated in the monad and we run the first compiled version on the training data with the purpose of changing these states. To accomplish dynamic re-compilation, we must enrich the monad M to include a profile state and alter the abstract machine (`compile`) to make (or respond to) changes in the profile state.

We want to make minimal changes to `compile` to make `adaptcompile` work. Amazingly enough, the only changes needed are changes to the monad and the mechanism that `compile` uses to map variable names to locations. The exact changes are:

1. Enriched the monad M with a profile state (`type Profile = (string*int*int) list`). Call this new monad M'. Each element of this list is a profile of the form (`var,addr,count`), where `var` is the program variable, `addr` is the address where it is stored, and `count` keeps track of the accesses to `var`. Define a function (`incUsageCount a : Value M'`) which when executed will increment the count component of a profile (`var,a,count`).

2. Include a call to (incUsageCount a) in the definitions of (read a) and (store a).

3. Change the definition of (AllocVars vars phi) so that it picks a single program variable x with a maximal usage count from the Profile state and allocates the general-purpose register Reg for x.

4. Alter compile so that it computes the variable which should be stored in Reg (and call the resulting compiler compile'):

```
fun compile' (Program (globals,main)) =
    Do M' { maxP <- maxProfile (* compute maximally-used variable *)
         ; fcode <- AllocVars (zip globals (upto (length globals - 1)))
                              maxP
                              (ccsrc main)
         ; Return M' <fn input => ~(fcode <input>)>  };
```

After Step 3, AllocVars looks like:

```
fun useReg x maxP = case maxP of Nothing => false | Just (v,u) => v=x;

fun var2reg x g = Do M' { r <- rdEnv ; inEnv (xEnv x Reg r) g };

fun AllocVars vars maxP phi =
case vars of
  [] => Do M' { body <- phi ; Return M' (fn input => body) }
| (x,n)::xs =>
      if (useReg x maxP) then
          var2reg x
              (Do M' { fcode <- (AllocVars xs Nothing phi)
                   ; (Return M' (fn input =>
                                 <Do M' { push (nth(~input,~(lift n)))
                                      ; loadReg
                                      ; ~(fcode input)}>))
                      })
      else
          var2loc x
              (Do M' { fcode <- (AllocVars xs Nothing phi)
                   ; (Return M' (fn input =>
                                 <Do M' { push (nth(~input,~(lift n)))
                                      ; ~(fcode input)
                                      ; pop
                                      }>))})});
```

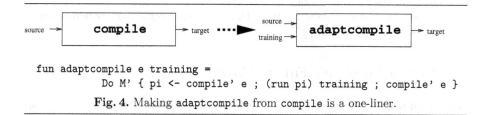

```
fun adaptcompile e training =
        Do M' { pi <- compile' e ; (run pi) training ; compile' e }
```

Fig. 4. Making adaptcompile from compile is a one-liner.

5   Example of Dynamic Recompilation

Figure 4 displays the compiler, adaptcompile, which dynamically recompiles its source program based on runtime profile information. Figure 3 shows "before and after" snapshots of compiling a program first without profiling and then with profiling information. Note first that the variable x is accessed most frequently in the sample program. In the "Before" snapshot, x is stored on the stack in location 0, and accesses to x (which are underlined in both snapshots) are either store or read instructions. In the "After" snapshot, x is stored in the register Reg. First, the 0-th member of the input list a is pushed onto the stack and loaded into Reg. Then, accesses to x are now performed with pushReg and loadReg instructions instead of read and store instructions. Finally, only one pop occurs at the end of the object code to deallocate y.

6   How to Add a Profile-Driven Optimization to Any Metacomputation-Based Compiler

Starting with compiler (C:(L -> (input -> Value D)S)):

1. Define M to be (S + D) incorporating all the operations of both monads. Use of monad transformers simplifies this step. Interpreting C within M has a different type, (L -> (input -> Value M) M), but produces identical results.
2. Stage C by adding MetaML staging annotations to produce a new metacomputation-based compiler (C' : L -> (<input -> Value M>) M) for language L and monad M.
3. Fix the type of profile data Profile for the specific optimization. To add usage counts for program variables as we do in the present work, this is the type (string*int*int) list.
4. Form a new monad M' combining all of the features of the monad M with Profile. Because M is assumed to be constructed with monad transformers [14], this is a simple task. In our case study, Profile is added with a state monad transformer.
5. The metacomputation-based compiler (C' : L->(<input -> Value M'>) M') behaves just as (C' : L -> (<input -> Value M>) M).
6. Alter the target language combinators to use Profile information. In our case, we change only (read a) and (store a).
7. Construct a new version of adaptC that observes profile data (when it exists) and compiles accordingly.

7   Conclusions and Future Work

How compiler optimizations are to be performed within a semantics-based approach to compilation has frequently been unclear. In this paper we have outlined a general technique for adding a whole class of compiler optimizations—those that are profile-driven—within a particular form of semantics-directed compiler. Adding profiling to the metacomputation-based reference compiler shown here was quite simple, mainly because the static and dynamic aspects of a metacomputation-based compiler can easily be combined. We did not include performance measures, as our goal was the development of a structure encapsulating dynamic adaptability rather than demonstrating the usefulness of any particular compiler optimization.

For the purpose of specifying and proving correctness, there is a significant advantage to keeping separate static and dynamic monads, S and D, instead of combining them into one monad (as we did here with the monad M). But this creates a complication in implementing the systems as we have in this paper in that a D computation is not immediately executable within a S computation. One approach is to introduce a "lift" morphism, which embeds a D computation into a S computation. In this setting, adaptcompile would look like:

```
compile : Program -> <input -> Value D> S;
lift : a D -> a S;
adaptcompile : Program -> training -> <input -> Value D> S
fun adaptcompile e training =
 Do S { pi <- compile e ; lift ((run pi) training) ; compile e }
```

We believe this technique is an instance of a general structure for modeling dynamically adaptable programs. If a staged programming language is used to implement both the compiler for a language, and the run-time system of the language, one essentially gets run-time re-compilation for free. This allows the expression of a whole range of dynamically adaptable behaviors at a very high level of abstraction.

Staged metacomputation-based compilers provide a high-level interface for describing adaptable systems. Suppose a system which evolves periodically, and for which significant speed-ups are possible if the source could be re-compiled to take advantage of configuration changes.

The system might be a network driver, and its configuration information may be the capacities of switches, lines, and the network topography. Or, the system might be an operating system service, and its configuration information may be the number, locations, and types of disk drives. Imagine that significant performance improvements can be made by compiling the code to take advantage of new configuration information. Several choices are possible:

1. One can pre-compile a number of anticipated configurations and dynamically switch between these when configurations change. The disadvantages of this mechanism are that it might be hard or impossible to anticipate all such changes.
2. Write an interpreter over the configuration states (with the consequent loss of performance that interpretation implies).
3. Bring down the system when configurations change for re-compilation. Obviously this involves human interference and significant loss of service.

The great thing about staged computation is that we can express at a high-level a single solution which incorporates the best aspects of all three of these solutions all at a modest cost. We take the second approach, choosing an interpreter because of its great flexibility. Staging it produces a compiler giving us the benefits of the first option. But there is no need to anticipate changes as new versions can be produced on demand. Merging the static and dynamic computations (and thereby enabling staging at the abstract machine level) captures in a high-level and concise manner both the kinds of policies implicit in the third option and the procedures that would be used to implement them. The approach outlined here brings together compilation, scripting languages, execution and monitoring abilities into one unified framework. For example, the high-level description of the above scenario is concisely described by:

```
adaptcompile prog config = Do M { code <- compile e config
                          ; handle (run code)
                                   (fn c => adaptcompile prog c) }
```

Here the monad has an exception mechanism which is raised when changes in the configuration occur. The function (handle body handler) runs body, which may raise an exception when the configuration state changes. At that point, handler continues execution until the next safe state is reached. Then, control is then passed to handler which, when supplied with the new configuration state, re-compiles and continues. Note that the configuration information config may contain a label specifying the entry (or re-entry) point in the code.

Acknowledgments. The work described here was supported by NSF Grant CDA-9703218, the M.J. Murdock Charitable Trust and the Department of Defense.

The authors would also like to thank Sam Kamin and Emir Pasalic for discussions of these ideas.

References

1. A. V. Aho, R. Sethi, and J. D. Ullman. *Compilers: Principles, Techniques, and Tools.* Reading, Mass.: Addison-Wesley, 1985.
2. C. Consel and F. Noël. A general approach for run-time specialization and its application to C. In ACM, editor, *Conference record of POPL '96, 23rd ACM SIGPLAN-SIGACT Symposium on Principles of Programming Languages: papers presented at the Symposium: St. Petersburg Beach, Florida, 21–24 January 1996*, pages 145–156, New York, NY, USA, 1996. ACM Press.
3. O. Danvy. Type-directed partial evaluation. In ACM, editor, *Conference record of POPL '96, 23rd ACM SIGPLAN-SIGACT Symposium on Principles of Programming Languages: papers presented at the Symposium: St. Petersburg Beach, Florida, 21–24 January 1996*, pages 242–257, New York, NY, USA, 1996. ACM Press.
4. O. Danvy and R. Vestergaard. Semantics-based compiling: A case study in type-directed partial evaluation. *Lecture Notes in Computer Science*, 1140:182–209, 1996.
5. R. Glück and J. Jørgensen. Efficient multi-level generating extensions for program specialization. In S. D. Swierstra and M. Hermenegildo, editors, *Programming Languages: Implementations, Logics and Programs (PLILP'95)*, volume 982 of *Lecture Notes in Computer Science*, pages 259–278. Springer-Verlag, 1995.

6. W. Harrison. *Modular Compilers and Their Correctness Proofs*. PhD thesis, University of Illinois at Urbana-Champaign, 2001.

7. W. Harrison and S. Kamin. Metacomputation-based compiler architecture. In *Mathematics of Program Construction – MPC200, Proc. 5th International Conference on the Mathematics of Program Construction, Ponte de Lima, Portugal*, volume 1837 of *Lecture Notes in Computer Science*, pages 213–229. Springer-Verlag, 2000.

8. W. L. Harrison and S. N. Kamin. Modular compilers based on monad transformers. In *Proceedings of the 1998 International Conference on Computer Languages*, pages 122–131. IEEE Computer Society Press, 1998.

9. P. Hudak, S. P. Jones, P. Wadler, B. Boutel, J. Fairbairn, J. Fasel, M. M. Guzman, K. Hammond, J. Hughes, T. Johnsson, D. Kieburtz, R. Nikhil, W. Partian, and J. Peterson. Report on the programming language haskell, version 1.2. *Sigplan*, 27(5), May 1992. Hudak, Wadler, Arvind, Boutel, Fairbairn, Fasel, Hughes, Johnsson, Kieburtz, Nikhil, Peyton Jones, Reeve, Wise, Young; Version 1.0: Functional Programming (Languages?) and Computer Architecture 89, pp123, 1989.

10. M. P. Jones. A system of constructor classes: Overloading and implicit higher-order polymorphism. In *Proceedings of the Conference on Functional Programming Languages and Computer Architecture*, pages 52–64, New York, NY, USA, June 1993. ACM Press.

11. N. D. Jones, C. K. Gomard, and P. Sestoft. *Partial Evaluation and Automatic Program Generation*. Prentice Hall International, International Series in Computer Science, June 1993. ISBN number 0-13-020249-5 (pbk).

12. P. Lee. *Realistic Compiler Generation*. Foundations of Computing Series. MIT Press, 1989.

13. M. Leone and P. Lee. A declarative approach to run-time code generation. In *Workshop on Compiler Support for System Software (WCSSS)*, Feb. 1996.

14. S. Liang, P. Hudak, and M. Jones. Monad transformers and modular interpreters. In ACM, editor, *Conference record of POPL '95, 22nd ACM SIGPLAN-SIGACT Symposium on Principles of Programming Languages: papers presented at the Symposium: San Francisco, California, January 22–25, 1995*, pages 333–343, New York, NY, USA, 1995. ACM Press.

15. S. S. Muchnick. *Advanced compiler design and implementation*. Morgan Kaufmann Publishers, 2929 Campus Drive, Suite 260, San Mateo, CA 94403, USA, 1997.

16. M. Odersky and K. Läufer. Putting type annotations to work. In ACM, editor, *Conference record of POPL '96, 23rd ACM SIGPLAN-SIGACT Symposium on Principles of Programming Languages: papers presented at the Symposium: St. Petersburg Beach, Florida, 21–24 January 1996*, pages 54–67, New York, NY, USA, 1996. ACM Press.

17. J. Peterson, K. Hammond, et al. Report on the programming language haskell, a non-strict purely-functional programming language, version 1.3. Technical report, Yale University, May 1996.

18. Calton Pu and Jonathan Walpole. A study of dynamic optimization techniques: Lessons and directions in kernel design. Technical Report OGI-CSE-93-007, Oregon Graduate Institute of Science and Technology, 1993.

19. C. Pu, H. Massalin, and J. Ioannidis. The synthesis kernel. *Usenix Journal, Computing Systems*, 1(1):11, Winter 1988.

20. J. C. Reynolds. The essence of algol. In J. W. de Bakker and J. C. van Vliet, editors, *Algorithmic Languages*, pages 345–372, Amsterdam, 1981. North-Holland.

21. T. Sheard, Z. El-Abidine Benaissa, and E. Pasalic. DSL implementation using staging and monads. In *Proceedings of the 2nd Conference on Domain-Specific Languages*, pages 81–94, Berkeley, CA, Oct. 3–5 1999. USENIX Association.

22. J. E. Stoy. *Denotational Semantics: The Scott-Strachey Approach to Programming Language Semantics*. MIT Press, Cambridge, Massachusetts, 1977.

23. W. Taha. *Multi-Stage Programming: Its Theory and Applications*. PhD thesis, Oregon Graduate Institute of Science and Technology, 1999.

24. W. Taha and T. Sheard. Multi-stage programming with explicit annotations. In *Proceedings of the ACM SIGPLAN Symposium on Partial Evaluation and Semantics-Based Program Manipulation (PEPM-97)*, volume 32, 12 of *ACM SIGPLAN Notices*, pages 203–217, New York, June 12–13 1997. ACM Press.

25. P. Wadler. Comprehending monads. *Mathematical Structures in Computer Science*, 2:461–493, 1992.

26. P. Wadler. The essence of functional programming. In ACM, editor, *Conference record of POPL '92, 19th ACM SIGPLAN-SIGACT Symposium on Principles of Programming Languages: papers presented at the Symposium: Albuquerque, New Mexico, January 1992*, pages 1–15.

27. P. Wadler. Monads for functional programming. *Lecture Notes in Computer Science*, 925:24–52, 1995.

28. M. Wand. Deriving target code as a representation of continuation semantics. *ACM Transactions on Programming Languages and Systems*, 4(3):496–517, July 1982.

A   MetaML Tutorial

MetaML is almost a conservative extension of Standard ML. Its extensions include four staging annotations. To delay an expression until the next stage one places it between meta-brackets. Thus the expression `<23>` (pronounced "bracket 23") has type `<int>` (pronounced "code of int"). The annotation, ~e splices the deferred expression obtained by evaluating e into the body of a surrounding Bracketed expression; and **run** e evaluates e to obtain a deferred expression, and then evaluates this deferred expression. It is important to note that ~e is only legal within lexically enclosing Brackets. We illustrate the important features of the staging annotations in the short MetaML sessions below.

```
-| val z = 3+4;
val z = 7 : int
```

Users access MetaML through a *read-type-eval-print* top-level. The declaration for z is read, type-checked to see that it has a consistent type (int here), evaluated (to 7), and then both its value and type are printed.

```
-| val quad = ( 3+4,   <3+4>,     lift (3+4), <z> );
val quad =    ( 7,     <3 %+ 4>, <7>,          <%z> ) :
              ( int * <int> *    <int> *       <int>)
```

The declaration for quad contrasts normal evaluation with the three ways objects of type code can be constructed. Placing brackets around an expression

(<3+4>) defers the computation of 3+4 to the next stage, returning a piece of code. Lifting an expression (lift (3+4)) evaluates that expression (to 7 here) and then lifts the value to a piece of code that when evaluated returns the same value. Brackets around a free variable (<z>) creates a new constant piece of code with the value of the variable. Such constants print with a % sign to indicate they are constants. We call this *lexical-capture* of free variables. Because in MetaML operators (such as + and *) are also identifiers, free occurrences of operators in constructed code often appear with % in front of them.

```
-| fun inc x = <1 + ~x>;
val inc = Fn  : ['a].<int> -> <int>
```

The declaration of the function inc illustrates that larger pieces of code can be constructed from smaller ones by using the escape annotation. Bracketed expressions can be viewed as *frozen*, i.e. evaluation does not apply under brackets. However, is it often convenient to allow some reduction steps inside a large frozen expression while it is being constructed, by "splicing" in a previously constructed piece of code. MetaML allows one to *escape* from a frozen expression by prefixing a sub-expression within it with the tilde (˜) character. Escape must only appear inside brackets.

```
-| val six = inc <5>;
val six =  <1 %+ 5> : <int>
```

In the declaration for six, the function increment is applied to the piece of code <5> constructing the new piece of code <1 %+ 5>.

```
-| run six;
val it = 6 : int
```

Running a piece of code, strips away the enclosing brackets, and evaluates the expression inside. To give a brief feel for how MetaML is used to construct larger pieces of code at runtime consider:

```
-| fun mult x n = if n=0 then <1> else < ~x * ~(mult x (n-1)) >;
val mult = fn  : <int> -> int  -> <int>
```

```
-| val cube = <fn y => ~(mult <y> 3)>;
val cube = <fn a => a * (a * (a * 1))> : <int  -> int>
```

```
-| fun exponent n = <fn y => ~(mult <y> n)>;
val exponent = fn  : int  -> <int  -> int>
```

The function mult, given an integer piece of code x and an integer n, produces a piece of code that is an n-way product of x. This can be used to construct the code of a function that performs the cube operation, or generalized to a generator for producing an exponentiation function from a given exponent n. Note how the looping overhead has been removed from the generated code. This is the purpose of program staging and it can be highly effective as discussed elsewhere [2,5,13, 18,24].

A.1   Monads in MetaML

We assume the reader has a working knowledge of monads [25,27]. We use the *unit* and *bind* formulation of monads [26]. In MetaML a monad is a data structure encapsulating a type constructor M and the *unit* and *bind* functions.

```
datatype ('M : * -> * ) Monad = Mon of
    (['a]. 'a -> 'a 'M) *                      (* unit function *)
    (['a,'b]. 'a 'M -> ('a -> 'b 'M) -> 'b M); (* bind function *)
```

This definition uses ML's postfix notation for type application, and two non-standard extensions to ML. First, it declares that the argument ('M : * -> *) of the type constructor Monad is itself a unary type constructor [10]. We say that 'M has *kind*: * -> *. Second, it declares that the arguments to the constructor Mon must be polymorphic functions [16]. The type variables in brackets, e.g. ['a,'b], are universally quantified. Because of the explicit type annotations in the datatype definitions the effect of these extensions on the Hindley-Milner type inference system is well known and poses no problems for the MetaML type inference engine.

In MetaML, Monad is a first-class, although *pre-defined* or *built-in* type. In particular, there are two syntactic forms which are aware of the Monad datatype: Do and Return. Do and Return are MetaML's syntactic interface to the *unit* and *bind* of a monad. We have modeled them after the do-notation of Haskell [9,17]. An important difference is that MetaML's Do and Return are both parameterized by an expression of type 'M Monad. Do and Return are syntactic sugar for the following:

```
(* Syntactic Sugar                        Derived Form      *)
    Do (Mon(unit,bind)) { x <- e; f }  =  bind e (fn x => f)
    Return (Mon(unit,bind)) e          =  unit e
```

In addition the syntactic sugar of the Do allows a sequence of x_i <- e_i forms, and defines this as a nested sequence of Do's. For example:

```
Do m { x1 <- e1; x2 <- e2 ; x3 <- e3 ; e4 }  =
    Do m { x1 <- e1; Do m { x2 <- e2 ; Do m { x3 <- e3 ; e4 }}}
```

Users may freely construct their own monads, though they should be very careful that their instantiation meets the monad axioms. The monad axioms, expressed in MetaML's Do and Return notation are:

```
Do {x <- Return e ; z}           = z[e/x]
Do {x <- m ; Return x}           = m
Do {x <- Do { y <- a ; b } ; c} = Do {y' <- a ; Do { x <- b[y'/y] ; c }}
                                 = Do {y' <- a ; x <- b[y'/y] ; c}
```

B   Executable Definition of Target Code

This appendix describes the executable specification of the abstract machine which is the target of the compiler in Figure 2.

We assume that the reader is familiar with monads [26,27,25,14]. The monads used in this paper are constructed from monad transformers [14]. A monad transformer creates a new monad from an existing monad and adds new data and operations to manipulate that data. The following table summarizes the monad transformers used in this paper:

M.T.	Associated Operation(s)	Meaning
$\mathcal{T}_{Env}$ T	rdT : T M	current T environment
	inT: T->a M->a M	(inT t x) evals x in T-env t
$\mathcal{T}_{St}$ S	updateS : (S->S)->S M	(updateS f) applies f to current S
		state, returning the resulting state
	getS : S M	getS = (updateS id) returns current S state
$\mathcal{T}_{CPS}$ A	CallCC:(a->A M)->A M	(CallCC f) passes f the current contin.

There are four monads used (sometimes implicitly) in this paper. They are:

S = $\mathcal{T}_{Env}$ Env ($\mathcal{T}_{Env}$ Addr ($\mathcal{T}_{St}$ Label Id))

D = $\mathcal{T}_{CPS}$ Value ($\mathcal{T}_{St}$ Sto ($\mathcal{T}_{St}$ Code Id))

M = $\mathcal{T}_{Env}$ Env ($\mathcal{T}_{Env}$ Addr ($\mathcal{T}_{CPS}$ Value ($\mathcal{T}_{St}$ Sto ($\mathcal{T}_{St}$ Label ($\mathcal{T}_{St}$ Code Id)))))

M$'$ = $\mathcal{T}_{Env}$ Env ($\mathcal{T}_{Env}$ Addr ($\mathcal{T}_{CPS}$ Value ($\mathcal{T}_{St}$ Sto ($\mathcal{T}_{St}$ Label ($\mathcal{T}_{St}$ Code ($\mathcal{T}_{St}$ Profile Id))))))

S and D are the static and dynamic monads, respectively, from the original metacomputation-based compiler for Src. One can recover this compiler from Figure 2 by replacing each occurrence of M occurring within <...> as D and all other occurrences with S. Erasing the staging annotations would then recover the original compiler. M arises as the combination S+D in step 1 on page 174. Finally, M$'$ is the monad S+D+Profile from step 3 on page 174.

For the monad M$'$ above:

```
Env = string -> Location (where Location = Loc of int | Reg)
Addr = Label = int
Value = code of <Value M'> | Z of int | Void
Sto = Addr*int*(Addr->Value)
Code = segm of Label -> Value M'
Profile = (string*int*int) list
```

In (sp,Reg,sigma):Sto, sp is the current stack pointer, Reg is the current contents of the general register, and sigma is the memory map (only integer values are stored in sigma). The code store Code is used to store continuations. Modeling jumps with a stored continuations is a common technique from denotational semantics [22].

B.1   Static Operations of M

The only static operation of the monad M not defined directly by the monad transformers is newlabel:

```
val newlabel = Do M { L <- updateLabel (fn l => l)
                    ; _ <- updateLabel (fn l => l+1) ; Return M L};
```

B.2   The Abstract Machine

All of the following are defined in terms of the operations provided by the above monad transformers. Except for read and store, their definitions in M' are identical.

Stack operations:

```
fun tweek l v sigma = fn l' => if l = l' then v else sigma l';
fun update f = Do M { _ <- updateSto f ; Return M Void};
fun writeLoc a i = update (fn (sp,reg,sigma) => (sp,reg,tweek a i sigma));
fun rdLoc a = Do M { (sp,reg,sigma) <- getSto ; Return M (Z (sigma a)) };
fun setSP sp = update (fn (_,reg,sigma) => (sp,reg,sigma));
fun setReg reg = update (fn (sp,_,sigma) => (sp,reg,sigma));
val SP = Do M { (sp,reg,sigma) <- getSto ; Return M sp };
val Reg = Do M { (sp,reg,sigma) <- getSto ; Return M reg };
fun push i = Do M { sp <- SP ; writeLoc sp i ; setSP (sp+1) };
val pop = Do M { sp <- SP ; setSP (sp-1) ; rdLoc (sp-1) };
val pushReg = Do M { reg <- Reg ; push reg };
val loadReg = Do M { (Z i) <- pop ; setReg i };
fun read a = Do M { Z i <- rdLoc a ; push i };
fun store a = Do M { (Z i) <- pop ; writeLoc a i };
```

Profiling operations:

```
fun incUsage a pl =  case pl of
   ((n,a',i)::prf) => if (a = a') then ((n,a',i+1)::prf)
                                  else  ((n,a',i)::incUsage a prf)
 | [] => [];

fun incUsageCount a = updateProfile (incUsage a);
fun read a = Do M' { Z i <- rdLoc a ; incUsageCount a ; push i };
fun store a = Do M' { (Z i) <- pop ; incUsageCount a ; writeLoc a i };
```

Arithmetic/Boolean operations:

```
val NEG = Do M { (Z i) <- pop ; push (neg i) };
val ADD = Do M { (Z i) <- pop ; (Z j) <- pop ; push (i + j) };
fun encode tf = if tf then 888 else 999;
fun decode i = (i=888);
val LEQ = Do M { (Z v1) <- pop ; (Z v2) <- pop ; push (encode (v2<=v1)) };
```

Control-flow operations:

```
fun rdSeg L = Do M { (segm Pi) <- getCode ; Pi L };
fun newSeg L x = updateCode (fn (segm Pi) => segm (tweek L x Pi));
fun endlabel L pi = CallCC (fn k => Do M { _ <- newSeg L (k Void) ; pi });
fun jump L = CallCC (fn _ => rdSeg L);
fun branch Lt Lf = Do M { (Z bv) <- pop
                        ; if (decode bv) then (jump Lt) else (jump Lf) };
```

MetaKlaim: Meta-programming for Global Computing[*]
Position Paper

Gianluigi Ferrari[1], Eugenio Moggi[2], and Rosario Pugliese[3]

[1] Dip. di Informatica, Univ. di Pisa, Italy
[2] Dip. di Informatica e Scienze dell'Informazione, Univ. di Genova, Italy
[3] Dip. di Sistemi e Informatica, Univ. di Firenze, Italy

Abstract. Most foundational models for global computing have focused on the *spatial* dimension of computations, however global computing requires also new ways of thinking about the *temporal* dimension. In particular, with no central control and the need to operate with incomplete information there is a compelling need to interleave meta-programming activities (like assembly and linking of code fragments), security checks (like type-checking at administrative boundaries) and normal computational activities. METAKLAIM is a case study in modeling both spatial and temporal aspects of computing by integrating METAML (an extension of SML for multi-stage programming) and KLAIM (a Kernel Language for Agents Interaction and Mobility). The staging annotations of METAML provide a fine-grain control of the temporal aspects, while KLAIM allows to model and program the spatial aspects of distributed concurrent applications. Our approach for combining these aspects is quite general and should be applicable to other languages/systems for network programming.

1 Introduction

The distributed software architecture (model) which underpins most of the wide area network (WAN) applications typically consists of a large number of heterogeneous computational entities (sometimes referred to as nodes or sites of the network) where components of applications are executed. The various nodes are handled by different authorities having different administrative policies and security requirements. Components of WAN applications are characterized by an highly dynamic behaviour. For instance, a component which acts as a server may become later a client asking for services to other components. Moreover, components have to deal with the unpredictable changes over time of the network environment (changes due to the availability of network connectivity, lack of services, node failures, network reconfiguration, and so on). Finally, nomadic or mobile components may detach from a node and re-attach later on a different

---

[*] Work supported by APPSEM WG and MURST projects SALADIN and TOSCA.

W. Taha (Ed.): SAIG 2001, LNCS 2196, pp. 183–198, 2001.
© Springer-Verlag Berlin Heidelberg 2001

node. Hence, components must be designed to support heterogeneity and inter-operability. Differently from traditional middle-wares for distributed programming, the structure of the underlying network is made manifest to programmers of WAN applications. We refer to Fuggetta, Picco and Vigna [16] and to Cardelli [5] for a comprehensive analysis of this issue.

The problems associated with the development of WAN applications has prompted the study of the foundations of programming languages with advanced features including mechanisms for agent mobility, for managing security, and for coordinating and monitoring the use of resources. Several foundational calculi have been proposed to tackle most of the phenomena related to WAN programming. We mention the Distributed Join-calculus [17], Klaim [9], the Distributed π-calculus [21], the Ambient calculus [3], the Seal calculus [34], and Nomadic Pict [30]. All these foundational models encompass a notion of location to reflect the idea of administrative domains, and computations at a certain location are under the control of a specific authority. In other words, they focus on the *spatial* dimension of WAN programming[1].

Another crucial aspect of WAN programming concerns the *temporal* dimension: the run-time system may interleave computational activities with structuring activities (e.g. the dynamic assembling of components). Components of WAN applications are often developed and maintained by different providers and may be downloaded on demand. Dynamic linking and dynamic enforcement of security checks (e.g. authentication and access control) increase the flexibility of WAN applications since it makes possible to reconfigure the application without having to restart the application. Several papers have addressed the problem of formally understanding dynamic linking (and separate compilation) [2,13,23, 29]; other approaches have tackled the problems of security in systems of mobile agents (see e.g. [12,20,22] and the references therein).

Hence, the spatial and the temporal dimension of WAN programming have been studied at considerable depth but in *isolation* and their interplay has not yet properly formalized and understood. This paper attempts to develop a foundational model which integrates together both the spatial and the temporal aspects of WAN programming. We have abstracted the basic feature of the problem in a calculus having primitives for programming agents which may migrate among sites, and primitives which support fine-grain control of dynamic linking and security checks.

Our calculus builds on the KLAIM language [9] and the MetaML functional language. The language KLAIM (Kernel Language for Agents Interaction and Mobility) is an experimental programming language, inspired by the Linda coordination model [19,6], specifically designed to model and to program WAN applications by exploiting mobility. KLAIM provides direct support for expressing and enforcing access control policies to resources and for authorizing migration and execution of mobile processes [12,11]. METAML [25] supports most features of SML and meta-programming constructs. Meta-programming provides

---

[1] The spatial dimension of WAN programming is often referred to as *network awareness*.

an ideal tool for describing customization and combination of software components. In other words, METAML enables programming of a variety of structural re-arrangements of code *directly* since the meta-programming constructs have the same status of the other programming constructs.

Sections 2 and 3 give an high-level overview of METAML and HOTKLAIM (a higher-order variant of KLAIM) introduced in Ferrari, Moggi and Pugliese [15]. Section 4 describes the formal development of METAKLAIM, a core language that integrates the meta-programming features of METAML with the programming constructs of KLAIM, and discusses how METAKLAIM may handle some of the most relevant issues raised by global computing. Section 5 gives few programming examples particularly relevant in a global computing scenario.

2   MetaML

METAML [25] is a substantial language, supporting most features of SML and a host of meta-programming constructs. In the current public release, safety is guaranteed only for programs in the pure fragment. Most of the theoretical work has gone into establishing type safety for larger subsets of the language. The key idea in multi-stage programming is the use of *annotations* to allow the programmer to breakdown the cost of a computation into distinct *stages*. METAML provides a type constructor $\langle \_ \rangle$ for code fragments with potentially unresolved links (represented by *dynamic variables*), and three basic staging annotations: Brackets $\langle \_ \rangle$, Escape ~ _ and Run run _. Brackets defers the computation of its argument (constructing code instead); Escape splices its code argument into the body of surrounding Brackets (combining code fragments into a larger fragment); and Run executes its code argument. The following examples illustrate more concretely how the staging annotation affects evaluation:

```
-| val a = <1>;
val a = <1> : <int>
-| val b = <~a+~a>;
val b = <1+1> : <int>
-| val c = run b;
val c = 2 : int
```

A distinguished feature of multi-stage (and multi-level) languages is the ability to "evaluate under a dynamic binder", and to manipulate values with free "dynamic variables" at run-time. For instance:

```
-| fun double x = <~x+~x>;
val double = fn ... :  <int> -> <int>
-| val f = <fn x => ~(double <x+1>)>;
val f = <fn x => (x+1)+(x+1)> : <int -> int>
```

the value <x+1> has a dynamic variable x free, and evaluation of double <x+1> is performed within the scope of a dynamic binder <fn x =>...>. Having values with free dynamic variables complicates the typing of *run* and of the three operations on references. In fact, the naive typing of such operations does not ensure type safety, as the following examples show:

```
-| <fn x => ~(run <x>;<x+1>)>;
(* x is an unresolved link, thus one cannot execute x *)
-| val l = ref <1>;
val l = ... : <int> ref;
-| val f = <fn x => ~(l:=<x>;<x+1>)>;
val f = <fn x => x+1> : <int -> int>
(* l contains <x>, so x is outside the scope of its binder *)
```

One of our starting points for designing METAKLAIM is the work by Calcagno, Moggi, Sheard and Taha [1], which exploits *closed types* to ensure type safety of METAML's staging annotations and cross-stage persistence in the presence of SML-style references. In fact, the authors conjecture that closed types provide a general solution for safely adding multi-stage programming constructs in the presence of computational effects. The key property of a term e of closed type is that "all free occurrences in e of dynamic variables are *dead code*", and therefore they can be ignored. The closed type constructor $[.]$, first introduced in Moggi, Taha, Benaissa and Sheard [26] for typing Run, maps a type t to the *biggest* closed type $[t]$ included in t.

Note 1. Hereafter, we use the following notations and conventions:

- Term equivalence, written $\equiv$, is α-conversion. $\mathrm{FV}(e)$ is the set of variables free in e. If E is a set of terms, then E_0 indicates the set of terms in E without free variables. Substitution of e_1 for x in e_2 (modulo $\equiv$) is written $e_2[x := e_1]$.
- m, n range over the set N of natural numbers, and $m \in \mathsf{N}$ is identified with the set of its predecessors.
- $\bar{e}$ denotes a sequence of terms and $|\bar{e}|$ indicates the number of its elements.
- $f : A \xrightarrow{fin} B$ means that f is a partial function from A to B with a finite domain, written $dom(f)$.
- $\mu(A)$ is the set of multisets with elements in A, and $\uplus$ denotes multiset union.
- Given an declaration of a grammar such as $e := P_1 \mid \ldots \mid P_m$, we write $e+ = P_{m+1} \mid \ldots \mid P_{m+n}$ as a shorthand for $e := P_1 \mid \ldots \mid P_{m+n}$.

Figure 1 summarizes the syntax of terms, types and closed types for the fragment of METAML considered in Calcagno, Moggi, Sheard and Taha [1]. Variables x range over an infinite set X (and locations l over an infinite set L).

The type system of METAML uses judgments of the form $\Delta; \Gamma \vdash_n e : t$, read "$e$ has type t at level n", where $\Delta : \mathsf{X} \xrightarrow{fin} (\mathsf{C} \times \mathsf{N})$ and $\Gamma : \mathsf{X} \xrightarrow{fin} (\mathsf{T} \times \mathsf{N})$ are type-and-level assignments. The level information is typical of type systems for multi-level languages (like $\lambda^\bigcirc$ of Davies [7]), in this context dynamic variables correspond to variables declared at level > 0. The splitting of type-and-level assignments in two parts (Δ and Γ) is borrowed from $\lambda^\square$ [8], and is needed for typing terms of type $[t]$. More formally, the difference between a declaration in

- Terms $e \in E ::= x \mid \lambda x.e \mid e_1 e_2 \mid$ let $x = e_1$ in $e_2 \mid$ fix $x.e$ functional fragment
  $\mid l \mid ref(e) \mid get(e) \mid set(e_1, e_2)$ references
  $\mid \langle e \rangle \mid \tilde{\ }e \mid \%e \mid run(e)$ meta-programming
  $\mid (x)e$ dead-code annotation

  Bind $(x)e$ declares that the free occurrences of x in e are *dead code*. Bind is used in the operational semantics for handling *scope extrusion*.
- Types $t \in T ::= \ldots \mid t_1 \to t_2 \mid [t] \mid$ ref $c \mid \langle t \rangle$
  Closed types $c \in C ::= \ldots \mid t_1 \to c_2 \mid [t] \mid$ ref c
  where ... stands for some unspecified base types, e.g. int.

Fig. 1. Syntax of METAML types and terms

Δ and the same declaration in Γ is expressed by the following substitution rules:

$$\frac{\Sigma; \Delta; \Gamma \vdash_m e_1 : t_1 \qquad \Sigma; \Delta; \Gamma, x : t_1^m \vdash_n e_2 : t_2}{\Sigma; \Delta; \Gamma \vdash_n e_2[x := e_1] : t_2} \qquad \frac{\Sigma; \Delta^{\leq m}; \emptyset \vdash_m e_1 : c_1 \qquad \Sigma; \Delta, x : c_1^m; \Gamma \vdash_n e_2 : t_2}{\Sigma; \Delta; \Gamma \vdash_n e_2[x := e_1] : t_2}$$

Figure 2 recalls the typing rules for the pure fragment, in particular:

- $\%e$ allows to use at higher levels a value defined at level n, this feature is called *cross-stage persistence*;
- $run(e)$ allows to execute the *complete* program (i.e. without unresolved links) represented by e. Since $run(e)$ is at the same the level of e, one could considered *run* as a constant of type $[\langle t \rangle] \to [t]$.

Given that one allows only references to values of a closed type, the three SML operations on references have the expected types, namely:

$$ref : c \to \text{ref } c \qquad get : \text{ref } c \to c \qquad set : \text{ref } c \to c \to \text{ref } c$$

Calcagno, Moggi, Sheard and Taha [1] adopt a small-step operational semantics, which eases the transfer of definitions and results to a concurrent setting. More precisely, there are transition relations $e \overset{n}{\longmapsto} e'$, one for each level, defined in terms of evaluation contexts [35] and two reductions $\overset{i}{\longrightarrow}$, one at level 0 (normal evaluation) and the other at level 1 (symbolic evaluation):

$$\frac{r \overset{i}{\longrightarrow} e'}{E_i^n[r] \overset{n}{\longmapsto} E_i^n[e']} \quad E_i^n \text{ evaluation context at level } n \text{ with hole at level } i$$

In fact, one is only interested in transitions $e \overset{0}{\longmapsto} e'$, where e is closed. However, the ability to evaluate under dynamic binders means that a redex r could have free dynamic variables even when $E_i^n[r]$ is closed. The following are the

$$\frac{}{\Delta; \Gamma \vdash_n x : t} \, (\Delta, \Gamma)(x) = t^n \qquad \frac{\Delta; \Gamma, x : t_1^n \vdash_n e : t_2}{\Delta; \Gamma \vdash_n \lambda x.e : t_1 \to t_2}$$

$$\frac{\Delta; \Gamma \vdash_n e_1 : t_1 \to t_2 \quad \Delta; \Gamma \vdash_n e_2 : t_1}{\Delta; \Gamma \vdash_n e_1 e_2 : t_2} \qquad \frac{\Delta; \Gamma \vdash_n e_1 : c_1 \quad \Delta, x : c_1^n; \Gamma \vdash_n e_2 : t_2}{\Delta; \Gamma \vdash_n \text{let } x = e_1 \text{ in } e_2 : t_2} \qquad \frac{\Delta; \Gamma, x : t^n \vdash_n e : t}{\Delta; \Gamma \vdash_n \text{fix } x.e : t}$$

$$\frac{\Delta; \Gamma \vdash_{n+1} e : t}{\Delta; \Gamma \vdash_n \langle e \rangle : \langle t \rangle} \qquad \frac{\Delta; \Gamma \vdash_n e : \langle t \rangle}{\Delta; \Gamma \vdash_{n+1} \tilde{\ } e : t} \qquad \frac{\Delta; \Gamma \vdash_n e : t}{\Delta; \Gamma \vdash_{n+1} \% e : t} \qquad \frac{\Delta; \Gamma \vdash_n e : [\langle t \rangle]}{\Delta; \Gamma \vdash_n \text{run } e : [t]}$$

$$\frac{\Delta; \Gamma \vdash_n e : t}{\Delta; \Gamma \vdash_n (x)e : t} \, x \text{ fresh} \qquad \frac{\Delta; \Gamma, x : t_1^m \vdash_n e : c}{\Delta; \Gamma \vdash_n (x)e : c} \, m > n \qquad \frac{\Delta, x : c_1^m; \Gamma \vdash_n e : c}{\Delta; \Gamma \vdash_n (x)e : c} \, m > n$$

$$\frac{\Delta; \Gamma \vdash_n e : c}{\Delta; \Gamma \vdash_n e : [c]} \qquad \frac{\Delta^{\le n}; \emptyset \vdash_n e : t}{\Delta; \Gamma \vdash_n e : [t]} \qquad \frac{\Delta; \Gamma \vdash_n e : [t]}{\Delta; \Gamma \vdash_n e : t}$$

Fig. 2. Type System for the pure fragment of METAML.

reductions for the pure fragment

$$((X)\lambda x.e) \, v^0 \xrightarrow{0} ((X)e)[x := v^0] \qquad \text{fix } x.e \xrightarrow{0} e[x := \text{fix } x.e]$$

$$\text{let } x = v^0 \text{ in } e \xrightarrow{0} e[x := \bullet v^0] \qquad run((X)\langle v^1 \rangle) \xrightarrow{0} (X)v^1 \downarrow_0$$

$$\tilde{\ }(X)\langle v^1 \rangle \xrightarrow{1} (X)v^1$$

where $(X)e$ is iterated Bind, $\bullet e$ is the Bind-closure of e (i.e. all free variables in e get bound by Bind in $\bullet e$), $v^{n+1} \downarrow_n$ is a Demotion operation which turns values at level $n + 1$ into terms, and v^n ranges over the set $\mathsf{V}^n \subset \mathsf{E}$ of values at level n

$$v^0 \in \mathsf{V}^0 ::= l \mid \lambda x.e \mid \langle v^1 \rangle \mid (x)v^0$$

$$v^{n+1} \in \mathsf{V}^{n+1} ::= \ldots$$

In the reduction let $x = v^0$ in $e \xrightarrow{0} e[x := \bullet v^0]$ we substitute x with $\bullet v^0$ rather than v^0. This can be done because the type of v^0 must be closed, and so all dynamic variables in v^0 are dead code. For the same reason, the reductions for $ref(v^0)$ and $set((X)l, v^0)$, which are the redexes that cause an update of the store, write to the store $\bullet v^0$ rather than v^0. In this way one ensures that the store contains only closed values, and that any free dynamic variable in v^0, that would go outside the scope of its dynamic binder, is re-bound by Bind.

3   Klaim

We now briefly reviews the main features of KLAIM by presenting a variant, called HOTKLAIM (for Higher-order typed KLAIM), which is more suitable for integra-

- Types $t \in \mathsf{T} ::= L \mid t_1 \rightarrow t_2 \mid (t_i | i \in m) \ (m \geq 0)$
- Terms $e \in \mathsf{E} ::= x \mid (mr_i | i \in n) \mid e_1 e_2 \mid \mathsf{fix}\ x.e$ functional fragment $(n > 0)$
  $\quad\quad\quad \mid (e_i | i \in m) \mid l \mid op(\overline{e}) \quad\quad (m \geq 0)$ and $(|\overline{e}| = \#op)$
  where op ranges over a set $\mathsf{Op} = \{nil, new, spawn, input, read, output\}$ of primitive operations. The arities of these operations are: $\#nil = 0$, $\#new = \#spawn = 1$ and $\#input = \#read = \#output = 2$.
  Patterns $p \in \mathsf{P} ::= x!t \mid e \mid (p_i | i \in m) \ (m \geq 0)$
  Match Rules $mr ::= p \Rightarrow e$
- Values $v \in \mathsf{V} ::= l \mid (vmr_i | i \in n) \mid (v_i | i \in m) \ (n > 0 \text{ and } m \geq 0)$
  Evaluated Patterns $vp \in \mathsf{VP} ::= x!t \mid v \mid (vp_i | i \in m) \ (m \geq 0)$
  Evaluated Match Rules $vmr ::= vp \Rightarrow e$

Fig. 3. Syntax of HotKlaim types, terms and values

---

tion with MetaML. Figure 3 summarizes the syntax of HotKlaim terms, which extends that of a core functional language with pattern matching[2].

The Klaim programming paradigm identifies *processes* as the primary units of computation, and *nets*, i.e. collections of *nodes*, as the coordinators of process activities. Each node has an address, called *locality*, and consists of a process component and a tuple space (TS), i.e. a multi-set of tuples. Processes are distributed over nodes and communicate asynchronously via TSs. The types of HotKlaim include the type L of localities and tuple types $(t_i | i \in m)$.

- *nil* is the deadlock process, while *spawn(e)* activates a process in a parallel thread. These operations have type $nil : t$ and $spawn : (() \rightarrow t) \rightarrow ()$ respectively.
- *output(l, v)* adds v to the TS at l (*output* is non-blocking). The type of *output* is $(L, t) \rightarrow ()$.
- *input(l, (vp_i \Rightarrow e_i | i \in m))* and *read(l, (vp_i \Rightarrow e_i | i \in m))* access the TS located at l. *input* checks each value pattern vp_i and looks in the TS at l for a matching v. If such a v exists, it is removed from the TS, and the variables declared in the matching pattern vp_j (i.e. those indicated by $x!t$) are replaced within e_j by the corresponding values in v. If no matching tuple is found, the operation is suspended until one becomes available (thus *input* is a blocking operation). *read* differs from *input* only in that the matching v is not removed from the TS. The type of *input* and *read* is $(L, t_1 \rightarrow t_2) \rightarrow t_2$. These are the only operations using dynamic type-checking (namely a matching v must be consistent with the types attached to variables declared in a pattern).
- *new(e)* creates a new locality l, activates process $e\ l$ at l, and returns the new locality. Therefore, the type of *new* is $(L \rightarrow t) \rightarrow L$.

In Klaim there is also an operation *eval(l, e)* for process mobility, which activates a process at locality l. The operation *eval* has not been included in HotKlaim. In fact, *eval* relies on dynamic scoping (a potentially dangerous

---

[2] The patterns are more general than those of SML, namely they include terms (that should evaluate to a locality).

mechanism), which is not available in HOTKLAIM, since in a functional language one can use (the safer mechanism of) parameterization. Moreover, the form of mobility underlying *eval* is "asynchronous", i.e. it involves only the sending node, this can be a source of security problems, because the target node has no control over the incoming processes. HOTKLAIM allows only "synchronous" process mobility. More precisely, a (sending) node can *output* a process abstraction in any TS, but the abstraction can become an active process only if (a process at) another (receiving) node does *input/read* it. Without *eval*, remote communication between nodes, like that provided by KLAIM primitives, is essential to implement mobility.

A HOTKLAIM *net* $N \in$ Net $\triangleq \mu(\mathsf{L} \times \mathsf{E}_0)$ is a multi-set of pairs consisting of a locality l (node name) and a term e (either a process running under the authority of that node or a value in the TS of that node). The dynamics of a net is given by a relation $N \Longrightarrow N'$ defined in terms of transition relations $e \overset{a}{\longmapsto} e'$ for terms, where a ranges over the set of *potential interactions*

$$a \in \mathsf{A} ::= \tau \mid l : e \mid s(e) \mid i(v)@l \mid r(v)@l \mid o(v)@l$$

For instance, $i(v)@l$ is the capability of *inputing* a value v from the TS at l, while $l : e$ is the (non-blocking) action of creating a new locality l running process e. The transitions relation $\overset{a}{\longmapsto}$ is defined in terms of evaluation contexts and a corresponding reduction $\overset{a}{\longrightarrow}$. The following is a sample of the reductions

$$(vp_i{\Rightarrow}e_i|i \in n)\ v \overset{\tau}{\longrightarrow} e_j[\rho] \qquad \text{if } j \in n \text{ and } match(vp_j, v) = \rho$$
$$\text{and } \forall i < j.match(pv_i, v) = fail$$

$$(vp_i{\Rightarrow}e_i|i \in n)\ v \overset{\tau}{\longrightarrow} fail \qquad \text{if } \forall i \in n.match(pv_i, v) = fail$$

$$input(l, (vp_i{\Rightarrow}e_i|i \in n)) \overset{i(v)@l}{\longrightarrow} e_j[\rho] \quad \text{if } j \in n \text{ and } match_t(vp_j, v) = \rho$$
$$\text{and } \forall i < j.match_t(pv_i, v) = fail$$

$$output(l, v) \overset{o(v)@l}{\longrightarrow} () \qquad spawn(v) \overset{s(v())}{\longrightarrow} () \qquad new(v) \overset{l:v\ l}{\longrightarrow} l$$

the functions $match(vp, v)$ and $match_t(vp, v)$ check the value v against the value pattern vp, and either return *the* matching substitution (if it exists) or $fail$, e.g. $match(v, v') = \emptyset$ if $v \equiv v' \in \mathsf{L}$, otherwise $fail$. The function $match_t$ does in addition dynamic type-checking, i.e. $match_t(x!t, v) = [x := v]$ when $\emptyset \vdash v : t$, otherwise $fail$.

4   MetaKlaim: A Proposal

This Section describes METAKLAIM, which integrates the meta-programming features of METAML with HOTKLAIM. The integration of types and terms is straightforward (see Figure 4). The typing judgments are those of METAML, and the type system extends that for the pure fragment of METAML (see Figure 2). The most critical design choice concerns the operational semantics:

- One choice is to have a sharp separation between symbolic evaluation and process interaction, namely to forbid process interaction during symbolic evaluation (i.e. within the scope of a dynamic binder).
- The other choice is to allow arbitrary interleaving of symbolic evaluation and process interaction.

We have opted for the second choice, since it offers a higher degree of flexibility, but one must be careful in typing the primitive operations $op \in \mathsf{Op}$, in order to prevent scope extrusion when process interaction occurs within the scope of a dynamic binder. The solution is similar to that for the SML operations on references, in certain cases one must use closed types instead of arbitrary types:

$$nil : t \qquad new : (L \to c) \to L \qquad spawn : (() \to c) \to ()$$
$$input, read : (L, c \to t) \to t \qquad output : (L, c) \to ()$$

The transition relations $e \overset{a,n}{\longmapsto} e'$ are defined in terms of evaluation contexts (see Figure 5) and reductions $r^0 \overset{a}{\longrightarrow} e'$ (for interactions) and $r^1 \overset{1}{\longrightarrow} e'$ (for symbolic evaluation), namely

$$\frac{r^0 \overset{a}{\longrightarrow} e'}{E_0^n[r^0] \overset{a,n}{\longmapsto} E_0^n[e']} \qquad\qquad \frac{r^1 \overset{1}{\longrightarrow} e'}{E_1^n[r^1] \overset{\tau,n}{\longmapsto} E_1^n[e']}$$

In fact, for defining the dynamics of a net only transition relations $\overset{a,n}{\longmapsto}$ with $n = 0$ are needed.

The reductions for the primitive operations $op(\bar{e})$ have to be modified as follows in order to prevent scope extrusion:

$$input(l, (vp_i^0 {\Rightarrow} e_i | i \in n)) \overset{i(v^0)@l}{\longrightarrow} e_j[\rho] \quad \text{if } j \in n \text{ and } match_t(vp_j^0, v^0) = \rho$$
$$\text{and } \forall i < j. match_t(pv_i^0, v^0) = fail$$

$$output(l, v^0) \overset{o(\bullet v^0)@l}{\longrightarrow} () \qquad spawn(v^0) \overset{s(\bullet v^0)()}{\longrightarrow} () \qquad new(v^0) \overset{l : \bullet v^0\; l}{\longrightarrow} l$$

The definition of net is like in HOTKLAIM, i.e. a multi-set $N \in \mathsf{Net} \overset{\Delta}{=} \mu(\mathsf{L} \times \mathsf{E}_0)$ of pairs. The following is a sample of the net transition rules

$$\frac{e \overset{i(v)@l_2,0}{\longmapsto} e'}{N \uplus (l_1 : e) \uplus (l_2 : v) \Longrightarrow N \uplus (l_1 : e') \uplus (l_2 : nil)}$$

$$\frac{e \overset{o(v)@l_2,0}{\longmapsto} e'}{N \uplus (l_1 : e) \Longrightarrow N \uplus (l_1 : e') \uplus (l_2 : v)} \quad l_2 \in L(N) \cup \{l_1\}$$

$$\frac{e \overset{l_2:e_2,0}{\longmapsto} e_1}{N \uplus (l_1 : e) \Longrightarrow N \uplus (l_1 : e_1) \uplus (l_2 : e_2)} \quad l_2 \notin L(N) \cup \{l_1\}$$

where $L(N) \overset{\Delta}{=} \{l | \exists e.(l : e) \in N\} \subseteq_{fin} \mathsf{L}$ is the set of nodes in the net N. We say that a net N is well-formed $\overset{\Delta}{\Longleftrightarrow}$ for every $(l : e) \in N$ exists $c \in \mathsf{C}$ s.t. $\emptyset; \emptyset \vdash_0 e : c$ and all localities occurring in e are in $L(N)$, i.e. are nodes of the net.

- Types $t \in \mathsf{T} ::= L \mid t_1 \to t_2 \mid (t_i|i \in m) \mid [t] \mid \langle t \rangle \ (m \geq 0)$
  Closed types $c \in \mathsf{C} ::= L \mid t_1 \to c_2 \mid (c_i|i \in m) \mid [t] \ (m \geq 0)$
- Terms $e \in \mathsf{E} ::= x \mid (mr_i|i \in n) \mid e_1 e_2 \mid \text{let } x = e_1 \text{ in } e_2 \mid \text{fix } x.e \quad (n > 0)$
  $\qquad \mid (e_i|i \in m) \mid l \mid op(\overline{e}) \qquad\qquad (|\overline{e}| = \#op \text{ and } m \geq 0)$
  $\qquad \mid \langle e \rangle \mid \tilde{\ }e \mid \%e \mid run(e) \mid (x)e$
  Patterns $p \in \mathsf{P} ::= x!t \mid e \mid (p_i|i \in m) \ (m \geq 0)$
  Match Rules $mr ::= p \Rightarrow e$
- Values $v^n \in \mathsf{V}^n \subset \mathsf{E}$ at level $n \in \mathsf{N}$
  $\quad v^0 ::= l \mid (vmr_i^0|i \in n) \mid (v_i^0|i \in m) \mid \langle v^1 \rangle \mid (x)v^0$

  $v^{n+1} ::= x \mid (vmr_i^{n+1}|i \in n) \mid v_1^{n+1}v_2^{n+1} \mid \text{let } x = v_1^{n+1} \text{ in } v_2^{n+1} \mid \text{fix } x.v^{n+1}$
  $\qquad \mid (v_i^{n+1}|i \in m) \mid l \mid op(\overline{v}^{n+1})$
  $\qquad \mid \langle v^{n+2} \rangle \mid \%v^n \mid run(v^{n+1}) \mid (x)v^{n+1}$

  $v^{n+2}+ = \tilde{\ }v^{n+1}$

  Evaluated Patterns $vp^n \in \mathsf{VP}^{\cdot} := x!t \mid v^n \mid (vp_i^n|i \in m)$
  Evaluated Match Rules $\quad vmr^0 ::= vp^0 \Rightarrow e$
  $\qquad\qquad\qquad\qquad\quad vmr^{n+1} ::= vp^{n+1} \Rightarrow v^{n+1}$

Fig. 4. Syntax of METAKLAIM types, terms and values

We expect that the two main results established in Calcagno, Moggi, Sheard and Taha [1], namely type safety for METAML and that METAML is a conservative extension of SML, extend smoothly to METAKLAIM. In particular, we have:

Theorem 1 (Type Safety). *If N is a well-formed net, then*

- $N \not\Longrightarrow \mathsf{err}$
- $N \Longrightarrow N'$ *implies that N' is well-formed and $L(N) \subseteq L(N')$.*

4.1   MetaKlaim and Global Computing

Global computing demands programming applications with different degrees of computational requirements and specific restrictions over resources. At the programming level, what is needed are constructs which permit programming and deploying a variety of computational policies to respond to the evolving demands of the run-time environment. In this paper, we outlined the development of METAKLAIM a basic core language for programming the temporal and spatial dimensions of global computing. The possibility of interaleaving metaprogramming activities with computational activities gives to METAKLAIM programmers the ability of programming policies without requiring a deep knowledge of the underlying system infrastructure. Indeed, the ability of directly accessing code fragments provides a high flexibility. For instance, one can program policies that constraint resource usages without rewriting the code of resource libraries. Moreover, platform independent code transformations can be programmed as well.

- Redexes $r^i \in \mathsf{R}^i$ at level $i \in \{0,1\}$

$$r^0 ::= x \mid v_1^0 v_2^0 \mid \mathsf{fix}\ x.e \mid \mathsf{let}\ x = v^0\ \mathsf{in}\ e$$
$$\mid op(\overline{v}^0) \qquad op \not\equiv nil\ \text{and}\ |\overline{v}^0| = \#op$$
$$\mid\ \tilde{}\ e \mid \mathsf{run}\ v^0 \mid \%e$$

$$r^1 ::=\ \tilde{}\ v^0$$

- Evaluation Contexts $E_i^n \in \mathsf{EC}_i^n$ at level $n \in \mathsf{N}$ with hole at level $i \in \{0,1\}$

$$E_i^n ::= (\overline{vmr}^n, Ep_i^n \Rightarrow e, \overline{mr}) \mid E_i^n e \mid v^n E_i^n \mid \mathsf{let}\ x = E_i^n\ \mathsf{in}\ e$$
$$\mid (\overline{v}^n, E_i^n, \overline{e}) \mid op(\overline{v}^n, E_i^n, \overline{e}) \qquad |\overline{v}^n| + 1 + |\overline{e}| = \#op$$
$$\mid \langle E_i^{n+1} \rangle \mid \mathsf{run}\ E_i^n \mid (x)E_i^n$$

$$E_i^{n+1} + = (\overline{vmr}^{n+1}, vp^{n+1} \Rightarrow E_i^{n+1}, \overline{mr}) \mid \mathsf{let}\ x = v^{n+1}\ \mathsf{in}\ E_i^{n+1} \mid \mathsf{fix}\ x.E_i^{n+1}$$
$$\mid\ \tilde{}\ E_i^n \mid \%E_i^n$$

$$E_i^i + = []$$

Evaluation Contexts for patterns $Ep_i^n ::= E_i^n \mid (\overline{vp}^n, Ep_i^n, \overline{p})$

- Interactions $a \in \mathsf{A} ::= \tau \mid l : e \mid s(e) \mid i(v^0)@l \mid r(v^0)@l \mid o(v^0)@l$
  with $\mathrm{FV}(e) = \mathrm{FV}(v^0) = \emptyset$

Fig. 5. METAKLAIM's redexes and evaluation contexts

There are several aspects, that are very important for global computing, which are not adequately handled in this preliminary proposal, e.g. genericity of SW components and security for systems of mobile components.

Genericity. In a global computing scenario most SW components available on the network are expected to be highly parameterized. Functional abstraction is not enough to express the desirable forms of parameterization. Also a limited form of polymorphism, like that supported by SML, appears inadequate. For instance, the full power of system F [18] is needed for expressing the type of mobile process abstractions used in the more sophisticated implementations of the *nomadic data collector* as we will briefly discuss in Section 5.

Security. The dynamic type-checking performed by the *input* and *read* primitives of KLAIM provide a simple and effective mechanism to ensure that a value fetched from a TS meets certain requirements. However, the expressiveness of this mechanism is directly related to the expressiveness of the type system. For instance, one would like to check that a process abstraction fetched from a TS does not perform unwanted interactions (e.g. communication with a certain locality) or meta-programming activities (e.g. symbolic evaluation or code execution). We believe that a promising approach is to adopt a type-and-effect system [32,33,27].

5   Examples

We have already pointed out components available on the network are expected to be highly parameterized, in order to accommodate a multiplicity of applications and to adapt to a variety of platforms and environments. A way to reconcile genericity and efficiency is to use *generative* components, which embody a method for constructing efficient object-code, once most of the parameters for the component have been fixed. Kamin, Callahan and Clausen [24] give numerous examples of components for generating object-code (for instance Java). These components are described as higher-order macros in a *functional* meta-language with Bracket and Escape constructs similar to those of METAML. We give two specific examples, a linker and a nomadic data collector, that make use of the process operations of HOTKLAIM and exemplify the additional advantages of METAKLAIM over HOTKLAIM.

5.1   Dynamic Linking and Loading

In global computing programming one important issue is the ability to control the loading policy of SW components. For instance, the JVM supports dynamic linking and loading of classes [28,14]. In some cases (localities with good connectivity or thrusted localities) one wants to load components just-when-needed, in other cases one may prefer to fetch in advance all components requested by a certain application. The naive solution is to parameterized applications w.r.t. a linker, and call the linker whenever a component (or service) is needed. This does not ensure enough flexibility, a better approach is to define a generative component parameterized w.r.t. a meta-linker. The meta-linker can decide whether to load a requested component at code-generation-time or to postpone the loading at run-time, namely by generating code for a call to the naive linker.

In the following example we assume that an application is parameterized w.r.t. a linker, which given a name of a service either succeeds in establishing a connection between the service and the application by returning an authorization key, or raises an exception. We are not interested in the details of the linker, but an abstract behavior could be: check whether the service (or its proxy) is present locally, if not search for it remotely and copy it locally (or create a proxy). We make use of the following types:

```
L        localities
Proc     processes (* e.g. the datatype with no values *)
Name     service names
Key      authorization keys
(* parameterized applications *)
Linker = Name -> Key       (* linkers *)
App = Linker -> Proc
(* parameterized application code *)
MLinker = Name -> <Key>    (* meta-linkers *)
CApp = MLinker -> <Proc>
```

The following process fetches applications from the local tuple place and execute them by passing a linker

```
execute (self:L, linker:Linker): Proc =
fix exec:Proc. input(self, fn x!App => spawn(x linker, exec))
```

If during execution the application calls the linker `link n` and the linker fails to make a connection to the service named `n`, then an exception is raised (and the application stops). The following process works similarly, but fetches application code and use a meta-linker:

```
Mexecute (self:L, mlinker:MLinker): Proc =
fix exec: Proc.
   input(self, fn x![CApp] => spawn(run(x Mlinker), exec))
```

An invocation of the meta-linker will be of the form `<...~(mlinker n)...>`. Using the meta programming facilities, the meta-linker can decide whether to invoke the linker immediately, i.e. `mlinker n = <%(linker n)>`, or whether to generate code for invoking the linker, i.e. `mlinker n = <%linker %n>`. In the first case, when the linker fails to make a connection, the code will not be executed at all.

5.2   Nomadic Data Collector

In this section, we exemplify the use of *mobile code* by means of a simple distributed information retrieval application. We assume that each node of a distributed database contain tuples of the form `(i,d)`, where `i` is the search key and `d` is the associated data, or of the form `(i,l)`, where `l` is a locality where more data associated to `i` can be searched. We give three implementations: two in HOTKLAIM, and the third in METAKLAIM. Hereafter we make use of the previously introduced types and of the following additional types:

```
Data      search keys and data
(* simple process abstractions *)
PA = L -> Proc
(* polymorphic types of process operations *)
Read = Input = V X:C. V Y:T. (L,X->Y) -> Y
Output = V X:C. V Y:T. (L,X,Y) -> Y
Spawn = V X:C. V Y:T. (X,Y) -> Y
Nil = V Y:T. Y
(* process abstractions with security checks *)
EnvK = (L,Key->Read,Key->Input,Key->Output,Nil,Spawn)
PAK = EnvK -> Proc
(* polymorphic types of process meta-operations *)
MSpawn = V X:C. V Y:T. (<X>,<Y>) -> <Y>
            (* and similarly for the other types *)
(* code abstractions with static security checks *)
MEnvK = (<L>,Key->MRead,Key->MInput,Key->MOutput,MNil,MSpawn)
CAK = MEnvK -> <Proc>
```

Simple process abstraction in HOTKLAIM. `ppa(i,u)` is a process abstraction activated by a process `execute`. `execute` fetches process abstractions from the local tuple space and activate them by providing the locality of the node. The parameter i is a search key, while u is the locality where all data associated to i should be sent. After activation ppa(i,u) removes data locally associated to i and forwards it to u, moreover ppa(i,u) sends copies of itself to localities that may contain data associated to i:

```
ppa(i:Data, u:L) : PA =
fix pa:PA. fn self!L =>
 spawn(fix p:Proc. input(self, fn (i, x!Data) => output(u, x, p)),
       fix p:Proc. input(self, fn (i, l!L) => output(l, pa, p)))


execute (self:L) : Proc =
fix exec:Proc. input(self, fn X!PA => spawn(X env, exec))
```

Process abstraction with security checks in HOTKLAIM. This implementation uses more complex process abstractions, namely a process is abstracted also w.r.t. surrogate process operations. Moreover, the surrogate communication primitives require an extra parameter (an authorization key):

```
ppa(k:Key, i:Data, u:L) : PAK =
fix pa:PAK. fn (self', _, in' , out', _, spawn'):EnvK =>
  spawn'(fix p:Proc.
              in' k (self', fn (i, x!Data) => out' k (u, x, p)),
          fix p:Proc.
              in' k (self', fn (i, l!L) =>  out' k (l, pa, p)))


execute (self:L, env:EnvK) : Proc =
fix exec:Proc. input(self, fn (X!PAK) => spawn(X env, exec))
```

Code abstraction with static security checks in METAKLAIM. This implementation refines the previous one by exploiting the meta-programming constructs of METAKLAIM, and has advantages similar to those offered by a meta-linker. For instance, depending on the key k, the meta-operation in' k could generate an input with no run-time overhead, or a deadlock nil (when the key does not allow to read anything), or some customized run-time checks on what is read.

```
pca(k:Key, i:Data, u:L) : CAK =
fix ca:CAK. fn (self', _, in' , out', _, spawn'):MEnvK =>
  spawn'(<fix p:Proc. ~(in' k (self', <fn (%i, x!Data) =>
                                     ~(out' k (<%u>, <x>, <p>))>))> ,
         <fix p:Proc. ~(in' k (self', <fn (%i, l!L) =>
                                     ~(out' k (<l>, <%ca>, <p>))>))>))


execute (self:L, env:[MEnvK]) : Proc =
fix exec:Proc. input(self, fn (X![CAK]) => spawn(run(X env), exec))
```

6   Conclusion

We introduced METAKLAIM as a basic calculus for handling the temporal and the spatial dimensions of global computing. Our preliminary results demonstrate that METAKLAIM can support programming of a variety of policies abstracting from the underlying system infrastructure. The meta programming primitives take care of describing how code manipulations is reflected in the underlying infrastructure. As the work outlined in this paper will progress, we believe to be able to demonstrate the full potentialities of METAKLAIM to address the peculiar aspects raised by global computing.

References

1. C. Calcagno, E. Moggi, T. Sheard, W. Taha. Closed types for safe imperative MetaML. submitted for publication, 2001.
2. L. Cardelli. Program Fragments, Linking, and Modularization. In *Proc. of the ACM Symposium on Principles of Programming Languages*, ACM Press, 1997.
3. L. Cardelli and A. Gordon. Mobile Ambients. *Theoretical Computers Science*240(1), Elsevier 2000.
4. L. Cardelli, A. Gordon. Types for Mobile Ambients. In *Proc. of the ACM Symposium on Principles of Programming Languages*, pp.79-92, ACM Press, 1999.
5. L. Cardelli, Abstractions for Mobile Computing, In In *Secure Internet Programming: Security Issues for Distributed and Mobile Objects* (J. Vitek, C. Jensen, Eds.), LNCS State-Of-The-Art-Survey, *LNCS* 1603, Springer, 1999.
6. N. Carriero, D. Gelernter. Linda in Context. *Communications of the ACM*, 32(4):444-458, ACM Press, 1989.
7. R. Davies. A temporal-logic approach to binding-time analysis. In *11*[th] *Annual IEEE Symposium on Logic in Computer Science (LICS)*, pages 184–195, New Brunswick, 1996. IEEE Computer Society Press.
8. R. Davies, F. Pfenning. A modal analysis of staged computation. In *23rd Annual ACM Symposium on Principles of Programming Languages (POPL)*, pages 258–270, St. Petersburg Beach, 1996.
9. R. De Nicola, G. L. Ferrari, R. Pugliese. KLAIM: A Kernel Language for Agents Interaction and Mobility, *IEEE Transactions on Software Engineering*, 24(5):315-330, IEEE Computer Society, 1998.
10. R. De Nicola, G. L. Ferrari, R. Pugliese. Types as Specifications of Access Policies. In In *Secure Internet Programming: Security Issues for Distributed and Mobile Objects* (J. Vitek, C. Jensen, Eds.), LNCS State-Of-The-Art-Survey, *LNCS* 1603, Springer, pp.117-146, 1999.
11. R. De Nicola, G. Ferrari, R. Pugliese. Programming Acess Control: The KLAIM Experience, In *Proc. CONCUR'2000, LNCS* 1877, 2000.
12. R. De Nicola, G. L. Ferrari, R. Pugliese, B. Venneri. Types for Access Control. *Theoretical Computers Science*, 240(1):215-254, special issue on Coordination, Elsevier Science, July 2000.
13. S. Drossopoulou. Towards an Abstract Model of Java Dynamic Linking and Verification. In *Proc. Types in Compilation*, 2000.
14. S. Drossopoulou, S. Eisenbach, D. Wragg. A fragment calculus - towards a model of separate compilation, linking and binary compatibility. In *14th Symposium on Logic in Computer Science (LICS'99)*, pages 147–156, Washington - Brussels - Tokyo, July 1999. IEEE.
15. G. Ferrari, E. Moggi, R. Pugliese. Global Types and Network Services. In Proc. *ConCoord: International Workshop on Concurrency and Coordination*, ENTCS 54 (Montanari and Sassone Eds), Elsevier Science, 2001.

16. A. Fuggetta, G. Picco, G. Vigna. Understanging Code Mobility, *IEEE Transactions on Software Engineering*, 24(5), IEEE Computer Society, 1998.
17. Fournet, C., Gonthier, G. Levy, J-J., Maranget, L., Remy, D. A Calculus of Mobile Agents, In Proc. CONCUR'96, *LNCS* 1119, Springer, 1996.
18. J-Y. Girard. Interprétation fonctionelle et élimination des coupures de l'arithmétique d'ordre supérieur. PhD. Thesis, Université Paris VII, 1972.
19. D. Gelernter. Generative Communication in Linda. *ACM Transactions on Programming Languages and Systems*, 7(1):80-112, ACM Press, 1985.
20. R. Gray, D. Kotz, G. Cybenko and D. Rus. D'Agents: Security in a multiple-language, mobile-agent system. In G. Vigna, editor, Mobile Agents and Security, *Lecture Notes in Computer Science*, Springer-Verlag, 1998.
21. M. Hennessy, J. Riely. Distributed Processes and Location Failures, *Theoretical Computers Science*, to appear, 2001.
22. M. Hennessy, J. Riely. Resource Access Control in Systems of Mobile Agents, *Information and Computation*, to appear, 2001.
23. M. Hicks and S. Weirich. A Calculus for Dynamic Loading, Technical report, MS-CIS-00-07, University of Pennsylvania, 2000, (available on line http://www.cis.upenn.edu/ mwh/papers/loadcalc.pdf).
24. S. Kamin, M. Callahan, L. Clausen. Lightweight and generative components II: Binary-level components. In *[31]*, pages 28–50, 2000.
25. The MetaML Home Page provides source code and online documentation http://www.cse.ogi.edu/PacSoft/projects/metaml/index.html.
26. E. Moggi, W. Taha, Z. Benaissa, T. Sheard. An idealized MetaML: Simpler, and more expressive. In *European Symposium on Programming (ESOP)*, volume 1576 of *Lecture Notes in Computer Science*, pages 193–207. Springer-Verlag, 1999.
27. F. Nielson, H. R. Nielson, and C. L. Hankin. *Principles of Program Analysis.* Springer-Verlag, 1999.
28. Z. Qian, A. Goldberg, A. Coglio. A formal specification of JavaTM class loading. In *Proceedings of the Conference on Object-Oriented Programming, Systems, Languages and Application (OOPSLA-00)*, volume 35.10 of *ACM Sigplan Notices*, pages 325–336, N. Y., October 15–19 2000. ACM Press.
29. P.Sewell. Modules, Abstract Types and Distributed Versioning. In *Proc. ACM Symposium on Principles of Programming Languages*, ACM Press, 2001.
30. P. Sewell, P. Wojciechowski. Nomadic Pict: Language and Infrastructure Design for Mobile Agents. *IEEE Concurrency*, 2000.
31. W. Taha, editor. *Semantics, Applications, and Implementation of Program Generation*, volume 1924 of *Lecture Notes in Computer Science*, Montréal, 2000. Springer-Verlag.
32. J.-P. Talpin, P. Jouvelot. Polymorphic type, region and effect inference. *Journal of Functional Programming*, 2(3):245–271, 1992.
33. J.-P. Talpin, P. Jouvelot. The type and effect discipline. *Information and Computation*, 111(2):245–296, June 1994.
34. J. Vitek, G. Castagna. Towards a Calculus of Secure Mobile Computations. In *Workshop on Internet Programming Languages*, *LNCS* 1686, Springer, 1999.
35. A.K. Wright, M. Felleisen. A syntactic approach to type soundness. *Information and Computation*, 115(1), 1994.

A Transformational Approach which Combines Size Inference and Program Optimization
Position Paper

Christoph A. Herrmann and Christian Lengauer

Fakultät für Mathematik und Informatik,
Universität Passau, Germany

{herrmann,lengauer}@fmi.uni-passau.de
http://www.fmi.uni-passau.de/cl/hdc/

Abstract. We propose a calculus for the analysis of list lengths in functional programs. In contrast to common type-based approaches, it is based on the syntactical structure of the program. To our knowledge, no other approach provides such a detailed analysis of nested lists.

The analysis of lists is preceded by a program transformation which makes sizes explicit as program values and eliminates the chain of cons operations. This permits alternative implementations of lists, e.g., by functions or arrays. The technique is being implemented in an experimental parallelizing compiler for the functional language $\mathcal{HDC}$.

We believe that analysis and parallelization work best if higher-order functions are used to compose the program from functional building blocks, so-called skeletons, instead of using unrestrained recursion. Skeletons, e.g., data-parallel combinators come with a theory of sizes and parallelization.

1 Introduction

If functional programs are to be used for high-performance computing, efficient data representations and operations must be provided. Our contribution is a calculus for the analysis of the lengths of (nested) lists and a transformation into a form which is liberated from the chain of cons-operations and which sometimes permits array implementations even if the length depends on run-time values.

A major advantage of functional programs vs. imperative programs is that dependence analysis is much easier, due to the absence of reassignments. One severe disadvantage of functional programs as of yet is that efficient, machine-oriented data structures (like the array) –absolutely necessary for high-performance computing– play a minor role in many language implementations since they do not harmonize with functional evaluation schemata (like graph reduction), which are at a higher level of abstraction.

We propose to construct programs by composition of skeletons, i.e., functional building blocks with a predefined, efficient implementation [9]. From the view of the source program, they are higher-order functions which are instantiated

W. Taha (Ed.): SAIG 2001, LNCS 2196, pp. 199–218, 2001.
© Springer-Verlag Berlin Heidelberg 2001

with problem-specific, customizing functions. We implement skeletons in an imperative language close to the machine. In the compilation of the program parts which are not skeletons, functional concepts are successively eliminated such that these parts can be linked together with the skeleton implementations. In this process, the most important step is the replacement of functional arguments by data structures of the source language [1].

Aside from instantiation of skeletons, functional arguments should be used moderately since they incur overhead and might introduce undesired dependences. Recursion should be replaced by skeletons, e.g., the recursive function map, which applies a function to each element of a list, can be replaced by a data-parallel implementation. The need for a size analysis arises from the use of simple inductive data structures, e.g., the list. With knowledge of its length, the list might be implemented more efficiently as an array.

Our size analysis calculates information about the sizes of lists at compile time, in terms of structural parameters, i.e., symbolic names assigned to the lengths of lists in the input. Characteristic for our approach is that the size analysis also computes a function which maps indices to elements. The result of the analysis can then be used for optimization by program transformations, e.g., intermediate lists could be eliminated, similar to deforestation or map distribution over composition [3]. The transformations provide the basis for a renewed size inference and subsequent optimization, in an iterative process which terminates according to criteria specified by compiler settings or directives.

Our inference and transformation rules are based on a view of lists which abstracts from the chain of elements present in many standard representations. Due to the absence of side effects, the compiler is not obliged to preserve a particular representation of data structures, i.e., a list may be eliminated, fused with some other list, represented by an array, reproduced by a function, etc. Data aggregates treated in such an abstract fashion are known as data fields [15, 24].

As far as we know, we are the first to derive compile-time information about each element of a list in terms of its position. This is possible by a symbolic representation of a function mapping indices to elements – a technique which provides the potential for a precise size analysis of nested lists and for their flat implementations [30]. Flat structures can lead to efficiency increases in memory allocation and release, access and update of elements and marshaling for communication.

Through size inference, the program can become amenable to further transformation, since compile-time information becomes visible at points where it was not visible before. With this kind of compilation, the efficiency of the generated code becomes sensitive to small changes in the program and, thus, small actions of program maintenance may have dramatic effects. Note that we aim for high performance of selected program parts, achieved with the programmer's interaction, not for a compiler which produces good code fully automatically in the average case. The novice programmer can interact by setting compiler switches and providing program annotations. The advanced (parallel) programmer can add skeleton implementations which capture computation schemata not previously known to the compiler.

Sect. 2 reviews related approaches to size inference. As a motivation for size inference, we present our experimental compiler in Sect. 3. Sect. 4 presents a transformation of the list data type which makes size expressions explicit in the program. In Sect. 5, we discuss the simplification of size expressions in a little auxiliary language, which need not –and, indeed, does not– contain lists, because size expressions have been disentangled from the list contents by the transformation in Sect. 4. Sect. 6 presents an example for which an exact treatment of the sizes of nested lists is useful: the multiplication of polynomials with coefficients represented by lists of digits. In Sect. 7, we summarize our statements and point to future work.

2   Related Work

The data field approach of Hammarlund and Lisper [15] inspired us to abstract from actual representations of aggregate data objects, in favor of minimizing dependences between data and increasing the potential for parallelism. By using an indexing function to refer to elements of an aggregate structure, many *arrangement* operations can be performed without visiting the data at all, just by modification of the indexing function: permutation, broadcast, partitioning, etc. We apply the data field approach to the parallelization of lists. As far as we know, the list is the most important aggregate data structure in functional programming, and it has a rich theory [3,28].

As Lisper and Collard [24] have pointed out, size inference can be viewed as a form of abstract interpretation [8]. One kind of abstract information of a list is its length. The length function is a monoid homomorphism that maps from the concrete domain of lists to the abstract domain of natural numbers. The empty list is mapped to zero and the function which adds an element to a list is mapped to the successor function. Unfortunately, this nice property of the list length is only one side of the coin. The power of abstract interpretation comes from the fact that the calculation is performed solely in the abstract domain. A complication with lists is that they can contain lists as elements. Applying the abstraction at the outer nesting level incurs a loss of information about the lengths of the lists at inner nesting levels, while an abstraction at an inner level means that the outer lists remain part of the abstract domain.

We employ a representation of lists which isolates the size information while preserving all other program information. Thus, we are doing something similar to abstract interpretation by performing a static analysis of the isolated size information. For nested lists, this means first to perform a static analysis of the lengths of the lists at the outer nesting level, then to continue with the analysis of the elements of that list, and so on.

The standard construction of lists is inductive and excludes a global view of the size or a possibility to access an element by index directly. Our new representation of lists has consequences for element access beyond program analysis.

In his *views* approach, Wadler [31] proposes pattern matching with constructors that do *not* form the representation of the data structure. We apply this principle to lists: the representation is subject to optimization by the compiler, while the standard list constructors are still available for user programs. In addition, a new list constructor is introduced internally, which permits symbolic pattern matching of a list against its size and its indexing function. We took the idea of such non-standard list constructors from cons-snoc lists and distributable homomorphisms [13] and powerlists [26]. In contrast to them, our approach strictly separates length and content of a list, with the need to add auxiliary functions to the program, mapping list indices to elements. Later in the compilation process, inlining of these functions can improve efficiency.

Our approach differs significantly from others in three aspects: (1) the impact of the success of the analysis and the way it is integrated into a compilation, (2) the role of types for size inference and (3) the restrictions of the source language:

1. Our size analysis is an optional part of the compilation. Its success –more precisely, the degree of its success– determines the efficiency of the target code but cannot lead to a failure of the compilation or a rejection of the program.

   Size inference or size checking appears in other approaches at the front end of a compilation process, even in transformational approaches [12]. Our size analysis is located in the middle of the back end of the compilation, inside an optimization loop. The analysis and subsequent program transformations are performed in a cycle and, thus, functions are analyzed that never existed in the source program.

2. Other researchers base size analysis, be it inference or checking, on types.

   a) Some groups draw a strong connection between types and sizes. Bellè and Moggi [2] apply size inference in an intermediate language with a two-level type system that distinguishes between compile-time and run-time values [27]. Xi and Pfenning [32] use dependent types and perform type checking modulo constraint satisfaction. Singleton types enable the generation of lists of a particular size, dependent on integer values. Jay and Sekanina [23] describe type checking in a language VEC on vectors, which distinguishes between so-called *shapely* types and *non-shapely* types. They distinguish two kinds of conditionals. The shapely conditional, which requires the condition to be of shapely type, is used to analyze recursive size functions but cannot deal with arbitrary program values. The non-shapely conditional can deal with all program values but cannot be used to define sizes. A surprisingly large class of programs can be handled with this approach: all usual array indexing operations and linear algebra. Hofmann [21] uses a linear type system to control the size of lists and permit an in-place update which is especially useful for sorting. Chin and Khoo [6] infer the sizes of recursive functions by a fixed-point calculation.

   b) Others perform type inference first, to keep it decidable, and then infer sizes based on the type information. Hughes, Pareto and Sabry [22] employ three separate, successive steps: (1) Hindley-Milner inference, (2) derivation of the size information and (3) constraint solving. Loidl and Hammond [25] followed this approach. Our initial attempts were similar [17], but we recognized that the treatment of nested lists in the type information leads to a formalism which is difficult to apply. Now, we are using types only to count the levels of nesting of the list, but do not tag type information with size information. As far as we know, the other groups are considering nested lists of rectangular shape only, i.e., those isomorphic to multi-dimensional arrays. This simplifies their treatment in the type system significantly. Fradet and Mallet [12] use predicates to restrict operations to a subset of this rectangular shape.

3. We do not impose restrictions on the source language to perform size analysis. As a necessary consequence, arbitrary size expressions may enter the analysis and, thus, conditions on sizes may be undecidable. Since our type inference happens in an earlier compiler phase and is completely unrelated to our static size analysis, the size analysis may fail but the program may still be typable.

In all other static approaches which we are aware of size inference is decidable. Chin and Khoo [6], Fradet and Mallet [12] and Xi and Pfenning [32] use linear inequalities for constraints, i.e., Presburger arithmetic. Bellè and Moggi [2], Jay and Sekanina [23] and Hofmann [21] achieve the decidability through their type system.

Limitation to Presburger arithmetic already rules out the following simple function f which is likely to appear in an N-body computation: f takes a list of size m as input and produces a list that contains all element pairs and whose size expression m^2 is not permitted in a Presburger formula.

Although formulas of number theory are, in general, undecidable, there is a good chance that one can solve more formulas than just those of Presburger arithmetic. Our approach is based on an extensible library of formula patterns and their simplifications, which are being consulted in size inference.

3 The $\mathcal{HDC}$ Compiler

Functional languages are well suited for program parallelization because of the simplicity of program analysis and transformation compared to imperative languages. However, if functional languages are to be competitive, their compilers must produce similar target code, without overhead for memory management or auxiliary data structures. This has motivated us to develop our own compiler for a functional language, with a strong focus on the code it produces. Skeletons are a suitable vehicle for achieving high efficiency [19].

We name our source language $\mathcal{HDC}$, for $\mathcal{H}$igher-order $\mathcal{D}$ivide-and-$\mathcal{C}$onquer, which reflects our belief in the productivity that higher-order functions lend to programming. We have focussed on divide-and-conquer because of its high potential for parallelism. Efficient parallel implementations of divide-and-conquer skeletons have been added to the compiler and have been used to express algorithms like Karatsuba's polynomial multiplication and the n-queens problem [20].

The syntax of $\mathcal{HDC}$ is a subset of Haskell [16], since we found language constructs like the list comprehension superior concerning notational convenience and style. In contrast to Haskell, the semantics of $\mathcal{HDC}$ is strict. This is to guarantee that the space-time mapping –that is, the assignment of operations to time and processors made at compile time– is respected in the actual execution.

Briefly, the $\mathcal{HDC}$ compiler [18] consists of the following parts:

1. front end: scanning, parsing, desugaring, λ-lifting, type inference/checking
2. back end, pre-optimization part: monomorphization, elimination of functional arguments, elimination of mutual recursion, **case**-elimination, generation of a directed acyclic program graph, tuple elimination
3. back end, optimization cycle:
   a) inlining (unfolding of function applications)
   b) rule-based optimizations by transformation (Sect. 4)
   c) size inference (Sect. 5)
4. back end, post-optimization part: abstract code generation, space-time mapping (parallelization), code generation, skeleton instantiation

In order to increase code efficiency, size inference and code optimizing transformations are performed alternatingly in several iterations. The size information can be used to control program transformations in the next iteration. Additionally, the size information is useful in the parallelization and for memory assignment in the code generation.

Due to the complexity of the task, the implementation of size inference is still at an early stage. Thus, the experimental results available to-date [18,20] do not reflect the impact of the methods presented here.

4   A List Transformation for Size Inference

This section is about the transformation which makes size information explicit for the later size analysis. In the source, lists are represented by the constructor nil ([ ]) for the empty list and the constructor cons (:) for appending a new element at the front of a list. The dependences introduced by cons rule out a constant-time access to all list elements and complicate the analysis. After the transformation, each list is represented by a pair of its size and a function mapping indices to elements. The transformation itself appears straightforward with the calculus presented in Sect. 4.2. The difficulty is simplifying the occurring expressions of the result to a closed form – in general, this is undecidable.

4.1   A New Representation for Lists

To maintain the list xs as a data object, its length ($\#xs$) and its indexing function ($\lambda i.xs!!i$) are not kept separate but are combined by a new constructor which we denote by Γ. In the new representation, ($\Gamma\, f\, n$) denotes a list of length n and its i-th element ($i \geq 0$) has the value $f(i)$, e.g., the indexing function f for the list $[0, 1, 4, 9, 16]$ is given by $f(i) = i^2$. The indexing functions of lists appearing as formal parameters and at the left side of **let**-definitions are referred to by fresh variables. For other lists, like the arithmetic sequence $[m..n]$, which contains all integers from m to n, a new auxiliary function is generated and its name is used in the Γ-expression. The indexing functions are inspected and simplified during the analysis. In the next iteration of the optimization cycle, they may disappear again due to inlining. We consider two distinct implementations of Γ-expressions: (1) preferably using an explicit indexing function and (2) alternatively using an array in the case that run-time values are to be stored.

In contrast to abstract interpretation, our transformation makes the information we want to reason about –the length– explicit without incurring a loss of information. To emphasize this fact, we call this change of representation a *change of basis*. We use the notion *basis* for a set of constructors that constitute a data type.

Lemma 1 (Existence of an index/length basis). *All finite lists can be expressed in a basis which makes their length and their indexing function explicit.*

Proof. By an isomorphism of types [11] induced by the functions **to-Γ** and **from-Γ** defined below. The domain of **to-Γ** is the set of all finite lists, the codomain is restricted to the image of **to-Γ** and is taken for the domain of **from-Γ**. map applies f to each element of this list. Γ can be defined as an algebraic data type (**data**).

data $\Gamma\alpha = \Gamma (\mathbb{N} \rightarrow \alpha)\, \mathbb{N}$

to-$\Gamma \in [\alpha] \rightarrow \Gamma\alpha$
to-Γ $xs = \Gamma (\lambda i.xs\,!!\,i)\ (\#xs)$

from-$\Gamma \in \Gamma\alpha \rightarrow [\alpha]$
from-Γ $(\Gamma\, f\, n) = $ map $f\ [0..n-1]$
$\square$

Due to this isomorphism, we identify the types $\Gamma\alpha$ and $[\alpha]$ and enable the compiler to apply **to-Γ** and **from-Γ** where an adaptation is required. The notation we use is adapted from the language Haskell [16].

4.2   Rewriting in the Γ-Calculus

The Γ-calculus is a set of rules that can be used for converting the standard list representation to Γ-form. Tab. 1 explains the notation used in the calculus. We split the rules into three classes. The top of Fig. 1 gives a complete specification of the semantics of Γ. In the middle part of the figure, we define the basic list functions in terms of Γ. Since pattern matching has been eliminated in an earlier compiler phase, we rely on a predicate for the empty list and two functions for selecting head and tail of a list, in addition to nil and cons. The rules for these basic functions are consistent with the definition based on the representation with nil and cons.

Table 1. Notation used in the calculus

$a \downarrow b$ / $a \uparrow b$	minimum/maximum of a and b
$a \updownarrow_{low}^{high}$	$= (a \uparrow low) \downarrow high$
$\otimes$	for an arbitrary binary operator of type $\alpha \to \beta \to \alpha$
$e \bigotimes\limits_{i=low}^{high} x_i =$	$\begin{cases} ((e \otimes x_{low}) \otimes \dots) \otimes x_{high}, & \text{if } low \leq high \\ e & \text{otherwise} \end{cases}$
$e[x := v]$	substitute every free occurrence of x in e by v
$\mu\, k\, x_i$	the highest j, for which $\sum_{i=0}^{j-1} x_i$ ($x_i \in \mathbb{N}$) does not exceed k

The rules in the lower part of Fig. 1 are derived from the basic list functions and simplified. Our strategy is to use as many rules as possible to accelerate the simplification of size information. Every list function, for which a rule is not stated, must be analyzed itself.

The following lemma states that these rules can be used to construct a terminating rewrite system. (We do not need confluence, since we do not compare the simplified program parts.)

Lemma 2 (Termination of the reduced rewrite system). *In the Γ-calculus without rule **intr-Γ**, rewriting terminates with an expression which contains neither the constructors nil and cons nor any list function on the left side of a rule.*

Proof sketch. The number of occurrences of nil, cons and list functions in an expression is finite. Each application of a rule strictly decreases this number by at least one. □

4.3 The List Transformation Algorithm

In many circumstances, the change of basis delivers a form of the function which expresses the lengths of the result lists in terms of the lengths of the argument lists. The difficulty is that this reduced form will likely inherit the recursion of the original. In Sect. 5, we tackle recursion elimination and other simplifications of size expressions in a little language. This language has only the value domains of numbers and Booleans, but contains symbolic reduction operators, e.g., summation. The symbolic calculation is necessary since the lengths of the argument lists are unknown at compile time and are, thus, represented by variables.

Our algorithm works on the syntax tree of the function. From an algorithmic point of view, the change of basis simplifies our transformation, since each list (in Γ-form) carries its (symbolic) length information along. If lengths were made

intr-Γ	$\{xs$ is a list$\}$	$xs \overset{\text{fresh } i}{\longrightarrow} \Gamma\,(\lambda i.xs!!i)\,(\#xs)$
elim-Γ.0		$\#\,(\Gamma\,\_\,n) \longrightarrow n$
elim-Γ.1		$(\Gamma\,f\,n)!!i \longrightarrow \text{\underline{if} } 0 \le i < n \text{ \underline{then} } f\,i \text{ \underline{else} } \bot$

null-Γ	$\text{null}\,(\Gamma\,\_\,n) \longrightarrow n = 0$
nil-Γ	$[\,] \longrightarrow \Gamma\,(\text{const } \bot)\,0$
cons-Γ	$x : \Gamma\,f\,n \overset{\text{fresh } i}{\longrightarrow} \Gamma\,(\lambda i.\text{\underline{if} } i = 0 \text{ \underline{then} } x \text{ \underline{else} } f\,(i-1))\,(n+1)$
head-Γ	$\text{head}\,(\Gamma\,f\,n) \longrightarrow \text{\underline{if} } n > 0 \text{ \underline{then} } f\,0 \text{ \underline{else} } \bot$
tail-Γ	$\text{tail}\,(\Gamma\,f\,n) \longrightarrow \text{\underline{if} } n > 0 \text{ \underline{then} } \Gamma\,(f \circ (+1))\,(n-1) \text{ \underline{else} } \bot$

sequence-Γ	$[a..b] \longrightarrow \Gamma\,(+a)\,((b-a+1)\uparrow 0)$
take-Γ	$\text{take}\,k\,(\Gamma\,f\,n) \longrightarrow \Gamma\,f\,(k\updownarrow_0^n)$
drop-Γ	$\text{drop}\,k\,(\Gamma\,f\,n) \longrightarrow \Gamma\,(f \circ (+(k\updownarrow_0^n)))\,(n-(k\updownarrow_0^n))$
map-Γ	$\text{map}\,g\,(\Gamma\,f\,n) \longrightarrow \Gamma\,(g \circ f)\,n$
foldl-Γ	$\text{foldl}\,\otimes\,e\,(\Gamma\,f\,n) \overset{\text{fresh } i}{\longrightarrow} {}^{e}\bigotimes_{i=0}^{n-1}(f\,i)$
scanl-Γ	$\text{scanl}\,\otimes\,e\,(\Gamma\,f\,n)$ $\overset{\text{fresh } i,j}{\longrightarrow} \Gamma\,(\lambda j.\,{}^{e}\bigotimes_{i=0}^{j-1}(f\,i))\,(n+1)$
append-Γ	$\Gamma\,f\,m \mathbin{+\!\!+} \Gamma\,g\,n$ $\overset{\text{fresh } i}{\longrightarrow} \Gamma\,(\lambda i.\text{\underline{if} } i < m \text{ \underline{then} } f\,i \text{ \underline{else} } g\,(i-m))\,(m+n)$
concat-Γ	$\text{concat}\,(\Gamma\,(\lambda i.(\Gamma\,(\lambda j.e_{i,j})\,n_i))\,m)$ $\overset{\text{fresh } k}{\longrightarrow} \Gamma\,(\lambda k.((e_{i,j}[i := \mu\,k\,n_i])[j := k - \sum_{i=0}^{\mu\,k\,n_i - 1} n_i]))\,(\sum_{i=0}^{m-1} n_i)$

Fig. 1. Rewrite rules

part of the type information, the correctness of the transformation could not be established solely by equational reasoning about the functional expressions. Also, nested lists can be treated precisely, since the length of an inner list can be expressed in terms of its index in the outer list. Algorithm LISTSIMP (Fig. 2) performs a complete change of basis on the lists in the expression given to it.

We demonstrate the algorithm on a tiny, non-recursive function. Function **rotate** performs a cyclic shift of the elements of a list. Application areas are hardware description/simulation or convolution.

The beauty of lists for this purpose is obvious: to rotate the first eight items of a list xs, we just write: **rotate** (**take** 8 xs) $\mathbin{+\!\!+}$ **drop** 8 xs.

INPUT: expression e and a set of constraints
OUTPUT: expression semantically equivalent to e which does not contain list operations in the standard basis

if e is a constant or variable
then if e is not of a list type
      then return e
      else substitute every occurrence of e by $(\Gamma\ f\ n)$
      where f and n are fresh names
else (e is a compound expression):
  1. apply LISTSIMP to each component of e; the result is called e'
  2. perform simplifications in the size language of all arithmetic expressions in e', yielding e''
  3. eliminate the standard list constructors and functions from the current node of the syntax tree by applying the rule of the Γ-calculus that matches, obtaining e'''
  4. if e''' is not of a list type then return e'''
     else (e''' is a list, represented by, say $(\Gamma\ h\ m)$):
     a) apply LISTSIMP to the expression m, getting m'
     b) apply LISTSIMP to the expression h using knowledge of m', yielding h'
     c) return $(\Gamma\ h'\ m')$

Fig. 2. Algorithm LISTSIMP

1. The initial function is as follows:

rotate $xs =$ if $\#xs < 2$ then xs else tail xs $+\!\!+$ $[\text{head } xs]$

Note that a straightforward compilation of this function would produce nasty code. On the one hand, the expression tail xs cannot be shared because $[\text{head } xs]$ has been appended at the end. On the other hand, it cannot be updated in-place, although it is not shared.

2. According to the algorithm, each occurrence of the list variable xs is replaced by $(\Gamma\ f\ n)$, where f and n are fresh variables:

rotate $(\Gamma\ f\ n) =$ if $\#(\Gamma\ f\ n) < 2$ then $\Gamma\ f\ n$
                       else tail $(\Gamma\ f\ n)$ $+\!\!+$ $[\text{head } (\Gamma\ f\ n)]$

3. Application of the rules for $\#$, tail and head:

rotate $(\Gamma\ f\ n) =$ if $n \mathop{\textrm{¡}} 2$ then $\Gamma\ f\ n$
                 else $\Gamma\ (\lambda i.f\ (i+1))\ (n-1)$ $+\!\!+$ $[f\ 0]$

4. Application of the rules for nil and cons to $[f\ 0]$:

rotate $(\Gamma\ f\ n) =$ if $n \mathop{\textrm{¡}} 2$ then $\Gamma\ f\ n$
         else $\Gamma\ (\lambda i.f\ (i+1))\ (n-1)$
                   $+\!\!+$ $\Gamma\ (\lambda i.\text{if } i = 0 \text{ then } f\ 0 \text{ else } \bot)\ 1$

5. Application of the append rule:

$$\text{rotate } (\Gamma\ f\ n) = \underline{\text{if }} n_!2 \text{ } \underline{\text{then }} \Gamma\ f\ n$$
$$\underline{\text{else }} \Gamma\ (\lambda i.\underline{\text{if }} i < n-1 \text{ } \underline{\text{then }} f\ (i+1) \text{ } \underline{\text{else }} f\ 0)\ n$$

6. Simplification of the conditional, using information about the length:

$$\text{rotate } (\Gamma\ f\ n) = \Gamma\ (\lambda i.f\ ((i+1) \bmod n))\ n$$

All rule applications aside from the simplification at the end are straightforward according to the rules. The success of the simplification enables further possibilities, e.g., an optimization of a sequence of k rotations, given by the following equality:

$$\text{rotate}^k\ (\Gamma\ f\ n) = \Gamma\ (\lambda i.f\ ((i+k) \bmod n))\ n$$

5   Simplification of Size Expressions

In the previous section, we have decomposed list data objects into two independent components: indexing function and length – both symbolic arithmetic expressions. Further simplifications need not resort to the list data type anymore.

The process of size inference abstracts temporarily from the program representation to focus on mathematical issues. Our intention is to handle constraint solving, simplification, etc. in a separate package which need not know anything about the syntax or semantics of the functional programming language. In this package, we use a small, first-order functional language, the *size* language. It consists of a set of (possibly recursive) function definitions and a single expression which defines a size dependent on symbolic names and which can use the set of functions.

The size language still needs to contain recursion. E.g., here is the size function obtained from a recursive reverse function:

$$\text{reverseSize } n = \underline{\text{if }} n = 0 \underline{\text{ then }} n \underline{\text{ else }} \text{reverseSize } (n-1) + 1$$

Simplification must solve this recursion. We will discuss that in Sect. 5.3.

5.1   The Syntax of Size Expressions

Atomic size expressions are constants and variables. Size expressions can be composed by arithmetic operators, conditionals, reduction operators (e.g., summation) and applications of size functions. Variables are used to represent unknown values and for indexing elements in a reduction.

Structural parameters are those unknowns which refer to input values of the function to be analyzed. Especially useful input values are list lengths and natural numbers which are decremented in recursive calls. However, the compiler may not always be able to decide which parameters are meant to be used as structural parameters. The user can point the compiler to a useful parameter –say n– for the problem size or depth of recursion by "branding" its name in the program: $n\bullet$. We believe that this kind of annotation is easier to use than annotations of the type language with size expressions.

The size information, expressed in terms of structural parameters, is derived by following the data flow of the function [4]. Our choice of a referentially transparent language enables a local analysis of each function. Where a function f is applied to an argument x, the size information of the result can often be computed by an application of the size function of f to the size information of x. We prefer to encode all functional closures by first-order data structures of the source language. Then, x will never be a functional closure.

In the calculation of sizes, rational numbers can appear as intermediate values. Exact rational arithmetic guarantees that no approximation errors will produce an incorrect integral size. Integers and natural numbers are treated as subtypes of the rational numbers. The integrality of decision variables can be enforced by subtype declarations. Boolean values are used for constraints.

```
type P = ([F],S)
type F = (Id,([Id],[S]))
type Id = String
data T = TBool | TNat | TInt | TRat
data S = Num Rational | SV Id T
       | BTrue | BFalse
       | S:+:S | S:-:S | S:*:S | S:/:S | S:^:S
       | Floor S | Ceil S | Frac S
       | Abs S | Sgn S | Min S S | Max S S
       | S:=:S | S:<:S | S:<=:S
       | IsRat S | IsInt S | IsNat S
       | Not S | S:&:S | S:|:S | S:<=>:S
       | Case [(S,S)] S
       | Let (Id,S) S
       | Apply Id [S] [Id] S
       | Reduce (ROp,Id,S,S,S) S
       | Recur [[S]] S [S]
data ROp = Sum | Prod | Minimum | Maximum | And | Or
```

Fig. 3. The size language

We present the abstract syntax of our size language in Fig. 3. Since we are working with syntax trees only and abstract from parenthesization, punctuation, etc. of a potential source language, we use algebraic data type definitions instead of BNF rules. Like BNF, these algebraic data types can be used to define context-free expressions and, in addition, constitute a set of patterns to be used in transformations.

- A size program P consists of a list of function definitions (F) and an expression S to be evaluated.

- In a function definition $(name,(as,rs))$ of type F, $name$ is the name of the function, as is a list of its parameter names and rs a tuple of result sizes. Functions can be defined recursively.
- Id represents identifiers.
- T is a collection of types assigned to variables: TBool (Booleans), TNat (natural numbers), TInt (integers) and TRat (rational numbers). There is the usual inclusion relation between the number types which allows coercing in evaluation. Thus, there need not be a specific integral division. The type information is used by solvers as constraint information.
- S is the type of syntax trees for size expressions. Each alternative on the right side corresponds to a particular kind of node, named by a constructor. There are two kinds of constructors: infix constructors are denoted with surrounding colons (e.g., :+:), the other constructors are prefix constructors (e.g., Floor). The parts of an alternative aside from the constructor either contain subtrees (S) or attributes (e.g., ROp).
- ROp describes the set of reduction operators, i.e., accumulated applications of a binary associative and commutative operator.

5.2   Semantics

The meaning of size expressions is defined by the following denotation, where $\mathcal{I}[\![\,exp\,]\!]$ is the interpretation of expression exp.

- $\mathcal{I}[\![\,\text{Num } r\,]\!] = r$: a number, represented by an exact rational number. Due to the number type inclusion, it can also carry a natural or an integer.
- (SV $name$ t) represents the variable $name$ of type t. The value of a variable may be used as a value of a superset but, in constraint solving, the obtained result must match the type.
- $\mathcal{I}[\![\,\text{BTrue}\,]\!] = \text{True}$ and $\mathcal{I}[\![\,\text{BFalse}\,]\!] = \text{False}$: the boolean constants.
- $\mathcal{I}[\![\,a:\circledast:b\,]\!] = \mathcal{I}[\![\,a\,]\!] \circledast \mathcal{I}[\![\,b\,]\!]$ for each binary operator $\circledast$.
- $\mathcal{I}[\![\,\text{Floor } x\,]\!] = \lfloor \mathcal{I}[\![\,x\,]\!] \rfloor$, $\mathcal{I}[\![\,\text{Ceil } x\,]\!] = \lceil \mathcal{I}[\![\,x\,]\!] \rceil$,
  $\mathcal{I}[\![\,\text{Frac } x\,]\!] = \mathcal{I}[\![\,x\,]\!] - \lfloor \mathcal{I}[\![\,x\,]\!] \rfloor$, $\mathcal{I}[\![\,\text{Abs } x\,]\!] = |\mathcal{I}[\![\,x\,]\!]|$,
  $\mathcal{I}[\![\,\text{Sgn } x\,]\!] = \text{signum}\,(\mathcal{I}[\![\,x\,]\!])$
- $\mathcal{I}[\![\,\text{Min } x\ y\,]\!] = \mathcal{I}[\![\,x\,]\!] \downarrow \mathcal{I}[\![\,y\,]\!]$, $\mathcal{I}[\![\,\text{Max } x\ y\,]\!] = \mathcal{I}[\![\,x\,]\!] \uparrow \mathcal{I}[\![\,y\,]\!]$
- $\mathcal{I}[\![\,\text{IsRat } x\,]\!] = (\mathcal{I}[\![\,x\,]\!] \in \mathbb{Q})$, $\mathcal{I}[\![\,\text{IsInt } x\,]\!] = (\mathcal{I}[\![\,x\,]\!] \in \mathbb{Z})$,
  $\mathcal{I}[\![\,\text{IsNat } x\,]\!] = (\mathcal{I}[\![\,x\,]\!] \in \mathbb{N})$
- $\mathcal{I}[\![\,\text{Not } x\,]\!] = \neg(\mathcal{I}[\![\,x\,]\!])$, $\mathcal{I}[\![\,a:\&:b\,]\!] = \mathcal{I}[\![\,a\,]\!] \wedge \mathcal{I}[\![\,b\,]\!]$,
  $\mathcal{I}[\![\,a:|:b\,]\!] = \mathcal{I}[\![\,a\,]\!] \vee \mathcal{I}[\![\,b\,]\!]$, $\mathcal{I}[\![\,a:\texttt{<=>}:b\,]\!] = \mathcal{I}[\![\,a\,]\!] \Leftrightarrow \mathcal{I}[\![\,b\,]\!]$
- $\mathcal{I}[\![\,\text{Case }[(c_0, v_0), ..., (c_n, v_n)]\ v_{n+1}\,]\!] = \mathcal{I}[\![\,v_j\,]\!]$, where j is smallest such that $\mathcal{I}[\![\,c_j\,]\!] = \text{True}$, with $\mathcal{I}[\![\,c_{n+1}\,]\!] = \text{True}$ by default.
- $\mathcal{I}[\![\,\text{Let }(x, v)\ e\,]\!] = \mathcal{I}[\![\,(e[x := v])\,]\!]$. The purpose of an auxiliary definition (Let) is to exploit common subexpressions.
- The semantics of (Apply f $[e_0,...,e_n]$ $[v_0,...,v_m]$ exp) is that the size function f is applied to the size expressions e_0 to e_n. f returns a tuple of size expressions which are bound to the variables v_0 to v_m. Then, the expression exp, defined in terms of these variables, is delivered.

- $\mathcal{I}[\![\,\text{Reduce}\,(\oplus, i, low, high, cond_i)\; elem_i\,]\!] \;=\; \bigoplus_{i \in I} elem_i$:
  a reduction with a commutative and associative binary operator $\oplus$, where
  $I = \{i \in \mathbb{Z} \mid \mathcal{I}[\![\,low\,]\!] \leq i \leq \mathcal{I}[\![\,high\,]\!] \wedge \mathcal{I}[\![\,cond_i\,]\!] = \text{True}\}$.
- $\mathcal{I}[\![\,\hat{A}\,\hat{n}\,\hat{e}\,]\!] = \pi_0 A^n e$, where A is an $m \times m$ matrix, $n \in \mathbb{N}$ and e an m-
  column vector. $A = \mathcal{I}[\![\,\hat{A}\,]\!]$, $n = \mathcal{I}[\![\,\hat{n}\,]\!]$ and $e = \mathcal{I}[\![\,\hat{e}\,]\!]$. Recur expressions
  provide a closed form for some recurrences without using roots. E.g., the
  Fibonacci number n can be expressed by $fib(n) = (1\ 0)\left(\begin{smallmatrix}1&1\\1&0\end{smallmatrix}\right)^n \left(\begin{smallmatrix}0\\1\end{smallmatrix}\right)$.

5.3   Simplification Heuristics

After the transformation of a recursive list function into Γ-form, length expressions may still be expressed recursively. Using knowledge about frequent
decomposition patterns, one can provide a heuristic procedure to find closed
forms.

Probably the patterns most often used are the decomposition of a list into
(1) head and tail and (2) the left part and the right part [13,26]. We discuss
briefly head/tail decomposition here. If we are lucky, we obtain a recursive size
function and its closed form of the following kind, where $a \in \mathbb{N}$ and $b \in \mathbb{N} \to \mathbb{N}$:

$$s(n) \;=\; \left\{ \begin{array}{ll} a & , \quad \text{if } n=0 \\ s(n-1) + b(n) , & \text{otherwise} \end{array} \right\} = a + \sum_{i=1}^{n} b(i)$$

If b is a polynomial or another simple kind of function, we can eliminate the
summation operator [14]. E.g., if the size function originates from flattening a
triangular matrix, we have $a = 0$ and $b(n) = n$. In this case, we obtain:

$$s(n) \;=\; 0 + \sum_{i=1}^{n} i = \frac{n(n+1)}{2}$$

We advocate the use of an extensible library of patterns. Unfortunately, we
cannot hope to find the pattern by a *syntactic* match. E.g., instead of the expression $s(n-1) + n$, we may encounter the expression $\lfloor n/2 \rfloor + s(n-1) + \lceil n/2 \rceil$
which is equal. Thus, we apply the following procedure:

1. Select a pattern which appears appropriate since it is known to be useful
   for the operators that appear in the expression. E.g., polynomials can be
   appropriate for expressions that contain only addition and multiplication.
2. Interpolate the expression with the pattern, obtaining values for the parameters of the pattern.
3. Run many tests with the instantiated pattern, to exclude a non-fitting pattern as quickly as possible.
4. Verify symbolically that the instantiated pattern equals the expression.
5. Simplify the pattern, exploiting properties gained by specialization.

We do not advocate interpolating the recursive function as a whole because a successful match will be very unlikely, even with a high number of attempts. Instead, we are looking for patterns for parts of the recursive function, which are (1) the condition that indicates the recursive case, (2) the value in the non-recursive case, (3) the expression which modifies the arguments for the recursive calls and (4) the expression which combines the result of the recursive calls. Then, we apply a recurrence elimination function according to the ensemble of patterns we obtained. A promising approach is to search for the power series of the generating function of the recursion [14]. The n-th coefficient of the power series carries the value of the recursive function for the input n. Chin and Khoo [5] developed a tupling method to reduce, in some cases, recursion in multiple variables to recursion in a single variable.

6   Example: Nested Lists in Multiple Precision Arithmetic

A major difference between our approach and those of others, e.g., [32], is that our size information can refer to the particular position in a surrounding data structure. Polynomial multiplication with multiple precision arithmetic makes use of this; here the bitsize of a coefficient in the result depends on its position.

6.1   Types and Representation

In order to make the maximal amount of information statically derivable, our programs resemble specifications of abstract digital designs [7,10,29]. The basic arithmetic functions –which are not presented here– are producing output lists that depend statically on the size of input lists. E.g., a function which adds two numbers delivers a sum whose size is the maximum of both inputs; a potential carry overflow is delivered in a separate component.

Each number is represented by a list of bits. Element i of each number represents the factor $(\in \{0,1\})$ of 2^i. We define the type `Polynomial`, whose values are polynomials in X, represented by their list of coefficients. Coefficients are themselves numbers. Element i of the polynomial represents the coefficient of X^i.

6.2   The Source Function

The upper part of Fig. 4 shows the definition of function `polymul`. The application of `sumN` sums, for each coefficient k, the products of the coefficients of the two polynomials xss and yss. low and $high$ are the index bounds of the coefficients of xss, in dependence of k. We define m as the length of xss and n as the length of yss. The degree of the product polynomial is the sum of the degree $m{-}1$ of xss and the degree $n{-}1$ of yss. Thus, it has $m{+}n{-}1$ coefficients, for X^0 to X^{m+n-2}. We use a Haskell [16] list comprehension to express this. A list comprehension has –in our case– the form $[~exp_i~|~i \leftarrow [lowbound..highbound]~]$ where the index variable i is taken from the integer range $[lowbound..highbound]$ and exp_i

```
polymul ∈ Polynomial → Polynomial → Polynomial
polymul xss yss =
  let m = #xss
      n = #yss
  in [ let low  = 0↑(k−n+1)
           high = (m−1)↓k
       in sumN [ mul (xss!!i) (yss!!(k−i)) | i ← [low..high] ]
     | k ← [0..m+n−2] ]
```

$$\text{polymul } (\Gamma\ (\lambda i.\Gamma\ (\lambda j.f_{i,j})\ p_i)\ m)\ (\Gamma\ (\lambda i.\Gamma\ (\lambda j.g_{i,j})\ q_i)\ n)$$
$$= \Gamma\ (\lambda k.\ \underline{\text{let}}\ \ low\ \ = 0{\uparrow}(k{-}n{+}1)$$
$$high\ = (m{-}1){\downarrow}k$$
$$r\ \ \ = high{-}low{+}\text{Reduce }(\text{Maximum}, i, 0, high{-}low, \text{BTrue})$$
$$(p_{(low+i)} + q_{(k-(low+i))})$$
$$(\Gamma\ h\ r) = \text{sumN }(\Gamma\ (\lambda i.\ \text{mul }(\Gamma\ (\lambda j.f_{i,j})\ p_i)\ (\Gamma\ (\lambda j.g_{k-i,j})\ q_{k-i}))$$
$$(high{-}low{+}1))$$
$$\underline{\text{in}}\ (\Gamma\ h\ r))$$
$$(m{+}n{-}1)$$

Fig. 4. Transformation of `polymul` into Γ-form

denotes the element of the list associated with index i. Note that list comprehensions can be desugared in an early compiler phase; our compiler performs a desugaring into the form map $(\lambda i.exp_i)$ $[lowbound..highbound]$.

6.3   Transformation into Γ-Form

The result of the transformation is shown in the lower part of Fig. 4. In Γ-form, we use m for the length of xss and n for the length of yss. The elements of xss and yss are expressed in terms of their position. $xss!!i$ is itself a list, in Γ-form: $(\Gamma\ (\lambda j.f_{i,j})\ p_i)$. Here, p_i is the length of $xss!!i$, and $f_{i,j}$ its element with index j. The representation of $yss!!i$ is analogous, with q instead of p and g instead of f. The analysis should infer a simplified Γ-expression for the body of `polymul` with respect to the following application, where xss and yss have been replaced by their Γ-form, as described above:

$$\text{polymul }\ (\Gamma\ (\lambda i.\Gamma\ (\lambda j.f_{i,j})\ p_i)\ m)\ (\Gamma\ (\lambda i.\Gamma\ (\lambda j.g_{i,j})\ q_i)\ n)$$

With this denotation of the parts of xss and yss, we analyze and transform the body of `polymul`. The first step is to transform the outer nesting level of the result list into Γ-form. We use exp_k as an abbreviation for element k of this list. Remember that the list comprehension

$$[\ exp_k\ |\ k \leftarrow [0..m+n-2]\ ]$$

has been desugared by an earlier compiler phase into:

$$\texttt{map } (\lambda k. exp_k) \ [0 . . m + n - 2]$$

Applying the rules of the Γ-calculus to the desugared form yields:

$$\Gamma \ (\lambda k. exp_k) \ (m + n - 1)$$

Next, we look at the transformation of exp_k and infer the length of:

$$\texttt{sumN } [\texttt{mul } (xss!!i) \ (yss!!(k-i)) \mid i \leftarrow [low . . high]]$$

After desugaring and translation into Γ-form, we have:

$$\texttt{sumN } (\Gamma \ (\lambda i.\texttt{mul } (\Gamma \ (\lambda j.f_{i,j}) \ p_i) \ (\Gamma \ (\lambda j.g_{k-i,j}) \ q_{k-i})) \ (high - low + 1))$$

We skip a lot of formal treatment here and present directly the size r of the result of the sumN application:

$$high - low + \texttt{Reduce } (\texttt{Maximum}, i, 0, high - low, \texttt{BTrue})(p_{(low+i)} + q_{(k-(low+i))})$$

6.4   Benefit of the Transformation

We have inferred that the result polynomial has $m + n - 1$ coefficients, and coefficient k can be represented by r digits with r as stated above. If r is not simplified, its value must be computed quickly at run time. Function h is based on the recursive function sumN and cannot be stated as a simple closed expression since it depends on many run-time values. Inlining of sumN could, in principle, be done after this transformation, but very likely sumN will not be inlined due to its complexity.

The computation of the digits of each coefficient k remains the task of function sumN. However, the size r is sufficient for our purpose, since we can allocate the memory for the coefficients of the result in advance:

1. In a parallel computation of the coefficients, the number of bytes to be allocated for each communication buffer is known in advance. Thus, an appropriate representation assumed, the final location of a coefficient can already be used to receive the message.
2. A simulator of a digital design can statically allocate the exact amount of memory cells required to store the values, i.e., no dynamic data structures are required. A compiler which produces a hardware design has knowledge of the exact amount of bits required for each coefficient, if the values of the structural parameters are fixed.

7   Summary and Perspectives

Size inference enhances the possibilities for a compilation of functional programs of high efficiency. Obviously, if a list can be represented by an array because its length is known in advance, at least the amount of space for chaining the elements can be saved. Loss of dependences increases the potential for parallelization.

Often, intermediate copies of data objects can be saved since the result can be put immediately at the place where it is required. This makes communication more efficient.

The analysis is inherently undecidable and must be based on heuristics, e.g., partial evaluation, constraint solving, solving of recurrence equations, simplification of symbolic expressions and pattern matching with unification. We are pursuing the following strategy, which we hold to be quite promising: iterate alternatingly through applying size inference and then exploiting the results via program transformations. Possible transformations are inlining, fusion, deforestation and program specialization. The iterative process propagates static information successively deeper into the program structure, until the effort to evaluate the symbolic expressions at run time exceeds the gain.

We are going to implement size inference and the list transformation into our compiler. We have not been able to find a tool which provides adequate support for simplification of size expressions as we require; we may have to implement the simplifier ourselves. Furthermore, the compiler is undergoing a redesign in which the front end is being replaced by the front end of the Glasgow Haskell compiler.

Acknowledgements. We are grateful to Peter Faber, Paul Feautrier, John O'Donnell and Gregor Snelting for fruitful discussions. Michael Mendler, Walid Taha and the anonymous referees gave us valuable hints about related work. The work was supported by the German Research Foundation (DFG).

References

1. Jeffrey M. Bell, Françoise Bellegarde, and James Hook. Type-driven defunctionalization. *SIGPLAN Notices*, 32(8):25–37, 1997.
2. Gianni Bellè and Eugenio Moggi. Typed intermediate languages for shape-analysis. In *Typed Lambda Calculi and Applications (TLCA'97)*, Lecture Notes in Computer Science 1210, pages 11–29. Springer-Verlag, 1997.
3. Richard S. Bird. Algebraic identities for program calculation. *The Computer Journal*, 32(2):122–126, 1989.
4. Siddharta Chatterjee, Guy E. Blelloch, and Allan L.Fisher. Size and access inference for data-parallel programs. Technical Report CMU-CS-91-118, Dept. Computer Science, Carnegie-Mellon Univ., 1991.
5. Wei-Ngan Chin and Siau-Cheng Khoo. Tupling functions with multiple recursion parameters. In Patrick Cousot, Moreno Falaschi, Gilberto File, and Antoine Rauzy, editors, *Static Analysis Third Int. Workshop (WAS'93)*, Lecture Notes in Computer Science 724, pages 124–140. Springer-Verlag, 1993.
6. Wei-Ngan Chin and Siau-Cheng Khoo. Calculating sized types. In *Proceedings of the 2000 ACM SIGPLAN Workshop on Evaluation and Semantics-Based Program Manipulation (PEPM-00)*, pages 62–72, N.Y., 2000. ACM Press.
7. Koen Claessen and Mary Sheeran. A tutorial on Lava: A hardware description and verification system. Technical report, Dept. of Computing Science, Chalmers University of Technology, August 2000.

8. Patrick Cousot and Radhia Cousot. Abstract interpretation: A unified lattice model for static analysis of programs by construction of approximation of fixed points. In *Proc. 4th ACM Symp. Principles of Programming Languages (POPL'77)*, pages 238–252. ACM Press, 1977.

9. John Darlington, Anthony Field, Peter Harrison, Paul Kelly, David Sharp, Qian Wu, and Ronald L. While. Parallel programming using skeleton functions. In Arndt Bode, Mike Reeve, and Gottfried Wolf, editors, *PARLE'93: Parallel Architectures and Languages Europe*, Lecture Notes in Computer Science 694, pages 146–160. Springer-Verlag, 1993.

10. Nancy A. Day, Jeffrey R. Lewis, and Byrin Cook. Symbolic simulation of microprocessor models using type classes in Haskell. Technical Report CSE-99-005, Pacific Software Research Center, Oregon Graduate Institute, 1999.

11. Roberto Di Cosmo. *Isomorphisms of Types: from λ-calculus to information retrieval and language design*. Progress in Theoretical Computer Science. Birkhäuser, 1995.

12. Pascal Fradet and Julien Mallet. Compilation of a specialized functional language for massively parallel computers. Technical Report 3894, Institut National der Recherche en Informatique et en Automatique (INRIA), 2000.

13. Sergei Gorlatch. Extracting and implementing list homomorphisms in parallel program development. *Science of Computer Programming*, 33(1):1–27, 1999.

14. Ronald L. Graham, Donald E. Knuth, and Oren Patashnik. *Concrete Mathematics*. Addison-Wesley Publishing Company, 1994.

15. Per Hammarlund and Björn Lisper. On the relation between functional and data parallel programming languages. In *Proc. Sixth Conf. on Functional Programming Languages and Computer Architecture (FPCA'93)*, pages 210–222. ACM Press, 1993.

16. haskell.org, 2000. http://www.haskell.org.

17. Christoph A. Herrmann and Christian Lengauer. Size inference of nested lists in functional programs. In Kevin Hammond, Tony Davie, and Chris Clack, editors, *Proc. 10th Int. Workshop on the Implementation of Functional Languages (IFL'98)*, pages 346–364. Dept. Computer Science, Univ. College London, 1998.

18. Christoph A. Herrmann, Christian Lengauer, Robert Günz, Jan Laitenberger, and Christian Schaller. A compiler for $\mathcal{HDC}$. Technical Report MIP-9907, Fakultät für Mathematik und Informatik, Univ. Passau, May 1999.

19. Christoph A. Herrmann. *The Skeleton-Based Parallelization of Divide-and-Conquer Recursions*. PhD thesis, Fakultät für Mathematik und Informatik, Univ. Passau. Logos-Verlag, Berlin, 2000.

20. Christoph A. Herrmann and Christian Lengauer. $\mathcal{HDC}$: A higher-order language for divide-and-conquer. *Parallel Processing Letters*, 10(2–3):239–250, 2000.

21. Martin Hofmann. A type system for bounded space and functional in-place update – extended abstract. In Gerd Smolka, editor, *Programming Languages and Systems (ESOP 2000)*, Lecture Notes in Computer Science 1782, pages 165–179. Springer-Verlag, 2000.

22. John Hughes, Lars Pareto, and Amr Sabry. Proving the correctness of reactive systems using sized types. In *Proc. 23rd Ann. ACM Symp. on Principles of Programming Languages (POPL'96)*, pages 410–423. ACM Press, 1996.

23. C. Barry Jay and Milan Sekanina. Shape checking of array programs. In J. Harland, editor, *Proc. Australasian Theory Seminar on Computing*, volume 19 of *Australian Computer Science Communications*, pages 113–121, 1997.

24. Björn Lisper and Jean-François Collard. Extent analysis of data fields. In Baudouin Le Charlier, editor, *Static Analysis (SAS'94)*, Lecture Notes in Computer Science 864, pages 208–222. Springer-Verlag, 1994.

25. Hans-Wolfgang Loidl and Kevin Hammond. A sized time system for a parallel functional language. In *Proc. 1996 Glasgow Workshop on Functional Programming*, 1996. Electronic publication: http://www.dcs.gla.ac.uk/fp/workshops/fpw96/Proceedings96.html.

26. Jayadev Misra. Powerlist: A structure for parallel recursion. *ACM Trans. on Programming Languages and Systems*, 16(6):1737–1767, November 1994.

27. Flemming Nielson and Hanne Riis Nielson. *Two-level functional languages*. Number 34 in Cambridge Tracts in Theoretical Computer Science. Cambridge University Press, 1992.

28. John T. O'Donnell. Bidirectional `fold` and `scan`. In *Functional Programming: Glasgow 1993*, Workshops in Computing, pages 193–200. Springer-Verlag, 1994.

29. John T. O'Donnell. From transistors to computer architecture: Teaching functional circuit specification in Hydra. In Pieter H. Hartel and Rinus Plasmeijer, editors, *Functional Programming Languages in Education*, Lecture Notes in Computer Science 1022, pages 195–214. Springer-Verlag, 1995.

30. James Riely and Jan Prins. Flattening is an improvement. In Jens Palsberg, editor, *Static Analysis (SAS'2000)*, Lecture Notes in Computer Science 1824, pages 360–376. Springer-Verlag, 2000.

31. Philip Wadler. Views: A way for pattern matching to cohabit with data abstraction. In *Proc. 14th ACM Symp. Principles of Programming Languages (POPL'87)*, pages 307–313. ACM Press, 1987.

32. Hongwei Xi and Frank Pfenning. Dependent types in practical programming. In *Proc. 26th ACM Symp. Principles of Programming Languages (POPL'99)*, pages 214–227. ACM Press, 1999.

Author Index

Lecture Notes in Computer Science

For information about Vols. 1–2086
please contact your bookseller or Springer-Verlag

Vol. 2127: V. Malyshkin (Ed.), Parallel Computing Technologies. Proceedings, 2001. XII, 516 pages. 2001.

Vol. 2129: M. Goemans, K. Jansen, J.D.P. Rolim, L. Trevisan (Eds.), Approximation, Randomization, and Combinatorial Optimization. Proceedings, 2001. IX, 297 pages. 2001.

Vol. 2130: G. Dorffner, H. Bischof, K. Hornik (Eds.), Artificial Neural Networks – ICANN 2001. Proceedings, 2001. XXII, 1259 pages. 2001.

Vol. 2132: S.-T. Yuan, M. Yokoo (Eds.), Intelligent Agents. Specification. Modeling, and Application. Proceedings, 2001. X, 237 pages. 2001. (Subseries LNAI).

Vol. 2133: B. Christianson, B. Crispo, J.A. Malcolm, M. Roe (Eds.), Security Protocols. Proceedings, 2001. VIII, 257 pages. 2001.

Vol. 2136: J. Sgall, A. Pultr, P. Kolman (Eds.), Mathematical Foundations of Computer Science 2001. Proceedings, 2001. XII, 716 pages. 2001.

Vol. 2138: R. Freivalds (Ed.), Fundamentals of Computation Theory. Proceedings, 2001. XIII, 542 pages. 2001.

Vol. 2139: J. Kilian (Ed.), Advances in Cryptology – CRYPTO 2001. Proceedings, 2001. XI, 599 pages. 2001.

Vol. 2141: G.S. Brodal, D. Frigioni, A. Marchetti-Spaccamela (Eds.), Algorithm Engineering. Proceedings, 2001. X, 199 pages. 2001.

Vol. 2142: L. Fribourg (Ed.), Computer Science Logic. Proceedings, 2001. XII, 615 pages. 2001.

Vol. 2143: S. Benferhat, P. Besnard (Eds.), Symbolic and Quantitative Approaches to Reasoning with Uncertainty. Proceedings, 2001. XIV, 818 pages. 2001. (Subseries LNAI).

Vol. 2144: T. Margaria, T. Melham (Eds.), Correct Hardware Design and Verification Methods. Proceedings, 2001. XII, 482 pages. 2001.

Vol. 2146: J.H. Silverman (Eds.), Cryptography and Lattices. Proceedings, 2001. VII, 219 pages. 2001.

Vol. 2147: G. Brebner, R. Woods (Eds.), Field-Programmable Logic and Applications. Proceedings, 2001. XV, 665 pages. 2001.

Vol. 2149: O. Gascuel, B.M.E. Moret (Eds.), Algorithms in Bioinformatics. Proceedings, 2001. X, 307 pages. 2001.

Vol. 2150: R. Sakellariou, J. Keane, J. Gurd, L. Freeman (Eds.), Euro-Par 2001 Parallel Processing. Proceedings, 2001. XXX, 943 pages. 2001.

Vol. 2151: A. Caplinskas, J. Eder (Eds.), Advances in Databases and Information Systems. Proceedings, 2001. XIII, 381 pages. 2001.

Vol. 2152: R.J. Boulton, P.B. Jackson (Eds.), Theorem Proving in Higher Order Logics. Proceedings, 2001. X, 395 pages. 2001.

Vol. 2153: A.L. Buchsbaum, J. Snoeyink (Eds.), Algorithm Engineering and Experimentation. Proceedings, 2001. VIII, 231 pages. 2001.

Vol. 2154: K.G. Larsen, M. Nielsen (Eds.), CONCUR 2001 – Concurrency Theory. Proceedings, 2001. XI, 583 pages. 2001.

Vol. 2157: C. Rouveirol, M. Sebag (Eds.), Inductive Logic Programming. Proceedings, 2001. X, 261 pages. 2001. (Subseries LNAI).

Vol. 2158: D. Shepherd, J. Finney, L. Mathy, N. Race (Eds.), Interactive Distributed Multimedia Systems. Proceedings, 2001. XIII, 258 pages. 2001.

Vol. 2159: J. Kelemen, P. Sosík (Eds.), Advances in Artificial Life. Proceedings, 2001. XIX, 724 pages. 2001. (Subseries LNAI).

Vol. 2161: F. Meyer auf der Heide (Ed.), Algorithms – ESA 2001. Proceedings, 2001. XII, 538 pages. 2001.

Vol. 2162: Ç. K. Koç, D. Naccache, C. Paar (Eds.), Cryptographic Hardware and Embedded Systems – CHES 2001. Proceedings, 2001. XIV, 411 pages. 2001.

Vol. 2164: S. Pierre, R. Glitho (Eds.), Mobile Agents for Telecommunication Applications. Proceedings, 2001. XI, 292 pages. 2001.

Vol. 2165: L. de Alfaro, S. Gilmore (Eds.), Process Algebra and Probabilistic Methods. Proceedings, 2001. XII, 217 pages. 2001.

Vol. 2166: V. Matoušek, P. Mautner, R. Mouček, K. Taušer (Eds.), Text, Speech and Dialogue. Proceedings, 2001. XIII, 452 pages. 2001. (Subseries LNAI).

Vol. 2170: S. Palazzo (Ed.), Evolutionary Trends of the Internet. Proceedings, 2001. XIII, 722 pages. 2001.

Vol. 2172: C. Batini, F. Giunchiglia, P. Giorgini, M. Mecella (Eds.), Cooperative Information Systems. Proceedings, 2001. XI, 450 pages. 2001.

Vol. 2176: K.-D. Althoff, R.L. Feldmann, W. Müller (Eds.), Advances in Learning Software Organizations. Proceedings, 2001. XI, 241 pages. 2001.

Vol. 2177: G. Butler, S. Jarzabek (Eds.), Generative and Component-Based Software Engineering. Proceedings, 2001. X, 203 pages. 2001.

Vol. 2181: C. Y. Westort (Eds.), Digital Earth Moving. Proceedings, 2001. XII, 117 pages. 2001.

Vol. 2182: M. Klusch, F. Zambonelli (Eds.), Cooperative Information Agents V. Proceedings, 2001. XII, 288 pages. 2001. (Subseries LNAI).

Vol. 2184: M. Tucci (Ed.), Multimedia Databases and Image Communication. Proceedings, 2001. X, 225 pages. 2001.

Vol. 2186: J. Bosch (Ed.), Generative and Component-Based Software Engineering. Proceedings, 2001. VIII, 177 pages. 2001.

Vol. 2188: F. Bomarius, S. Komi-Sirviö (Eds.), Product Focused Software Process Improvement. Proceedings, 2001. XI, 382 pages. 2001.

Vol. 2189: F. Hoffmann, D.J. Hand, N. Adams, D. Fisher, G. Guimaraes (Eds.), Advances in Intelligent Data Analysis. Proceedings, 2001. XII, 384 pages. 2001.

Vol. 2190: A. de Antonio, R. Aylett, D. Ballin (Eds.), Intelligent Virtual Agents. Proceedings, 2001. VIII, 245 pages. 2001. (Subseries LNAI).

Vol. 2191: B. Radig, S. Florczyk (Eds.), Pattern Recognition. Proceedings, 2001. XVI, 452 pages. 2001.

Vol. 2193: F. Casati, D. Georgakopoulos, M.-C. Shan (Eds.), Technologies for E-Services. Proceedings, 2001. X, 213 pages. 2001.

Vol. 2196: W. Taha (Ed.), Semantics, Applications, and Implementation of Program Generation. Proceedings, 2001. X, 219 pages. 2001.